“Books Most Needful to Know”

OLD ENGLISH NEWSLETTER SUBSIDIA

Volume XXXVI

Medieval Institute Publications is a program of
The Medieval Institute, College of Arts and Sciences

"Books Most Needful to Know"

Contexts for the Study of Anglo-Saxon England

Edited by

Paul E. Szarmach

Old English Newsletter Subsidia

MEDIEVAL INSTITUTE PUBLICATIONS
Western Michigan University
Kalamazoo

Library of Congress Cataloging-in-Publication Data
are available from the Library of Congress.

ISBN: 9781580441827
eISBN: 9781580441834

Printed and bound in Great Britain by CPI Group (UK) Ltd, Croydon, CR0 4YY

Contents

Preface vii

Anglo-Latin Literature in the Foreground 1
Rosalind Love

North Sea Currents: Old English and Old Norse in Comparison and in Contact 61
Richard Dance

Légend hÉrenn: "The Learning of Ireland" in the Early Medieval Period 85
Máire Ní Mhaonaigh

Preface

TO A 1978 LUNCHEON, Mr. John Pickles brought along a copy of W. W. Skeat's *An English—Anglo-Saxon Vocabulary*, which he suggested might reappear as a pamphlet under the auspices of the *Old English Newsletter.* The suggestion was friendly and the idea good. Despite some mild caution by elements of the SUNY–Binghamton administration, the *Old English Newsletter* Subsidia came forth, but more as a one-off than as the beginning of some grand new enterprise. OEN Subsidia, volume 1, was cast in the image and likeness of its older sibling: plain and unaffected—and above all cheap. But the technical and intellectual success of this first volume unearthed in the Anglo-Saxonist community a professional interest in accessible *ancillae* for research or teaching that over its nearly three decades in existence Subsidia has sought to serve the field by a variety genres. In its pre–Western Michigan incarnation, Subsidia published several special volumes. Perhaps the volume that best exhibited the potential of the Subsidia series was William Schipper's brilliant navigation of various bureaucracies and cultural expectations to produce *Old English Studies from Japan 1941–81* (vol. 14 [1988]). Schipper arranged for funding in Japan, collected representative essays, supervised the translation process, and edited the volume, which went out to some 1,100 plus individual and institutional subscribers as a free good in the interests of international scholarship. Others who consult the Subsidia series may have their own favorites. These might include Simon Keynes's *Anglo-Saxon Manuscripts in Trinity College* (vol. 18 [1992]) with its forty illustrations or the first printed version of his *Anglo-Saxon History: A Select Bibliography* (vol. 13 [1987]). The discerning Anglo-Saxonist will see from the appendix that the publishing history of Subsidia includes the support of Sources of Anglo-Saxon Literary Culture, various studies in meter, the programs of the Old English Division of the Modern Language Association, and of course the International Congress at Western Michigan University.

When Subsidia joined the *OEN* in its move to Western Michigan University in 1994, it became a sponsored program of the Richard Rawlinson Center and eventually a publication of Medieval Institute Publications. Subsidia took on a new life when Patricia Hollahan assumed the position of managing editor of Medieval Institute Publications in 2002. The volumes published under her general editorship showed new production values and a new professionalism, while developing the core missions of the series. Thus, Donald Scragg on canonized popes, Helmut Gneuss on Ælfric, and Robin Norris on interpolations in Ælfric's *Lives of Saints* represent current high points for the series, as does this special volume, *"Books Most Needful to Know": Contexts for the Study of Anglo-Saxon England*. Volume 36 derives from the 2006 Summer Seminar, "Holy Men and Holy Women," supported by the National Endowment for the Humanities. Rosalind Love and Máire Ní Mhaonaigh were faculty members in the seminar. Richard Dance generously stepped in to offer "North Sea Currents." And I should like to thank King Alfred for supplying the title of this volume from his Preface to the *Pastoral Care*.

While *OEN Subsidia* leaves its home at The Medieval Institute and Medieval Institute Publications at Western Michigan University, it will continue under a new editorial board directed by Prof. Stephen Harris (University of Massachusetts at Amherst). Send orders, inquiries, and submissions to Prof. Harris at sharris@english.umass.edu. The Western Michigan staff wishes its successors a successful future.

I should like to acknowledge the kind permission of the Master and Fellows of Corpus Christi College for the use of an image from Cambridge, Corpus Christi College 183, fol. 1v.

Anglo-Latin Literature in the Foreground

Rosalind Love

TO ONE OF THE volumes of the Short Oxford History of the British Isles, Andy Orchard contributed a chapter entitled, "Latin and the Vernacular Languages: The Creation of a Bilingual Textual Culture."[1] He describes the role of Latin in sub-Roman Britain, Wales, Ireland, Scotland, and finally Anglo-Saxon England, portraying it as a powerful influence and a catalyst for the vernacular languages. The notion of a "bilingual textual culture" is one galvanizing principle in the following, brief introduction to Anglo-Latin literature, used to explore the possibilities for bilingualism in genre, individual authors, and literary style. Since this volume is intended primarily as a guide for those engaged in the teaching and study of Old English language and literature, we may as well also direct the bilingual principle to the question of why such people should wish to know about Anglo-Latin.

Latin is often spoken of as the "background" to Old English; for example, the excellent survey by Michael Lapidge which heads up Greenfield and Calder's New Critical History of Old English Literature, is entitled, "The Anglo-Latin Background."[2] Yet there is something about the word "background" that does not quite capture the relationship of Anglo-Latin and Old English. We ought, of course, to distinguish between the wealth of Latin literature that the Anglo-Saxons inherited – patristic writings, the pagan classics, and so on – and the Latin which they wrote themselves. A swift and accessible way to gain an impression of the former is to spend some time exploring the online database of the Fontes Anglo-Saxonici project.[3] For anyone not already familiar with it, the database is a searchable catalogue of the literary sources for Old English and Anglo-Latin texts, fruits of a twenty-year project. It allows us a brief inquisitive rummage in the Anglo-Saxons' bookchests, and provides some sense of which were the most-thumbed books. Obviously another steadily-growing answer to the same question is afforded by the volumes emerging from SASLC. Add to that the monumental study by Michael Lapidge on the Anglo-Saxon library, and our picture of the "background" gains ever sharper focus.[4]

The Anglo-Saxons' own Latin, however, cannot so neatly be put aside as "background." For a picture of literary culture in England, Anglo-Latin texts are just as much the foreground as are texts in Old English. Indeed the enthusiasm and ostentation which characterizes a good deal of Anglo-Latin literature means that it leaps up and down in the foreground like an eager child desperate to be noticed. Our understanding of the Anglo-Saxon thought-world and its aesthetic values must be informed by consideration of both literatures, or it is an imperfect view. For example, while we struggle to prove that much extant Old English was composed by women, in Anglo-Latin there survives a scattering of women's writing, some of which has provoked intriguing comparisons with vernacular material. A great wealth of correspondence survives from the Anglo-Saxons' mission-field in Germany, letters reflecting the ups and, more particularly, the downs, of eighth-century missionary life, sent by Boniface and his colleagues.[5] Among them are letters written by women, and the tone of some of these has led commentators to see resonances with the Old English elegies.[6]

Another area in which we must keep an eye on developments in Anglo-Latin is the cult of saints and its literary manifestation, the Lives of the saints. Hagiography is the largest and most plentifully attested genre in medieval Latin, and that certainly applies to Anglo-Latin, too. This was an inherited genre to which there was a consistent and sustained response at every stage in the development of Anglo-Latin, from the eccentric Whitby Life of Gregory the Great to the sophisticated Winchester propaganda-machine that was Lantfred's account of the translation of Swithun in 917.[7] Given the popular nature of the cult of the saints, you might think that hagiography would also be prevalent in Old English. Yes and no, is the answer, it seems to me. In the tenth century Ælfric made a massive contribution to opening up access to the stories of the saints. His efforts apart, there are some thirty anonymous Old English Lives, of which most, like Ælfric's, are reworkings of Latin texts; but it is striking that precious few of these deal with home-grown saints and, when they do, with very few exceptions, are dependent on a pre-existing Latin source.[8] Thus Ælfric included just seven Insular saints – Cuthbert, Fursey, Æthelthryth, Edmund, Oswald and Swithun, and then also Alban – but in each case depended heavily on either Bede's Ecclesiastical History or some other Latin source. As for the anonymous Old English hagiography, just five native Anglo-Saxon saints are covered – Chad, Guthlac, Mildryth, Neot, and Seaxburh – and then two Italians whose cults were important to England, namely Augustine (a text only surviving as a fragment) and Paulinus, as well as the British saint, Machutus (Malo). Again, most of that material can be shown to depend on an earlier Latin source, with the fascinating exceptions of the poem Guthlac A, and the less familiar but fragmentary accounts of Mildryth and Seaxburh.[9]

I do not wish to suggest here that Old English renditions of pre-existing Latin hagiography are without their own profound interest or that they cannot be used to shed light on attitudes towards sanctity. My point is simply that for a full picture of the cult of the Anglo-Saxon saints, so central to contemporary spirituality, we must, indeed should, turn to Anglo-Latin. To judge from the surviving evidence, many Anglo-Saxon saints—especially women—were first commemorated by a Latin Life in the later eleventh century, at least partly in response to the changing circumstances of the post-Conquest church.[10] Many of the Lives written then discuss their sources, including oblique reference to materials in Old English, subsequently lost. Such claims do seem to have become a topos aimed at establishing authenticity, but could they hint at a body of vernacular hagiography that has since vanished?

A couple of examples will serve to highlight the complexity of the situation. A while back, I edited the mid-eleventh-century Latin Life of the ninth-century Mercian boy-martyr, Kenelm.[11] The text's prologue refers to *anglica scripta*—things written in English about the saint; yet all that survives is a lone couplet in English, incorporated into the Life in Latin translation: "In Clent Cowbatch under a thorn-tree, Lies Kenelm 'cynebearn' bereaved of his head," variously interpreted as a fragment of a lost Old English poem about the saint, or perhaps more likely, a refrain sung by pilgrims traveling to Kenelm's shrine.[12] It is impossible to know for sure now, but there is a great difference between that fragment of popular remembrance and the carefully-controlled Latin Life. The second example relates to a rather more famous and substantial figure, Dunstan, archbishop of Canterbury (959–88). There are few Anglo-Saxon saints at whom so much effort was directed by Latin hagiographers. Two Lives survive from the period immediately following his death, a highly eccentric account by the author known only as .B. (dateable to 995x1005), and then a shorter but no less important set of readings for the night office by Adelard of Ghent (written between 1006 and 1011).[13] After the conquest, the biography of Dunstan was then revisited first by Osbern of

Canterbury (in the early 1090s), and then in the early twelfth century by Eadmer of Canterbury and William of Malmesbury. In editing the last of these, Winterbottom and Thomson have picked over the evidence behind the claims of these five hagiographers concerning the sources they drew upon, and conclude that there must have been an Old English Life, now lost.[14] Whatever form it took, this Life has left only the faintest shadow, accounting for this or that discrepancy between the Latin versions, and the later authors' manner of reference to it is vague to the point of evasion. Osbern observes, "they say that some things about him survive that were translated into the native tongue, that is into English" [aliqua in patrium id est in Anglicum sermonem translata supersunt], and William refers to "writings, both in Latin and in English, that you had found in an ancient chest of yours" [scripta ... tam Latina quam Anglica in antiquissimo armario uestro reperta].[15]

Hagiography thus highlights the sort of complementarity between the two languages which means that we neglect the one or the other to our cost. Yet at the same time the genre does present some kind of match across the linguistic divide, in the sense that we have examples in both Latin and Old English which can be read side-by-side as distinct responses to the same tradition, prompting interesting questions about attitudes towards the relative status and function of the two languages. We may also feel enticed to wonder whether other literary genres offer something similar. Any attempt to address that question quickly meets a practical problem which is worth a brief digression here. At present there is no Anglo-Latin equivalent of the Cameron list – that is, Angus Cameron's List of Old English texts assembled as part of the Plan for the Toronto Dictionary. There is no repertory to give a comprehensive overview, no detailed seamless diachronic survey – the closest thing to that is Michael Lapidge's collected essays, which represent three decades of mapping the field. In the meantime, for named authors one can turn to two valuable resources: first Richard Sharpe's monumental *Handlist of the Latin Writers of Great Britain and Ireland*, and then also little by little the fascicles of *CALMA* (*Compendium Auctorum Latinorum Medii Aevi*), a comprehensive list of all medieval Latin authors and their works, 500–1500, of which the letters A to H are available so far. For an overview of anonymous texts, however, one is at present left very much high and dry. General medieval repertories can yield some information, and there are individual genre surveys (for example, on hagiography). On the whole, though, it is hard to get a confident sense of what survives.

Probably the most familiar example of a genre-match across the language divide is that of the Old English riddles in the tenth-century Exeter Book and the Anglo-Latin Enigmata of Aldhelm (abbot of Malmesbury and bishop of Sherborne, d. 709 or 710) and his later imitators. Here assumptions about what might be the background and what the foreground, as well as other quickly-formed impressions, all too easily get in the way of seeing such a match as a genuine reflex of Orchard's bilingual textual culture. The quickly-formed impressions are of the Old English Riddles as popular and accessible, fun, intended mainly for entertainment, and the Enigmata as dry, opaque, the humorlessly didactic stuff of the classroom. Such are the tropes of student essays on the subject. Orchard has recently tackled head-on the issue of the supposedly great difference between the lack of legible solutions to the Old English Riddles as preserved in the Exeter Book, and the transmission of the Latin Engimata with the solutions as titles or even concealed within the enigma, thus sapping them of their very life-blood as teasing riddles.[16] He musters plenty of evidence to show that the Anglo-Latin Enigmata did not always travel with their solutions, and my own personal wish-list of lost manuscripts includes a missing back page from the Exeter book providing all the answers to the Old English Riddles like the kind of puzzle-book for sale in airports. It is also instructive, in the case of the Latin Enigmata, to envisage the classroom context in which they might have been used, to judge, at any rate, from the ways in which they were glossed in the surviving later manuscripts.[17] If one supposes the teacher to have been the one in control of the manuscript copy of the Enigmata, dictating to the class for copying out, there is no reason why he could not have withheld the solution to begin with, until his pupils had wrestled a while with the conundrum before them. Another readily-observable difference between the Old English Riddles and the Enigmata is the presence among the former of bawdy double-entendre specimens. In these one salacious solution is naughtily dangled in front of another more innocent one so suggestively as to displace the latter almost completely.[18] We search in vain for anything of that nature among the more earnest Enigmata, a difference that cannot be readily put aside. Yet the Enigmata suffer first of all from our own sense of their stiltedness, because in order to appreciate them we have to strive with the Latin grammar and syntax first. But if we persevere, at least in one case that I can think of, it is possible to perceive a glimmer of the same fantasy world. Tatwine, who became archbishop of Canterbury in 731, wrote forty Enigmata that are very clearly inspired by those of Aldhelm.[19]

That they are seen as derivative of Aldhelm's means that Tatwine's Enigmata have not received the scholarly attention that they probably should have. Some of these poems demonstrate precisely the didactic perspective already mentioned, such as an Enigma on the four Latin prepositions that take two cases (that is, ablative, the case that "takes away," and accusative, the case used to express cause: the prepositions in question are "in, sub, subter, super"):

> Emerita gemina sortis sub lege tenemur:
> Nam tollenti nos stabiles seruire necesse est,
> Causantis contra cursus comitamur eundo;
> Sicque uicissim bis binae coniungimur ambit
> Quippe sorores; decreta stat legibus urna.[20]

> It is our fate that we are bound by a well-worn two-fold law: for we, immoveable, have to serve the one [i.e., the case] that takes away, but on the other hand, by moving we accompany the courses of the one that accuses; and thus by turns we twice-two sisters are joined to both; our lot is decreed by laws.

Yet there are others that open the window on a different world, of physicality, violence, even voyeurism: the parchment stripped of its skin by a savage plunderer ("efferus ... populator"), the pen robbed of its natural behavior and forced to toil, the pitiful anvil which must put up with every blow and may neither dodge aside nor retaliate, the table which is dressed up in fine clothes only to be stripped and left naked later on, and charcoal, invaded and murdered by a fierce enemy that enslaves it.[21] Particularly intriguing as a glimpse into the workings of Tatwine's vivid imagination is the riddle on the embroidery needle, whose suffering body is on display for the pleasuring of royalty (he also included the plain needle, which unless blinded in its single eye cannot go about its work):

> Reginae cupiunt animis me cernere, nec non
> Reges mulcet adesse mei quoque corporis usus;
> Nam multos uario possum captare decore.
> Quippe meam gracilis faciem iugulauerat hospes,
> Nobilior tamen adcrescit decor inde genarum.[22]

> Queens desire in their hearts to look upon me, and also the presence of my body's usings gives kings pleasure; for I can captivate many with my manifold beauty. A slender visitor had cut into my face, yet thereby the beauty of my cheeks grows still nobler.

Even his treatment of relatively dry abstract concepts teems with queenly mistresses and their boudoirs: so Wisdom, the mother of Faith, Hope and Charity, keeps to her sunny bed-chamber (*thalamus*), the four ways of interpreting the Scriptures keep watch on behalf of their *dominatrix*, Wisdom's sister, and Pride and the other seven vices are queens locked away with their swarm of offspring and attendants.[23] Such a fantasy world does not seem as far from that of the Old English riddlers as is sometimes contended, just as the rather detached and even skeptical tone with which "heroic" topics are handled in the Old English riddles may bespeak occasionally the same clerical world as that of Aldhelm and his successors. Indeed, what would prevent us from imagining that the same men composed their brain-teasers in both languages? In the case of Aldhelm, enquiring into such a possibility turns up tantalizing evidence, which brings us to a brief exploration of a bilingual literary culture as embodied in an individual author and his works.

Aldhelm has rightly been celebrated as "the first English man of letters" who was to have a lasting influence on the development of Anglo-Latin. His surviving works are quite remarkable yet, perhaps thanks to the way they have been made so accessible through the efforts of Michael Lapidge and Michael Herren in particular, they are too easily taken for granted as the earliest extensive body of Latin literature produced by an Anglo-Saxon.[24] By his own reckoning, Aldhelm was the first of the Germanic race to compose Latin verse or describe how to do so, an achievement of which he was justifiably proud.[25] He forged for himself a workable methodology for composing hexameters, which must always have remained something of a toilsome business, and it has been convincingly demonstrated that he brought a familiarity with vernacular verse composition to bear upon his efforts.[26] What spoils the picture is that we do not knowingly have anything that Aldhelm composed in Old English. All we can cling to is the story, told by William of Malmesbury, that King Alfred had recorded in his commonplace-book (*Handboc*) an anecdote about Aldhelm's habit of standing by the bridge at Malmesbury singing secular Old English poetry intermingled with biblical phrases, to entice his flock into church. One of his poems was still popular in Alfred's day, we learn, but alas William does not tell us what it was.[27]

What we would not give to have heard Aldhelm's Old English poetry, considering the kind of Latin he wrote; indeed, as Paul Remley has reminded us, some scholars would gladly have exchanged all Aldhelm's Latin for one bit of his Old English, and he points us in various directions for the best chances of recovering any of it.[28] Both our curiosity about what Aldhelm's Old English would have looked like and the distaste some readers have felt at his Latin stem from the fact that the latter has a reputation principally for its elaborate affectation, doubtless the chief reason why his works stayed popular from his own day to the eleventh century. The prose in particular is challenging to translate, chiefly because Aldhelm cultivated an expansive style that built sub-clause upon sub-clause seeking endlessly to vary and elaborate, thereby producing sentences several lines long. The quest for variation also led him to seek out unusual vocabulary, whether archaisms or grecisms, in order to add lustrous learnedness to the tone. Many see this supposedly fearsome and tedious Latin merely as a barrier to accessing what Aldhelm wrote *about*, which is a great pity.[29] Because his Latin style is actually what defines Aldhelm, central to what he wanted to say: Orchard calls his prose style "a triumph of form over content,"[30] and Aldhelm himself refers proudly to "the verbose garrulity or garrulous verbosity of my dissertation."[31] One view would be that Aldhelm was an unbearable show-off who, having mastered Latin, was so pleased with himself that he wanted readers to wallow up to their necks in his verbiage; but in his enthusiasm, putting them through that kind of intellectual work-out was also an important part of the message he wished to convey. That this was Aldhelm's view of book-learning is evident from the way in which he complimented the group of nuns to whom he dedicated his treatise on virginity (the prose *De uirginitate*), by comparing their intellectual endeavors to those of athletes, in a remarkable sequence of bracingly vivid images that reads like a day's reportage on the Olympic games.[32] Furthermore, the complex train of Aldhelm's argumentation at this point in his treatise suggests that he viewed scholarship, a day's wrestling with a juicy bit of Latin, as an important part of the means by which his addressees might gain a spiritual virginity that would transcend their corporeal virginity, or, lack thereof. The corporeal is attainable by many, according to Aldhelm, the spiritual by very few.[33]

To give some impression of the qualities that simultaneously attract and repel, we may as well head straight for the opening of Aldhelm's most notoriously wrigglesome (and possibly the most intensively studied) work, his *Letter to Heahfrith* (Letter 5).

> Primitus pantorum procerum praetorumque pio potissimum paternoque praesertim priuilegio panagericum poemataque passim prosatori sub polo promulgantes stridula uocum simphonia et melodiae cantilenaeque carmine modulaturi ymnizemus, praecipue quia

> tandem almae editum puerperae sobolem ob inextricabile sons protoplaustorum piaculum priscorumque cirografum oblitteraturum terris tantundem destinare dignatus est, luridum qui linguis celydrum trisulcis rancida uirulentaque uomentem per aeuum uenena torrentia tetrae tortionis in tartara trusit et, ubi pridem eiusdem nefandae natricis ermula ceruulusque cruda fanis colebantur stoliditate in profanis, uersa uice discipulorum gurgustia, immo almae oraminum aedes architecti ingenio fabre conduntur.[34]

> Principally, with particularly pious and paternal privilege, publicly proffering beneath the pole panegyric and poems promiscuously to the Procreator of "la plupart des" princes and praetors, let us hymnize in measured rhythms with a stridulous "symphonisme" of voices and with song of melody and ballad, especially because He who thrust into Tartarus of terrible torture the ghastly "vipère" with three-forked tongues who vomits torrents of rank and virulent poisons through the ages, deigned in like measure to send to earth the offspring begotten of a dear child bearer in order to obliterate the offense of the "premier-creés" and the autograph of the ancients on account of their inextricable sin; and because, where once the "colonne" of that same abominable asp, and the stag, were culted with coarse stupidity in unholy holies, in their place hovels for students, not to mention holy houses of prayment, are constructed skillfully by the talents of the architect.

Here are fifteen plosives in a row, tantamount to spitting in the listener's eye, or perhaps a trumpet fanfare to herald the orchestral praise that follows. The alliteration continues insistently through the passage and is a conspicuous feature of Aldhelm's style, in both prose and verse, in the former often serving to highlight a significant sense-break. The second word, *pantorum,* is a reasonable latinization of the Greek adjective meaning "all" – for our purposes it is of interest to note that particular grecism otherwise crops up in a hymn preserved in the late seventh-century Antiphonary of Bangor (Milan, Biblioteca Ambrosiana C.5.inf.)[35] and in the utterly mad but fascinating group of texts known as the *Hisperica Famina,* also possibly connected with seventh-century Bangor.[36] Other grecisms are *panagericum*, *poemata*, *simphonia*, *ymnizemus*, *protoplaustorum*, *cirografum*, *celydrum*, *tartara*, and *ermula*, though it is important to emphasize that unlike *pantorum*, most of these had already effectively been absorbed into Christian Latin before Aldhelm's day.

As well as the rich polysyllabic texture, of which the grecisms are but one strand, Aldhelm also employs complex word order, that is, hyperbaton, which interlaces pairs of nouns and adjectives in various patterns (for example, "luridum ... linguis celydrum trisulcis" and "torrentia tetrae tortionis ... tartara") presumably to create a poetic tone rather than necessarily to infuriate the reader. It should also be evident from this passage how he built up layer upon layer—by using pairs of synonyms ("procerum praetorumque" and "panagericum poemataque") or complementary descriptors ("pio ... paternoque" and "rancida uirulentaque"), by parallel phrases that restate a point ("stridula uocum simphonia / melodiae cantilenaeque carmine"). That such building blocks can be quite readily identified and separated out (despite what generations of struggling students of Insular Latin may feel) is a feature of Aldhelm's prose style which led Michael Winterbottom to characterize it most aptly as "ostentation, perhaps, but not obfuscation."[37] From all this tangled verbiage emerges the simple message "let us praise God because he sent his son to redeem our sins and because we now have churches instead of pagan shrines."

Aldhelm once described himself as someone known for an inclination to read between the lines. Acknowledging letters received from the female dedicatees of his treatise on virginity, he observes "when I looked over the words of your letters with the swift dartings of my eyes and mulled over them with a certain natural curiosity (as is said to be innate in me) about the things that lie hidden."[38] Thus taking our cue from the author himself, we may justifiably extract from this opening to the *Letter to Heahfrith* not so much the simple message just outlined, as the loudly ostentatious blare of Aldhelm blowing his own trumpet.

If scholars have looked to Old English verse for influences upon Aldhelm's metrical verse, the one rhythmical poem which survives from his hand—the so-called *Carmen rhythmicum*, a wonderfully breathless rhyming account of a journey through the stormy West Country[39]—points towards another cultural connection, namely that between Anglo-Saxon England and Ireland, discussed elsewhere in this volume. Andy Orchard has pointed to the strong likelihood that Aldhelm was familiar with the Irish tradition of rhythmical hymnody exemplified by the extraordinary seventh-century octosyllabic poem known as *Altus prosator*, believed to have been composed on Iona.[40]

It is worth lingering a little longer over the question of Aldhelm's debt to Irish literary culture, in particular because scholars are continuing to reframe the answer. Earlier commentators were tempted to draw parallels between his difficult prose style and certain trends in Hiberno-Latin. But in an article published in 1977, Michael Winterbottom showed in compelling fashion that the style can just as readily—indeed more readily—be accounted for by stylistic trends on the continent.[41] Until quite recently, moreover, it was thought that Aldhelm's earliest studies were with an Irishman, whose name supposedly lies behind the place-name Malmesbury. William of Malmesbury's biography of Aldhelm, in the fifth book of his *Gesta pontificum*, is the beginning and the end of this notion. A cursory reading of chapter 189 suggested to successive commentators that one Maelduib ("quidam Meldum, qui alio nomine uocatur Meildulf, natione Scottus") had become a hermit at Malmesbury and was Aldhelm's teacher, but once William's words are spelt out, it becomes clear that he does not quite say quite as much:

> when he [Maelduib] ran short of what he needed to live, he took on boys as pupils, so that their generosity might make good the slenderness of his means. As time went on they followed in their master's footsteps by becoming monks instead of students, and came to form a sizable convent. Aldhelm, prompted to further study by their example and fellowship, added the liberal arts to his repertoire of knowledge.[42]

Aldhelm himself seems on the face of it not to mince his words on the subject of Irish learning. One of his more challenging works, the letter whose opening we have already examined, which was addressed to an otherwise unknown Heahfrith, seemingly a former pupil, deliberately polarizes the difference between two places of learning, Canterbury and Ireland.[43] We know from two other letters written by Aldhelm that he had studied for an indeterminate time at the famed school at Canterbury presided over by the Greek-speaking monk Theodore (archbishop of Canterbury from 667) and his colleague Hadrian. Bede later raved about this school ("some of their students still survive who know Latin and Greek just as well as their native tongue"), and named a handful of its eminent alumni, though interestingly enough did not include Aldhelm in that list.[44] Aldhelm's own praise for Theodore and Hadrian, spelt out for the benefit of Heahfrith, is deliberately at the expense of Irish scholars, whom he imagines as hounds sent yelping into retreat in the face of the well-honed tusks of the fierce boar that was Theodore.[45] He professes himself at a loss to understand why so many ferry-loads of Anglo-Saxon students, teeming like a swarm of bees, continue to make the trip across the Irish Sea in the quest for learning.[46]

In another sadly fragmentary but colorful letter, Aldhelm seems to lay sarcasm as thick as the honey produced by his beloved bees over the wish of another otherwise unknown correspondent, Wihtfrith, to study in Ireland.[47] He warns that there is too much emphasis on Classical Latin literature and its pagan stories and too many prostitutes; the hyperbolic terms in which the latter are described, weighed down with as much metal-work as a souped-up road-racer ("prostitutes with luxury as their pander, who are adorned with the flashing burnish of leg-bands and with smooth arm-bracelets, just as ornamented chariots are adorned with metal bosses"), suggest more bluff than known reality.[48] Current research, however, may suggest that there is more than a little irony in Aldhelm's admonitions about Irish scholarship. Michael Lapidge has proposed that Aldhelm may have studied for a time on Iona and that one of the things he pored over there was Vergil's *Eclogues*.[49] Such a possibility would imply that the scornful views aired in Aldhelm's letters to Wihtfrith and Heahfrith were founded on personal experience, even if they do have the ring of the puffed-up, self-preening college student who thinks he knows it all after a tutorial with a particularly inspiring don and looks back with contempt upon the humble schoolmaster who drummed in the sturdy foundations of arithmetic, Latin grammar or a serviceable knowledge of Vergil.

The densely oozing honey of Aldhelm's prose contrasts with the more austere Latin of his later contemporary, Bede (d. 735), who, as a dedicated teacher, was concerned with instructing his readers, and to make accessible digests of inherited learning; as George Brown observed in his 1996 Jarrow Lecture, "what Bede wanted to do and did superbly was educate, soberly, quietly, discreetly."[50] Like Aldhelm, he was in a position to gain both from the tradition of Irish scholarship that had flowed into Northumbria in an earlier generation, but also from the barrow-loads of books which were brought into England from Italy, in this case by the founder of his home community, Benedict Biscop, and by the first abbot, Ceolfrith.[51] On the face of it, though, Bede's response to that inheritance was quite unlike that of Aldhelm, with none of the pomposity and self-advertisement of the latter's utterances and style, presenting instead what has recently been described as a style "showing a deliberate neutrality ... avoiding any kind of idiosyncrasy, even of personality."[52] Of the two, Bede wrote far more, in particular commentaries on the Scriptures and other aids for their study. It is an important corrective to our primary focus upon Bede as the author of his Ecclesiastical History that access to his commentaries has gradually opened to a wider audience thanks to a steady stream of translations into English, as well as a rich vein of recent scholarship which reframes him as, first and foremost, a monk and a preacher, and only secondly as a historian.[53] His own view of his contribution in writing these commentaries was that they provided a synthesis of the wealth he found in the library to which he was fortunate to have access: "I have taken care to make brief notes from the works of the venerable Fathers for my own benefit and that of my brothers."[54] Bede has been praised for his self-restraint and modesty, yet recently one scholar has suggested that like Aldhelm, he had his own sense of pride in achievement.[55] The second half of the scholarly manifesto just quoted: "... or to add notes of my own to clarify their sense and meaning" (siue etiam ad formam sensus et interpretationis eorum superadicere), suggests sufficient confidence to step right over the tracks left by one's forebears and run on ahead to places where they never trod, as Bede did indeed do in some of his works.[56]

Much has been made of Bede's clarity of expression, maybe at times too much, as Richard Sharpe has shown with his analysis of some really knotty samples from the biblical commentaries.[57] Bede's prose is at its most testing, he concludes, when, perhaps in an effort to emulate the expository rhetoric of Jerome, he piles up ever deeper layers of clause and sub-clause, with overlapping explanations and qualification; and it is interesting to see that in the exegesis produced towards the end of his life, the average number of words per sentence ramped up quite significantly.[58] Long, seemingly rambling sentences are what students hold against Aldhelm, as we have seen: but Bede can present just as much of a challenge, also for reasons of ambition, though of quite another kind. The crucial difference between them seems to be that Aldhelm's long-windedness was born mainly of the desire for elaboration, which merely varies the tone without necessarily saying anything new, thereby raising the texture of the prose to a higher poetic plane. As Michael Winterbottom observed, "for an author so keen to pile up synonyms and show off width of vocabulary, there just were not enough common words to serve his turn."[59] That is why Aldhelm's style is strongly flavored with out-of-the-way vocabulary and Bede's is not: Aldhelm was seeking not so much to puzzle with the arcane, as to dazzle with glistering variety and overwhelm with quantity.[60] If Bede wrote long complex sentences in his commentaries it was not because he said the same thing several times with different words, but because he was anxious to explain everything, qualify every statement, leave no room for ambiguity; quite simply, he had a lot of content to pack in.

The literary bilingualism we have been pursuing is again, in Bede's case, attested only anecdotally. Apart from the five-line *Death Song*, itself of uncertain attribution, we have no Old English verse or prose written by Bede, even though his pupil Cuthbert observes, "he was familiar with English poetry," and describes him toiling over a translation into English of St John's Gospel right up until the moment he died.[61] That he took the trouble to include the story of Caedmon in the *HE* also suggests more than a passing interest in the composition of Old English verse.

In the earliest writings that survive from seventh-century England it is possible to identify an effort to synthesize the treasury of learning that was imported from various directions, whether it be Bede's biblical commentaries purveying what he had gleaned from the meadow of the Fathers, or Aldhelm's summary of exemplary virgins and his one hundred enigmatic examples of how to compose hexameters. Yet neither Aldhelm nor Bede stopped at the passivity of synthesis, and can be seen as confident innovators in almost everything they undertook. One might argue that Anglo-Saxon England never again produced anyone to match their ambitious range and prolific abilities. It is striking that the eighth-century missionaries in Germany, Boniface and his colleague Lul, wrote home asking for copies of Biblical texts – understandably enough – but also for the works of Aldhelm and, particularly, of Bede, "who has lately shone in your midst like an ecclesiastical candle."[62] Their correspondents also sometimes allude to such requests[63] and, in meeting them, may in some cases have done their bit to protect works from being lost to us forever through the destruction or theft of books that seems to have happened from the late eighth century onwards. The proof of this lies in the Anglo-Latin works preserved in manuscripts written on the continent but then imported back into England in the later ninth, tenth and eleventh centuries.[64]

Aldhelm found imitators among his pupils, contemporaries, and in succeeding generations.[65] The diligent studying of his style—in both prose and verse—left a clear imprint, for example, on the literary products of the expatriate community in Germany.[66] From time to time, the scarcely-concealed impulse to show off is quite unmistakeable in that milieu. A particularly intriguing example is a pair of saints' Lives, celebrating the brothers Willibald and Wynnebald, composed at Heidenheim in about 778 by the Anglo-Saxon nun, Hygeburc, whose work is best-known for incorporating an account of Willibald's whistle-stop tour of the Holy Land, the so-called *Hodoeporicon*.[67] The oldest surviving manuscript of the *Vitae* (Munich, Bayerische Staatsbibliothek, clm 1086, from the late eighth or early ninth century) shows that Hygeburc hid her name in a cryptogram, only to be unmasked in 1931 in an article with the unforgettable title "Wer ist die Nonne von Heidenheim?"[68] Such coyness seems consonant with the self-deprecating qualifications Hygeburc includes in the preface to the *Vita Willibaldi*—"I, unworthy woman, the very last of those of the Saxon race to come here, and not only in years, but also in character ... as it were a weak little woman," and "I, a woman, corruptible through the frail foolishness of my sex."[69] Yet, as Peter Dronke has pointed out, the over-toppling stylistic pretensions of her prose (she had read too much Aldhelm) and her flagrant disregard for the rules of Latin morphology (she liked nouns and their matching adjectives to *rhyme* even when they should not with the correct case endings), coupled with the cryptogram, actually tell rather a different story.[70]

If there is just one other figure who can vie with the ability and range of Aldhelm and Bede, it must surely be Alcuin of York, who was born around the time of Bede's death, as if somehow the baton of scholarship were being invisibly passed on. He was an extraordinarily productive author whose works covered biblical exegesis, theology, liturgy, moral instruction, philosophy, dialectic, rhetoric, orthography, metrics, arithmetic, hagiography, and, not forgetting the things for which he is best known, some 270 letters and over 120 poems.[71] Alcuin's influence was also significant and lasting in many areas.[72] His vast surviving correspondence can easily convey the impression of a lonely old man, desperate not to be overlooked, with his repeated requests for a letter in return, or to be remembered in prayers. However, it is also the case that he wrote with a confident sense of his own influence, as teacher and advisor to many, doling out admonitions that he envisaged being read and re-read.[73] Just to pick out one well-known example, in a letter to the pupil he calls Dodo (no. lxv), having doled out a pretty stiff telling-off and then good practical advice for amendment, he says,

> whatever the quality of this letter, have it as a witness to my advice. And every time you read it through, recognize my voice speaking in your heart, and if you care about my teaching, do not shrink from reading it through often. I believe that by God's grace constancy of virtues can grow in your heart from reading it regularly.[74]

Alcuin never felt the need for the kind of lexical ostentation we find characteristic of Aldhelm, but he had his own way of showing off what he could do and what he knew. This inclination was doubtless fostered by the spirit of one-upmanship which shows itself in the verses batted to and fro by the gifted poets whom Charlemagne had drawn into his orbit,[75] among whom Alcuin seems to have been something of a queen bee, "the glory of our poets."[76] That Alcuin's ostentation could be a feather's touch compared with the heavily plosive pounding of Aldhelm's big guns, is readily shown by a brief look at just a few lines of verse, from *Carmen* xxxii, written upon returning from a visit back to England, to admonish a drunken pupil:[77]

> En tuus Albinus, saeuis ereptus ab undis,
> uenerat, altithrono nunc miserante Deo,
> te cupiens apel- peregrinis -lare camenis,
> O Corydon, Corydon, dulcis amice satis.
> Quid, quid tu uolitas per magna palatia regum,
> ut ludens pelago aliger undisono,
> qui sophiae libros primis lac ore sub annis
> suxisti et labris ubera sacra tuis?

> See now your Albinus had come back, snatched from the wild waves by the mercy of high-throned God, longing to (with poems from abroad) greet you, O Corydon, Corydon, sweet friend. Why, oh why, do you flit through the great palaces of kings like a bird on the wing playing in the wave-sounding ocean, you who from your earliest years sucked in as milk in your mouth the books of Wisdom, your lips on the holy teats?

Here, and throughout the rest of the poem, Alcuin plays about with Vergil's second *Eclogue* (from which line 4 is a direct quotation), in which the country bumpkin Corydon broods on the departure of his townie lover-boy Alexis. But he also pretends that his disembarkation from the cross-channel journey is like the end of Aeneas's epic voyage, since "saeuis ereptus ab undis" conjures up that hero's words to Dido, in Vergil's Aeneid I.596 ("adsum / Troius Aeneas, Libycis ereptus ab undis"). The deliberate splitting of the verb *apellare* by tmesis (line 3) is open to a number of different interpretations. Perhaps it is parody of the fancy word-order beloved of the likes of Aldhelm, or the stammering of an exile freshly returned from speaking his native tongue again, or simply a broken call across the noisy waves. Alcuin then moves on to allude to the biblical image of the nourishment offered by the Word, which must be tailored to the needs of each palate. Much more that is skillfully rich follows—Alcuin effectively doles out a stern message to the inebriated waster Corydon, "put to sleep by Bacchus. Naughty old Bacchus!" But the detox pill is sweetened by the prevailing humor and lightness of the poem's tone.

Although most of Alcuin's output was written after he had left England for the Continent soon after making Charlemagne's acquaintance in 781, Alcuin maintained a lively interest in the affairs of his homeland.[78] Many must have been the new impressions upon entering the Frankish court: impressions gained both from books that had not been accessible in England and from the wide circle of personal contacts which Alcuin built up and fostered. Yet in terms of outlook and attitude, it is surely fair to say that you can take the boy out of Anglo-Saxon England, but... Alcuin's writings certainly have plenty to offer the student of Old English, whether it be his witty use of the riddling tradition in a very explicitly classroom-based setting, recently highlighted by Andy Orchard,[79] or the tantalizing resonance with the Old English elegies in his most famous poem, "O mea cella." Ostensibly a lament for a beloved place or, perhaps, more accurately, for a lost era, "O mea cella" channels the emotional energy of nostalgia into emphasizing the didactic point that the love of Christ, and the hope He offers, transcends the care for material things.[80]

If Alcuin ever composed verse in Old English, it has not survived, or at any rate, not with his name on it. In fact, he is probably most famous to Anglo-Saxonists as the man supposed to have scolded the monks of Lindisfarne for enjoying their native poetry, with the words, "What has Ingeld to do with Christ?"[81] So much for our bilingual literary culture! More recent scholarship has, however, abandoned not only the notion that the letter containing this rhetorical question was addressed to Higbald, abbot and bishop of Lindisfarne, but even that it refers at all to the performance of Old English verse. Mary Garrison has deftly argued for the allusion to Ingeld as, instead, more relevant to the propagandist recitation of royal genealogies in a Mercian context.[82]

Alcuin is also famous for his poem lamenting the Vikings' sack of Lindisfarne in 793.[83] This shocking event was the start of a difficult period for Anglo-Saxon England, which caused a hiatus in the history of Anglo-Latin literature, of which very little was composed for several decades thereafter.[84] For an audience of Anglo-Saxonists, there is little need to rehearse King Alfred's own view of the perilous state of learning in England as he inherited it, or the measures that he put in place to remedy the situation. In large measure the revival of Latin learning was due to the galvanizing agency of scholars like those whose services Alfred had called in from outside his kingdom.[85] But in the tenth century, a close reading of Aldhelm's showy Latin was also one of the things which set the tone for the direction Anglo-Latin took when it began to be written again in earnest, as if to summon up the spirit of that confidently adventurous era. His writings were intensively studied, to judge from the heavily-glossed copies which survive from the tenth and eleventh centuries.[86] Scott Gwara's edition of the *De uirginitate* with all the accompanying glosses nicely lays bare the mechanisms of that intensive attention, much in the same way Nancy Porter Stork's earlier focus on one extensively-annotated manuscript containing the *Enigmata* had done.[87]

From this studying, together with other influences from northern France, grew the literary trend that has come to be known as the "hermeneutic style," first defined distinctly by Michael Lapidge—the term comes from the name for certain Greek-Latin glossaries (*hermeneumata*) which were one of the sources for the lexical enormities committed in this period.[88] Specimens of this style are marked by their ostentatious use of Greek loanwords, Latin archaisms, polysyllabic coinages, and the like, producing texts which, at their most extreme, tax the reader considerably, sometimes defying interpretation altogether. Combined, these elements certainly make clear that learned culture in England had risen again to its full potential, like a glittering phoenix from the ashes of the ninth century. Some of these authors stretched Latin to its limits (to the breaking-point, some might say), experimenting, borrowing and blending, enjoying words and the ability to play about with them, striving for a high tone: like Aldhelm, one might say, though in truth his tenth-century imitators were in some cases significantly heavier-handed than their model. What was the intention behind such stuff: sheer enjoyment of acquired competence, a striving for high art, exclusivity, or simply the wish to show off?

It is worth looking at few examples, from the two places, Canterbury and Winchester, where learned culture probably reached the highest levels in the tenth century. The first comes from the prose preface to the versification of the Life of St Wilfrid of Ripon, whose relics were stolen and taken to Canterbury in 948. Supposedly by Oda, archbishop of Canterbury (941–58), who had overseen the "translation" of the relics, the prefatory letter may well have been composed by the author of the epic poem (just under 1400 lines long) that then follows, commissioned from a Frankish scholar named Frithegod, who was active in Canterbury at this time.

> Igitur uenerabillimas beati confessoris Christi Wilfridi reliquias indecenti senticosae uoraginis situ marcidas, immo, quod dictu quoque meticulosum est, praelatorum <u>horripilatione</u> neglectas, cum inde, fauente Deo, scilicet a loco sepulchri eius, quidam transtulissent, reuerenter excepi, atque intra ambitum metropolitanae, cui gratia Dei praesideo, ecclesiae collocaui ... Itaque tantae tamque Deo

dignae affinitatis delectatus uicinitate, et editiore eas entheca decusare, et excerptis de libro uitae eius flosculis, nouo opere pretium duxi carmine uenustare ... Porro acerbae ceruicositatis aporias, iniectaeque deperationis angilogias intrito uniuersalitatis epithemate, et ambrosio dictionalitatis collemate indulcabo, ringens cum giganticida Domino, "ego in Domino speraui."[89]

Therefore when certain persons brought the venerablest relics of the blessed confessor of Christ Wilfrid, which were mouldering in an unbefitting site of a thornous abyss, nay rather—which is also awe-full to tell—neglected by the horripilation of the men-at-the-top, thence, by God's favor, to wit from the place of his tomb, I received them reverently, and placed them within the confines of the metropolitical church, over which by the grace of God, I preside ... Therefore, delighting in the proximity of such a great intimacy, and so worthy of God, I had taken the trouble both to englorify them with a more lofty "cerceuil" [coffin] and to beautify them in song, with blossomettes plucked from the book of his life ... Furthermore, I shall ensweeten the "épreuves" [trials] of hard neck-bendery, and the "anguisheries" of additional plunderment with the rubbed-in "poultice" of universality, and the ambrosial "bétonnerie" [cement] of dictionary-speak, snarling out to the Lord with the giganticide [i.e. David]: "I have trusted in the Lord!"

I hope that the affected pomposity of the Latin will be evident from my deliberately eccentric translation. At times the polysyllabic texture of the diction becomes almost overwhelming, for example in the final sentence of the passage quoted above. One can pick out grecisms (*entheca*, *aporias*, *epithema*, *collema*), of which two (along with the invented verb *decusare*) can be traced to one particularly influential gold-mine for would-be bombasts, book 3 of the early tenth-century poem by Abbo of Saint-Germain-des-Prés, *Bella Parisiacae Urbis*, studied and glossed in England.[90] The word *angilogias* represents a hybrid, bolting a greek suffix on to a Latin stem; and then one can but admire the piled-up syllables of the abstract nouns *horripilatio*, *affinitas*, *uicinitas*, *ceruicositas*, *deperatio*, *uniuersalitas*, and *dictionalitas*, gleaned from various sources or made up on the spot and wrapped around each other in different combinations.

Now consider a couple of samples from the poem itself, in the first of which Frithegod describes Wilfrid as a boy, and in the second recounts the saint's decision not to be detained in France on the way to Rome:[91]

Iam quia mellito dulcescit nectare gutur,
prosequar arguta iuuenem modulando cicuta.
Hic membris etenim compto glaucomate firmis,
aequeuos habitu studuit superare uenusto,
nil puerile gerens, facundae munia linguae
aspirante Deo gestis explebat apertis.
at perfecta uirum postquam perfecerat aetas,
natales statuit functa genitrice penates
linquere, et assiduis Domino famularier horis.

tiro dehinc agilis, uoti non immemor, infit:
"ardent excoctis fibrarum omenta laternis
abdita, conceptis dum detrahor, optime, uotis.
Thetis cur tumidas Zephiro minitante saliuas
expetii? Frustra me saeua Salatia pressit,
cosmica si spreto repetam contagia Christo.
Sedis apostolicae uiso primum cliothedro
aeria merear si longule uescier aura,
te, pater, ex animo soboles deuota, uidebo."

Now since the throat sweetens up with honeyed nectar I shall pursue the youth, playing on my trilling hemlock-pipe. For he with sturdy limbs, and tidy "nuagerie" (or "violetterie") strove to outdo his peers with their glamorous garb; doing nothing infantile, he executed the offices of an eloquent tongue, by God's in-breathing, in his public deeds. And after completed years had made him a man complete, his mater deceased, he determined to relinquish his natal household gods, and to serve Ye Lord with regular hours.

Henceforth the agile tyro, not unmindful of his scheme, quoth: "the hidden membranes of my entrails burn with well-baked lamps, O best one, so long as I delay the schemes I conceived. Why did I seek out the spittle of Neptune's daughter tumid with Zephyr's menace? In vain Neptune's brute wife has pressed upon me, if I return to the infections "du monde" having spurned Christ. Having once gazed upon the "siege-célèbre" of the apostolic see, if I deserve to enjoy Ye aery airs for the littlest bit longer, you, father, shall I see, offspring devoted in heart."

The diction offers a sprinkling of grecisms (here *cicuta*, *glaucomate*, *cosmica*, *cliothedro*), and references to Classical mythology (*Thetis*, *Zephyro*, *Salatia*), to name a few, but it should be evident that there is also something extraordinarily oblique about Frithegod's manner of expression. Of all the known specimens of tenth-century Anglo-Latin, Frithegod's poem offers the most sustained challenge to the reader. The editor Campbell did not offer a translation, there is not yet one in print, and it is easy to see why, considering that some lines of the poem leave one utterly bereft of even the beginnings of an explanation—a choice example being the sentence "extorres statuunt agio incassum palinodo / quos sacer electis gradibus formarat adelphos / dulsos coenosi lichinos audititidestos" (lines 1116–18), where the last word seems, if anything, to be a corruption (yet is present in what may have been a copy annotated by the author himself).[92] Arguably to translate the *Breuiloquium* into English would be to miss the point of Frithegod, where content seems truly to take second place to form.

Now on to Winchester, and to a poem composed by Bishop Æthelwold's chaplain, Godeman, who in about 973 wrote one of Anglo-Saxon England's most lavishly illuminated manuscripts, the Benedictional of Æthelwold (now in the British Library, Addit. 49598). The style was clearly meant to be the literary equivalent of the gold-leaf capitals in which it was written.

> quemdam subiectum monachum circos quoque multos
> in hoc precepit fieri libro bene comptos,
> completos quoque agalmatibus uariis decoratis
> multigenis miniis pulchris necnon simul auro
> craxare hunc sibi prescriptis fecit boanerges
> idcirco ut soteris populum in biblo potuisset
> sanctificare ....

> he instructed a certain monk under his rule to make many very elegant markings in this book also accompanied by various decorated "dessins" with manifold beautiful "rouges" and also gold the Son of Thunder had this stylussed in aforementioned fashion so that he might sanctify the people in this "livre du Sauveur."

For us, this is peculiar stuff, maybe off-putting to the taste of some, like Liberace at his piano. Yet it was too prevalent to be an isolated eccentricity, and we have to accept this style of writing as an important facet of the Anglo-Saxon literary aesthetic. These poems may seem restricted to an elitist intellectual world, trumpeting arcanely to a tiny audience, like donnish chortlings at a caricature Oxbridge high table. But in the article which first defined this style of Latin, Michael Lapidge drew attention to another context wherein comparable literary ambition found its expression, namely Anglo-Saxon royal diplomas, which on the face of it one might have expected to see as work-a-day formulaic documents, recording a grant of land or privileges to an individual or an institution.[93] Even before the *Breuiloquium* was a twinkle in Frithegod's eye, the charter draftsman known as "Æthelstan A," who produced a stream of documents through King Æthelstan's reign (924–39), was strutting his stuff, just to say that the king makes his gift because over-love of perishable material things leads to hell, whereas giving them away buys heaven:[94]

> Fortuna fallentis saeculi procax non lacteo immarcescibilium liliorum candore amabilis, sed fellita heiulandae corruptionis amaritudine odibilis, foetentis filios valle in lacrimarum carnis rictibus debacchando venenosis mordaciter dilacerat; quae quamvis arridendo sit infelicibus adtractabilis Acherontici ad ima Cocyti, ni satus alti subveniat boantis, impudenter est decurribilis; et ideo quia ipsa ruinosa deficiendo tanaliter dilabitur, summopere festinandum est ad amoena indicibilis laetitiae arva, ubi angelica ymnidicae iubilationis organa, mellifluaque vernantium rosarum odoramina a bonis beatisque naribus inestimabiliter dulcia capiuntur, sineque calce auribus clivipparum suavia audiuntur; cuius amore felicitatis illectus, fastidiunt iam infima, dulcescunt superna, eisque pro percipiendis semperque specie indefectiva fruendis, ego Æðelstanus rex Anglorum ....

> The wanton fortune of this fallacious world, not lovable with the milky whiteness of unwitherable lilies but hateful with the gall-steeped bitterness of lamentable decay, in a wild rage tears bitingly with poisonous jaws at the sons of the stinking flesh in this vale of tears; although with her false smiles she can entice the unblessed down to the depths of Acherontic Cocytus, if the seed of the High-thundering One does not intervene, she is shamelessly slippery; and so because she slithers off in fashion "fatale," by sliding down into a ruinous wreck, we should most especially hasten towards the pleasant pastures of inexpressible joy, where the angelical instruments of hymnodic jubilation and the honey-laden odors of fresh-grown roses, unguessably sweet, are caught by good and blessed nostrils, and without end the lovely sounds of the "clivippae" are heard in their ears [or lovely things are heard by the ears of the "clivippae"]; drawn by love of the blessed estate – now base things sicken, heavenly things sweeten – and for the sake of acquiring the latter and enjoying their undiminishable beauty for ever, I Æthelstan, king of the English ....

It is impossible to convey adequately in English, even with the most eccentric of translations, all of the alliteration and rhyme, the extensive use of interlaced noun-adjective pairs, not to mention the pompous polysyllabic texture of this passage. There is not space here for the kind of extended commentary it warrants, but worthy of note, for example, are Classical references (to two of the rivers of the underworld, Acheron and Cocytus) used to refer to hell, the extremely rare form *tanaliter*, an adverb possibly based upon the Greek word *thanatos* (death),[95] as well as the mysterious *clivipparum* which still awaits its doubtless coruscatingly brilliant decoder. The same draftsman followed this up with a fierce sanction, or anathema, a standard feature of diplomas, by which a curse was laid on anyone presuming to meddle with the terms of the grant. Here it is, in a particularly ambitious rendition:[96]

> Si autem, quod absit, aliquis typo supercilii turgens hanc mee emptionis ac confirmationis breuiculam elidere uel infringere temptauerit, sciat se nouissima ac tremenda concionis die classica archangeli clangente bucina, somatibus tetra postponentibus poliandria, cum Iuda impie proditionis compilatore, infaustis quoque Iudeis Christum ore sacrilego ara in crucis blasphemantibus, eterna confusione, edacibus fauillantium tormentorum ignibus, sine fine poenaliter arsurum.
>
> If anybody—which heaven forfend!—o'erblown with the "orgueuil" of arrogance has tried to break or weaken this little note of my transaction and confirmation, let him know that on the very last and terrible day of assembly, when the archangel's battle-trumpet blares, when the "cadavres" turn away from their noisome "tombeaux," along with Judas the perpetrator of wicked treachery and the ill-starred Jews who blasphemed Christ with sacrilegious lips on the altar of the cross, in everlasting dismay he will burn punishingly without end in the voracious fires of hot-glowing tortures.

Again there is alliteration, interlaced word-order, a preference for pompous vocabulary, including the grecisms *typhos* (pride), *buccina*, *soma* (body), and *polyandrion* (cemetery). With the phrase "classica archangeli clangente buccina," the draftsman gives away the likely source of inspiration for his ostentatious style, since Aldhelm was particularly fond of the multiple possibilities for referring onomatopoeically to trumpets; for example, in his *Carmen de uirginitate*, "salpix classica clangit" (line 1549), but also "clangente euangelica bucina," in the prose *De uirginitate* c. 21. Although in many ways this particular draftsman was a particularly gifted one-off, both before him (even in the later ninth century) and throughout the tenth century, charters continued to be a showcase for significant talent, exhibiting specimens of carefully-crafted Latin. "Æthelstan A" and others like him appear to have used the same broad outline for the text of charter more than once, perhaps for several different documents produced in the same year, even in the same week. Thus, we end up with something extremely rare in Anglo-Latin (or for that matter Old English), namely successive re-performances of roughly the same composition, in which one can see the draftsman subtly altering the odd phrase here and there, substituting synonyms and the like.[97] Quite another can of worms is opened up by asking the question of how such ostentatious pieces of Latin relate to the physical act of making the grant in the presence of witnesses (was the pompous Latin read aloud with much rolling of r's, not to mention eyes?), and who was meant to be impressed by it. To revert to our theme of bilingual literary culture, another matter of great interest is the fact that diplomas such as S 425, discussed above, pass unfalteringly from Latin to Old English (for describing the boundaries which define the land being granted) and back again.

Even though widely espoused, this richly poetic style may not have been everybody's cup of tea. It was at its height of popularity when Ælfric of Eynsham was active. Everything he strove for seems to fly in the face of a literary trend that can only have been accessible to a learned clique. One wonders which was more representative of contemporary taste and attitude – Ælfric, who was a pupil of Bishop Æthelwold at Winchester, or Godman, Æthelwold's chaplain; simple but elegant utility or grandiose display. Here and there in the prefaces to his writings, Ælfric passed comment upon the necessity to cultivate "not obscure words but plain English" (nec obscura ... verba, sed simplicem Anglicam) and to avoid "garrulous verbosity and unfamiliar diction" (garrula verbositate aut ignotis sermonibus). He also observed, most tellingly, that his own motivation was a desire "rather to profit the listeners through straightforward expression than to be praised for the composition of an artificial style, which our simplicity has by no means mastered."[98] Such sentiments, not least because of the clear nod in the direction of Aldhelm (recall that "garrula uerbositas" was his own cheery description of his style), can easily be interpreted as a gentle rebuke to the practitioners of an inflatedly baroque Latin style.

That said, as Michael Lapidge has observed, it may then seem contradictory that specimens of the style can be found fairly close to home:[99] the Latin translation of the Anglo-Saxon Chronicle by Ælfric's powerful lay patron, Æthelweard, offers very many examples of unusual Latin words and grecisms in the manful quest for variation.[100] One might argue that

Æthelweard would have every justification for wanting to show off his knowledge of Greek words in particular, if we accept Lapidge's conjecture that he may have learnt them—especially some rather specialised naval terminology—directly from a Greek bishop, Nikephoros (alias Sigewold), living in exile in England.[101] Ælfric's pupil, Ælfric Bata also evinced an interest in passing on to his own pupils not only some wicked lavatorial humor, but also an enthusiasm for recondite vocabulary. Of the two sets of often hilarious classroom colloquies that he composed sometime in the early eleventh century, the second set, his *Colloquia Difficiliora* (Harder Colloquies), incorporates some fairly florid diction, including a wonderful encapsulation of the sheer enjoyment of stretching Latin to its limits: "O diligibillime scolastice, heri nos lusitauimus ad inuicem latialibus rematibus" (Oh, most belovedest scholar! Yesterday we both played about together avec les mots de Latium).[102]

Lapidge suggested that perhaps the trend for using *obscura verba* was so influential that, however vigorous he may have been, Ælfric remained a lone and unattended voice of sanity, to which even those closest to him paid no attention. One might also think in terms of a significant difference of agenda: as the years went by Ælfric became increasingly concerned with the need to offer accessible orthodox teaching and the popularity, and thus preservation, of his work allows us to see him going about that very practical task.[103] If you have an urgent message you are desperate to communicate, there is little point in shouting it in "double dutch." On the other hand, while the ostentation of some Latin works that display a florid style had an arguably utilitarian function as propaganda, intended specifically to impress (thinking, for example, of Frithegod's *Breuiloquium* and the charters drafted by "Æthelstan A," or Godeman's poem in the Benedictional of Æthelwold), others can only have been composed for the sheer unbridled pleasure of being able to do so. These were intended for the plaudits of a like-minded audience, whose attention was far from millennial fears, the correction of sin, or the like: this might apply, for example, to the poems Michael Lapidge first published in 1972, as the products of Æthelwold's school at Winchester, or Dunstan's intentionally challenging acrostic, "O pater omnipotens."[104] As with Aldhelm, the ostentatious style thus becomes part of the message being conveyed by such texts, indeed sometimes the primary one.

An interesting challenge is to come up with something in Old English that shares the same show-off vein as this kind of ornate Latin. One particular name comes to mind: Byrhtferth, monk of Ramsey (in the

Fens), an almost exact contemporary of Ælfric. Like Aldhelm and Bede, Byrhtferth and Ælfric were chalk and cheese. Byrhtferth was an enthusiastic exponent of ostentatious Latin, of which his tour-de-force was a *Vita* of St. Ecgwine (bishop of Worcester, d. *circa* 717), written just after the year 1000.[105] Little is known about Ecgwine—indeed Byrhtferth himself knew hardly anything, but did not let that put him off. The eccentric *Vita* is full of red herrings, paraded learning, and high-spirited capering through the Latin language—Byrhtferth was an attentive student of Aldhelm's writings, sprinkling grecisms and coinages liberally, some of them borrowed directly from the master. Rather ironically, Lapidge has shown that Byhrtferth's stylistic pretension outstripped his grasp of some aspects of Latin grammar, so that solecisms (notably a dire confusion between the passive and active infinitive) almost vie with grecisms on the page.[106]

Here is the opening of the *Vita*—comically enough, Byrhtferth called it his "epilogus"—and again I hope that my translation conveys a little of the flavor. It is very eccentric, both in content and style—verbiage for verbiage's sake, to sound deeply learned.

> INCIPIT EPILOGVS VITAE ECGWINI EPISCOPI ET CONFESSORIS. Cum furor saeuus imperatoris Chaldaici regni innocuos detruderet uiros flammis, que gloria illis? Tum gymnosophiste sagaci mente ludebant et, uelut in gymnasio constituti, lusibus plaudebant, ymnizantes cum triumpho Deo, sollerter opera eius ad laudem prouocantes. Quid uerax euuangelice relationis tetrarcha? Nonne ymeneos despexit et Pathmos dilexit? Cumque in hac quiem haberet quanta inibi in oromate conspexit, quis urbana fretus eloquentia potest pleniter inuestigare? Nichil contulit cursus Nemroth uagus per mundi clymata sancte ecclesie, nec magna scientia Stoicorum et philosophorum, nec aurea facundia Omeri; sed peruigilis custodis fidelium animarum Gregorii antistitis Romulee urbis dicta uel facta inedicibiliter proficuerunt, ceterorumque heroicorum uirorum quorum sollicitudine totus orbis extat decoratus uelud supernus aer densis ornatus stellis, quem aureus sol et uaga lucina perornant, diuidentes mundum quadratum communi lege. Denique, cum quietorum perspicerem uirorum sollicitudinem, cogitaui sagaciter quid Deo muneris quiuissem offerri; et hec cogitans statim inrupi in uitam pretiosi uiri Ecgwini, qui tertius fuisse presul in regione Merciorum dinoscitur et primus abbas loci ipsius qui dicitur Eoueshamm.

> HERE BEGINS THE EPILOGUE OF THE LIFE OF ECGWINE, BISHOP AND CONFESSOR. When the savage rage of the emperor of the Chaldean kingdom thrust the harmless men into the flames, what glory was in it for them? Then "les philosophes-nus" [naked philosophers] with wise mind made merry and as if in a "gymnase," clapped their hands in their merriment, singing hymns of triumph to God, carefully proclaimed His works to his praise. What about the truthful tetrarch of the evangelic story? [i.e., John the Evangelist] Did he not despise "les noces" [i.e., marriage] and love Pathmos? Which person, relying on urbane eloquence can fully discern what great things he saw in his "rêve" [dream]? The course of wandering Nemroth across "les frontières" of the world brought no benefit to the church, nor the great wisdom of the Stoics and philosophers, nor the golden fluency of Homer; but the words and deeds of the ever-watchful guardian of faithful souls, Gregory bishop of the Romulean city, were inexpressibly beneficial, and also those of the other heroic men by whose care the whole world is decorated like the upper air is dotted with dense stars, which the golden sun and wandering Lucina [the moon] adorn, dividing the four-square world by a common law. So then, when I gazed upon the care of men now at rest, I wisely thought out what gift I might offer [actually he writes, "I might be offered"] to God; and thinking upon this on a sudden I broke in upon the life of the precious man Ecgwine, who is denoted as third bishop of the Mercians and first abbot of this same place which is called Evesham.

And here at last we may have hit upon an author for whom we have surviving work that yokes up a two-horse chariot, for Byrhtferth's Enchiridion is a marvelous rag-bag of arithmetic, theology, and grammar written in 1011, in a mixture of Latin and English.[107] If we then ask whether there is any carry-over of his ornately obscure Latin into Byrhtferth's Old English, the answer seems to be in the affirmative. Malcolm Godden, in assessing Byrhtferth's Old English observes, "the combination of exaggerated word-play, poetic and esoteric vocabulary, extravagant imagery and extensive intermingling of Latin words, produces the most extreme case of high style in Old English prose, matching the extravagance of the same author's Latin prose."[108] Like Aldhelm, as well as being a profoundly gifted scholar, Byrhtferth was a bit of a show-off and a genuine eccentric, but in him we seem to meet an embodiment of Orchard's bilingual textual culture.

NOTES

[1] Charles-Edwards, ed., *After Rome*, pp. 191–219.

[2] Greenfield and Calder, eds., *A New Critical History of Old English Literature*, pp. 5–37. The survey is reprinted in a slightly revised form under the title, "Anglo-Latin Literature," in the first volume of Lapidge's collected essays, *ALL 600–899*, pp. 1–35.

[3] *Fontes Anglo-Saxonici: A Register of Written Sources used by Anglo-Saxon Authors*, accessible online at http://fontes.english.ox.ac.uk.

[4] Lapidge, *The Anglo-Saxon Library*.

[5] The correspondence can be read in the edition by Tangl, *Die Briefe des Heiligen Bonifatius und Lullus*, Epistolae Selectae 1. Selected letters were also translated by Emerton, trans., *The Letters of Saint Boniface* (1940); reprinted with an introduction and bibliography by T. F. X. Noble (2000).

[6] See Peter Dronke, *Women Writers of the Middle Ages* (Cambridge: Cambridge University Press, 1984), pp. 30–33; A. Classen, "Frauenbriefe an Bonifatius: Frühmittelalterliche Literaturdenkmäler aus literarischer Sicht," *Archiv für Kulturgeschichte* 72 (1990): 251–73; Schaefer, "Two Women in Need of a Friend," pp. 491–524; and Orchard, "Old Sources, New Resources," pp. 15–38.

[7] For a full survey, see M. Lapidge and R. C. Love, "The Latin Hagiography of England and Wales," III.203–325.

[8] I follow here the useful summary of vernacular hagiography by Gordon Whatley, "Late Old English Hagiography, ca. 950–1150," in *Hagiographies: International History of the Latin and Vernacular Hagiographical Literature in the West from its Origins to 1550*, ed. G. Philippart, 4 vols. (Turnhout: Brepols, 1994–2006) II, 429–99.

[9] M. Swanton, ed., "A Fragmentary Life of St. Mildred and Other Kentish Royal Saints," *Archaeologia Cantiana* 9 (1975): 15–27; and see the discussion of these fragments by Stephanie Hollis, "The Minster-in-Thanet Foundation Story," *ASE* 27 (1998): 41–64; and in my *Goscelin of Saint-Bertin*, pp. xxx–xxxii and cv–cvi.

[10] A measured assessment of the situation, earlier interpreted as simple Norman antagonism to saints with outlandish names, is given by Ridyard, "Condigna Veneratio," pp. 179–206; and see also Paul Hayward, "Translation Narratives in Post-Conquest Hagiography," pp. 73–85.

[11] Love, ed. and trans., *Three Eleventh-Century Anglo-Latin Saints' Lives*, pp. 50–89.

[12] Love, ed. and trans., *Three Eleventh-Century Anglo-Latin Saints' Lives*, pp. cxvii–cxix.

[13] Lapidge and Winterbottom, eds., *The Early Lives of Dunstan*.

[14] Winterbottom and Thomson, eds. and trans., *William of Malmesbury*, pp. xviii–xx.

[15] Osbern, *Vita S. Dunstani* c. 1, p. 70; and Winterbottom and Thomson, eds. and trans, *William of Malmesbury*, pp. 168–69 (Book I, Prol. 7).

[16] Orchard, "Enigma Variations," I.284–304.

[17] See, for example, the detailed study of one particular extensively glossed tenth-century manuscript by Porter Stork, *Through a Gloss Darkly*.

[18] For some thoughts about the role of these Riddles, see D. K. Smith, "Humour in Hiding: Laughter Between the Sheets in the Exeter Book Riddles," in *Humour in Anglo-Saxon Literature*, ed. Jonathan Wilcox (Cambridge: CUP, 2000), pp. 79–98.

[19] Glorie, ed., *Collectiones Aenigmatum Merovingicae Aetatis*, I.143–208.

[20] *Enigma* XVI, CCSL 133, p. 183.

[21] *Enigmata* V, "De membrano," and VI, "De penna," CCSL 133, pp. 172–73; XXVIII, "De incude," p. 195; XXIX "De mensa," p. 196; and XXXVIII, "De carbone" p. 205.

[22] *Enigma* XIII, "De acu pictili," CCSL 133, p. 180.

[23] *Enigmata* II, "De spe, fide et caritate," and III, "De historia et sensu et morali et allegoria," CCSL 133, pp. 169–70; and XXV, "De superbia," p. 192.

[24] The most accessible assessments of Aldhelm's career and writings remain those provided in the introductions to Lapidge and Herren, trans., *Aldhelm: The Prose Works*; Lapidge and Rosier, trans., *Aldhelm: The Poetic Works*; see also Lapidge's entry on Aldhelm in *WBEASE*, pp. 27–29.

[25] He makes this claim in his long composite treatise known as the *Epistola ad Acircium*, in the section entitled, "De pedum regulis," c. 142, MGH, AA 15, p. 201; and Lapidge and Herren, trans., *Aldhelm: The Prose Works*, p. 45: "no one born of the offspring of our race and nourished in the cradles of a Germanic people has toiled so mightily in a pursuit of this sort before our humble self."

[26] The evidence was first laid out by Lapidge in the article, "Aldhelm's Latin Poetry and Old English Verse," pp. 249–314. Andy Orchard then extended the range of the question and provided a good deal of detailed analysis in *The Poetic Art of Aldhelm*, especially chapter 3.

[27] William of Malmesbury, *Gesta Pontificum Anglorum* V.190, ed. and trans. M. Winterbottom, with R. M. Thomson, OMT (2007), I.506–07: "Filled full of letters as he was, he did not neglect the poetry of his native tongue either. Indeed, as we are told in the book by Alfred I mentioned before, no one has ever in any age rivalled him in the ability to write poetry in English, to compose songs, and to recite or sing them as occasion demanded. For instance, Alfred relates that Aldhelm was the author of a popular song still current today."

[28] Remley, "Aldhelm as Old English Poet," I.90–108.

[29] Cf., for example, the observation made by Clare Lees and Gillian Overing, *Double Agents: Women and Clerical Culture in Anglo-Saxon England* (Philadelphia, PA: University of Pennsylvania Press, 2001), at p. 115: "Such a structure ... remains buried beneath the inscrutable workings of Aldhelm's rhetorical wizardry."

[30] Orchard, *The Poetic Art of Aldhelm*, p. 15.

[31] "propriae disputationis verbosa garrulitas aut garrula verbositas." Ehwald, ed., "De uirginitate," c. 19, MGH, AA 15, p. 249; Lapidge and Herren, *Aldhelm: The Prose Works*, p. 76.

[32] Ehwald, ed., "De uirginitate," c. 2, MGH, AA 15, p. 230; Lapidge and Herren, *Aldhelm: The Prose Works*, p. 60.

[33] These observations about spiritual and corporeal virginity come in the very opening inscription to his female addressees, and thus seem crucial to unlocking Aldhelm's message: "To the most reverend virgins of Christ ... to be celebrated not only for the distinction of corporeal chastity, which is the achievement of many, but also to be glorified on account of their spiritual purity, which is the achievement of few." Ehwald, ed., "De uirginitate," c. 2, MGH, AA 15, p. 228; Lapidge and Herren, trans., *Aldhelm: The Prose Works*, p. 59.

[34] Ehwald, ed., "Epistola V," MGH, AA 15, pp. 488–89. Lapidge and Herren, trans., *Aldhelm: The Prose Works*, pp. 160–61, with some modifications.

[35] F. E. Warren, *The Antiphonary of Bangor*, 2 vols., Henry Bradshaw Society 4 and 10 (London, 1893–95); and M. Curran, *The Antiphonary of Bangor and the Early Irish Monastic Liturgy* (Dublin, 1984), pp. 81–82 (on the hymn "Audite pantes ta erga").

[36] J. H. Jenkinson, ed., *The Hisperica Famina* (Cambridge: Cambridge University Press, 1908); and Herren, ed. and trans., *The Hisperica Famina I: The A-Text* [with discussion of "pantes," p. 139]; on locating the *Hisperica Famina* see Stevenson, "Bangor and the *Hisperica Famina*," pp. 202–16; and further contextualization by Orchard, "The *Hisperica Famina* as Literature," pp. 1–40.

[37] Winterbottom, "Aldhelm's Prose Style and its Origins," p. 40.

[38] Prose "De uirginitate," c. 2, MGH, AA 15, p. 229 ("cumque singulos epistolarum textus recitans pernicibus pupillarum obtutibus specularer atque naturali quadam, ut mihi insitum fertur, latentium rerum curiositate contemplarer..."). Lapidge and Herren, trans., *Aldhelm: The Prose Works*, p. 59 lightly modified.

[39] Ehwald, ed., "Carmina rhythmica," MGH, AA 15, pp. 524–28; Lapidge and Rosier, trans., *Aldhelm: The Poetic Works*, pp. 177–79.

[40] Orchard, *The Poetic Art of Aldhelm*, pp. 54–60; *Altus Prosator* can be found in C. Blume, ed., *Analecta Hymnica Medii Aevi* 51 (Leipzig: Fues, 1908), pp. 271–83; and with a translation in T. O. Clancy and G. Márkus, *Iona: the Earliest Poetry of a Celtic Monastery* (Edinburgh: Edinburgh University Press, 1995); and see the very full discussion of it by J. Stevenson, "Altus Prosator," *Celtica* 23 (1999): 326–70.

[41] Winterbottom, "Aldhelm's Prose Style and its Origins."

[42] Winterbottom and Thomson, eds., *Gesta pontificum Anglorum*, V.189.3: "Defitientibusque necessariis, scolares in discipulatum accepit, ut eorum liberalitate tenuitatem uictus corrigeret. Illi procedente tempore, magistri sequaces, ex scolaribus monachi effecti, in conuentum non exiguum coaluere. Horum exemplo et consortio Aldelmus informatus ad studium, liberales artes plenitudini scientiae adiecit."

[43] Ehwald, ed., "Epistola V," MGH, AA 15, pp. 488–94; Lapidge and Herren, trans., *Aldhelm: The Prose Works*, pp. 160–64.

[44] Bede, *Historia ecclesiastica*, IV.2.

[45] Ehwald, ed., "Epistola V," MGH, AA 15, p. 493; Lapidge and Herren, trans., *Aldhelm: The Prose Works*, p. 163. His "Epistola III" similarly seems to scorn Irish scholarship for being misdirected; see Ehwald, ed., "Epistola III," MGH, AA 15, p. 479; Lapidge and Herren, trans., *Aldhelm: The Prose Works*, pp. 154–55.

[46] Lapidge and Herren, *Aldhelm: The Prose Works*, p. 163: "Why, I ask, is Ireland, whither assemble the thronging students by the fleet-load, exalted with a sort of ineffable privilege, as if here in the fertile soil of Britain, teachers who are citizens of Greece and Rome cannot be found?"

[47] Ehwald, ed., "Epistola III," MGH, AA 15, pp. 479–80; Lapidge and Herren, trans., *Aldhelm: The Prose Works*, pp. 154–55.

[48] Lapidge and Herren, *Aldhelm: The Prose Works*, p. 155

[49] Lapidge, "The Career of Aldhelm," pp. 15–69; he also lays out the evidence for the link between Aldhelm, Iona and Vergil in, Lapidge, "Aldhelm and the Epinal-Erfurt Glossary," in *Aldhelm and Sherborne*, pp. 129–63.

[50] Brown, "Bede the Educator," (1996), p. 1.

[51] For accounts of the achievements of these two men, see the Jarrow Lectures which focused upon them: Fletcher, *Benedict Biscop* (1981), and Wood, *The Most Holy Abbot Ceolfrid* (1995); and see the assessment of Bede's library in Lapidge, *Anglo-Saxon Library*, pp. 34–37 and 191–228.

[52] Sharpe, "The Varieties of Bede's Prose," pp. 339–55.

[53] See the list of translated texts in the bibliography below, and the recent collection of essays edited by DeGregorio, *Innovation and Tradition in the Writings of the Venerable Bede*.

[54] *Historia ecclesiastica*, V.24 ("meae meorumque necessitati ex opusculis uenerabilium patrum breuiter adnotare ... curaui").

[55] Roger Ray, "Who Did Bede Think He Was?" in DeGregorio, *Innovation and Tradition in the Writings of the Venerable Bede*, pp. 11–35.

[56] In addition to Ray's article just cited, see also, Scott DeGregorio, "Footsteps of His Own: Bede's Commentary on Ezra-Nehemiah," in the same volume, pp. 143–68.

[57] Sharpe, "The Varieties of Bede's Prose," pp. 343–50.

[58] See the tables presented in "The Varieties of Bede's Prose," pp. 352–53.

[59] Winterbottom, "Aldhelm's Prose Style and Its Origins," p. 45.

[60] For a discussion of poetic diction in Anglo-Latin, see Lapidge, "Poeticism in Pre-Conquest Anglo-Latin Prose," pp. 321–37.

[61] "Epistola de obitu Baedae" in Colgrave and Mynors, eds. and trans., *Bede's Ecclesiastical History*, pp. 582–83.

[62] In Letters 75 and 76 Boniface asks Archbishop Ecgbert and then Hwætberht, abbot of Wearmouth-Jarrow, for copies of Bede's works (ibid., pp. 158–59) and Letter 91 again asks Ecgbert for Bede's homilies and commentary on Proverbs (p. 207); in Letter 71, Lul asks Dealwine for "any works of Aldhelm, whether prose or metrical or rhythmical" (p. 144); in Letter 125 he asks Coena,

archbishop of York, for Bede's commentaries on I Samuel, Ezra, Nehemiah, and on the Gospel of Mark (p. 263); in Letter 126 he asks Gutberht, abbot of Wearmouth-Jarrow, for Bede's "De templo," his commentary on the Song of Songs and his book of epigrams; Gutberht's reply, with a copy of "De templo," follows immediately (pp. 264–65).

[63] Bugga mentions the "the passions of the martyrs which you asked to be sent to you," in Letter 15 (ibid., p. 27); in Letter 116, Abbot Gutberht sends Lul Bede's prose and verse *Vitae* of Cuthbert and promises further works (pp. 251–52); Letter 124, Archbishop Coena responds to a query about a shipment of books (p. 261).

[64] A list of these manuscripts of continental origin is provided by Lapidge as Appendix D of his *The Anglo-Saxon Library*, pp. 167–73.

[65] For an assessment of the influence of Aldhelm's poetry, see Orchard, *The Poetic Art of Aldhelm*, ch. 5.

[66] Orchard, "Old Sources, New Resources," shows the extent of the debt to Aldhelm.

[67] T. Tobler and A. Molinier, eds., *Itinera Hierosolymitana et Descriptiones Terrae Sanctae* (Geneva: J. G. Fick, 1879), I.243–81; Holder-Egger, ed., "Vita SS. Willibaldi et Wynnebaldi," MGH, Scriptores 15.1, pp. 86–106; partly translated in Talbot, *The Anglo-Saxon Missionaries in Germany*.

[68] B. Bischoff, "Wer ist die Nonne von Heidenheim?" *Studien und Mitteilungen zur Geschichte des Benediktinerordens* 49 (1931): 387–88.

[69] "ego indigna Saxonica de gente, istinc venientium novissima, et non solum annis, sed etiam moribus ... quasi homuncula;" and "ego femina fragilique sexus imbecillitate corruptibilis." Holder-Egger, ed., "Vita SS. Willibaldi et Wynnebaldi," MGH, Scriptores 15.1, p. 86.

[70] Dronke, *Women Writers of the Middle Ages*, pp. 33–35. For a detailed analysis of Hygeburc's flouting of the rules of Latin morphology, see E. Gottschaller, *Hugeburc von Heidenheim: philologische Untersuchungen zu den Heiligenbiographien einer Nonne des achten Jahrhunderts* (Munich: Arbeo-Gesellschaft, 1973).

[71] For a comprehensive list of Alcuin's works, including those now lost, see the entry by Lockett in *Compendium Auctorum Latinorum Medii Aevi*, I.2, pp. 145–53; the list certainly makes Aldhelm's list, on p. 154 of the same fascicule, seem puny.

[72] An assessment of Alcuin's modern reputation, as well as of his immediately posthumous one, forms the early section of Bullough's detailed study, *Alcuin: Achievement and Reputation*; on p. 12 he cites Ludwig Traube as having claimed in the late nineteenth century that Alcuin "became and long remained the intellectual leader of Europe."

[73] Bullough cautions against assuming that Alcuin's view of himself and the importance of his advice projected in his letters was necessarily shared by his addressees (given that we do not have the letters they wrote by way of reply, for the most part); *Alcuin: Achievement and Reputation*, p. xix. For a fascinating assessment of Alcuin's epistolary persona, see Garrison, "An Aspect of Alcuin."

[74] Dümmler, ed., "Letter LXV," MGH, Epist. IV: Epist. Karolini Aevi 2, p. 109; Allott, trans., *Alcuin of York*, pp. 132–33.

[75] For snap-shots of this poet's bitchy world, see Godman, ed. and trans., *Poetry of the Carolingian Renaissance*, pp. 9–14; and also Garrison, "The Emergence of Carolingian Latin Literature," pp. 111–40.

[76] The title bestowed upon Alcuin by Theodulf of Orléans, in his poem on Charlemagne's court (Dümmler, ed., "Ad Carolum regem," MGH, PLAC 1, pp. 483–89; also, with facing translation, Godman, *Poetry of the Carolingian Renaissance*, pp. 150–63); the probably mocking irony behind it is discussed by Orchard, "Wish You Were Here," pp. 21–43, esp. 38.

[77] Dümmler, ed., "Carmen XXXII," MGH, PLAC 1, pp. 249–50; also, with facing translation, Godman, *Poetry of the Carolingian Renaissance*, p. 122.

[78] Alcuin's affection for home is explored in Orchard, "Wish You Were Here;" and for an insightful analysis of Alcuin's view of events in England in the 790s, see Garrison, "The Bible and Alcuin's Interpretation of Current Events," pp. 68–84.

[79] Orchard, "Enigma Variations," pp. 285–86, 288–89.

[80] Dümmler, ed., "Carmen XXIII," MGH, PLAC 1, pp. 246–47; also, with facing translation, Godman, *Poetry of the Carolingian Renaissance*, pp. 124–27. For two opposing views of what Alcuin was lamenting, see Godman, "Alcuin's Poetic Style and the Authenticity of 'O mea cella'," pp. 555–83; Newlands, "Alcuin's Poem of Exile," pp. 19–45; and Pucci, "Alcuin's Cell Poem," pp. 839–49.

[81] Dümmler, ed., "Epistola CXXIV," MGH, Epistolae IV: Epistolae Karolini Aevi 2, pp. 181–84.

[82] M. Garrison, "'Quid Hinieldus cum Christo?'" in O'Brien O'Keeffe, and Orchard, *Latin Learning and English Lore*, I:237–59. The letter's link with Lindisfarne was put aside by Donald Bullough, "What Has Ingeld to Do With Lindisfarne?" *ASE* 22 (1993): 93–125.

[83] Dümmler, ed., "Carmen IX," MGH, PLAC 1, pp. 229–35; also, with facing translation, Godman, *Poetry of the Carolingian Renaissance*, pp. 126–39.

[84] On this break in the tradition, see Lapidge, "Latin Learning in Ninth-Century England," pp. 409–54; also, for one of the few notable literary products of the ninth century, Aediluulf's *Carmen de abbatibus*, in Lapidge, "Aediluulf and the School of York," pp. 381–98.

[85] See the first three essays in the second volume of Lapidge's collected works on the men whom Alfred enlisted to inaugurate a cultural revival (Werferth, Plegmund, Asser, Grimbald and John the "Old Saxon"), and then on the presence of the Breton scholar, Israel the Grammarian, at the court of King Æthelstan.

[86] See Gwara, "Manuscripts of Aldhelm's *Prosa de Virginitate*," pp. 101–59; and for another viewpoint, Kiff-Hooper, "Classbooks or Works of Art?," pp. 15–26.

[87] Porter Stork, *Through a Gloss Darkly*.

[88] Lapidge, "The Hermeneutic Style in Tenth-Century Anglo-Latin Literature," pp. 67–111, reprinted in *ALL 900–1066*, pp. 105–49, which should be read in conjunction with Lapidge's own more recent thoughts on this literary trend, "Poeticism in Pre-Conquest Anglo-Latin Prose," pp. 321–37.

[89] Campbell, ed., *Frithegodi Monachi*, p. 1.

[90] See P. Lendinara, "The Third Book of the Bella Parisiacae Urbis by Abbo of Saint-Germain-des-Prés and its Old English Gloss," *ASE* 14 (1986): 73–89.

[91] Frithegod, "Breuiloquium uitae Wilfredi," lines 49–57 and 121–29 (pp. 6 and 9).

[92] See the analysis of the surviving manuscripts of the *Breuiloquium*, which include a possible autograph; M. Lapidge, "Autographs of Insular Latin Authors," in *Gli autografi medievali: Problemi paleografici e filologici*, ed. P. Chiesa and L. Pinelli (Spoleto, 1994), pp. 103–44.

[93] Lapidge, "The Hermeneutic Style," pp. 99–100.

[94] S 425, Brooks and Kelly, eds., *Charters of Christ Church Canterbury*, II.866–70 (no. 106), dated 28 May 934, and records Æthelstan's grant of land in Sussex and Kent to his thegn, Ælfwald. On the group of charters identifiable as the work of "Æthelstan A," see Simon Keynes, *The Diplomas of King Æthelred "the Unready" 978–1016: A Study in Their Use as Historical Evidence* (Cambridge: CUP, 1980), pp. 43–44; and a much fuller account forthcoming as the published version of Keynes's 2001 Toller Lecture, "The Charters of King Æthelstan (924–39) and the Kingdom of the English."

[95] *Tanaliter* is only otherwise known in a Breton-Latin poem, the "Saint-Omer Hymn," certainly known in England in time to be incorporated into a mid-eleventh-century manuscript known as the "Canterbury class-book" (Cambridge, University Library, Gg.5.35, written at St. Augustine's, Canterbury); on the hymn, and an alternative, more complex explanation for "tanaliter" as derived from the Old Irish word *tonna* (death's), see Herren, *The Hisperica Famina II*, pp. 104–111 and 171–72; on the means by which it might have reached England during Æthelstan's reign, see M. Lapidge, "Israel the Grammarian in Anglo-Saxon England," reprinted in *ALL 900–1066*, pp. 87–104, esp. 94–95. See also D. A. Woodman, "Æthelstan A and the Rhetoric of Rule," *ASE* 42 (2013): 217–48.

[96] S 407 (dated 7 June 930, but originally meant to be 934), recording the king's grant of Amounderness to St. Peter's, York, preserved in a fourteenth-century cartulary in the archives of York Minster, edited by D. A. Woodman, Charters of Northern Houses, Anglo-Saxon Charters 16 (Oxford: OUP-British Academy, 2012), no. 1.

[97] Another glimpse of an author's workings is Lapidge's analysis of how the manuscripts of Frithegod's *Breuiloquium* may incorporate revision: "A Frankish Scholar in Tenth-Century England."

[98] Ælfric's prefaces are conveniently collected together by Jonathan Wilcox in a little book by that name in the Durham Medieval Texts Series, no. 9 (Durham, 1994, reprinted 1996); see pp. 107 (Latin preface to the First Series of Catholic Homilies) and 111 (Second Series of Catholic Homilies), with translations at pp. 127–28.

[99] Lapidge, "The Hermeneutic Style," p. 139.

[100] Campbell, ed., *Chronicon Æthelweardi*; see also, Winterbottom, "The Style of Æthelweard," pp. 109–18.

[101] M. Lapidge, "Byzantium, Rome and England in the Early Middle Ages," in *Roma fra Oriente e Occidente*, Settimane di Studio XLIX (Spoleto, 2002), pp. 363–400, at 386–98.

[102] Gwara and Porter, eds. and trans., *Anglo-Saxon Conversations*, pp. 192–93 (though the silly translation I offer here – of frankly silly Latin – is mine not theirs, which runs, more sensibly: "Most beloved student! Yesterday we played together with Latin words").

[103] It is interesting to observe the plain straightforwardness of the Latin composed by that other gifted preacher in Old English, Archbishop Wulfstan, in the material recently edited by Hall, "Wulfstan's Latin Sermons," pp. 93–109.

[104] Respectively, "Three Latin Poems from Æthelwold's School at Winchester," pp. 225–78, and "The Hermeneutic Style," pp. 146–47.

[105] Lapidge, ed. and trans., *Byrhtferth of Ramsey*. The translation that follows here is my own idiosyncratic rendition, written before the publication of a rather better one in that volume.

[106] Lapidge, *Byrhtferth: The Lives of St Oswald and St. Ecgwine*, intro. and ch. 3.

[107] Baker and Lapidge, eds., *Byrhtferth's Enchiridion*.

[108] M. Godden, "Literary Language," in *The Cambridge History of the English Language I: The Beginnings to 1066*, ed. R. M. Hogg (Cambridge: CUP, 1992), p. 534.

Abbreviations

ActaS	[Bollandists] Acta Sanctorum
ALL 600–899	M. Lapidge, *Anglo-Latin Literature 600–899* (London and Rio Grande, OH: Hambledon Press, 1996)
ALL 900–1066	M. Lapidge, *Anglo-Latin Literature 900–1066* (London and Rio Grande, OH: Hambledon Press, 1993)
ASE	*Anglo-Saxon England* (Cambridge: CUP)
CCSL	*Corpus Christianorum: Series Latina* (Turnhout: Brepols)
CSASE	Cambridge Studies in Anglo-Saxon England (Cambridge: CUP)
CUP	Cambridge University Press
LUP	Liverpool University Press
MGH	*Monumenta Germaniae Historica*
MGH, AA	*Monumenta Germaniae Historica*, Auctores Antiquissimi
MGH, PLAC	*Monumenta Germaniae Historica*, Poetae Latini Aevi Carolini
OEN	*Old English Newsletter*
OMT	Oxford Medieval Texts (Oxford: Clarendon Press)
OUP	Oxford University Press
PIMS	Pontifical Institute of Mediaeval Studies (Toronto)
PL	J.-P. Migne, *Patrologia Latina*, 221 vols. (Paris, 1857–66)
S	P. H. Sawyer, *Anglo-Saxon Charters: An Annotated List and Bibliography* (London, 1968)
WBEASE	*The Wiley-Blackwell Encyclopaedia of Anglo-Saxon England*, ed. M. Lapidge, J. Blair, S. Keynes, and D. Scragg (Chichester: Wiley-Blackwell, 2014)

Bibliography

Introduction to Anglo-Latin Literature

Compendium Auctorum Latinorum Medii Aevi (*CALMA*). Fascicles I.1 onwards (A–). Edited by M. Lapidge, G. Garfagnini, R. C. Love, and L. Lanza. Florence: SISMEL-Edizioni del Galluzzo, 2000– .

Howlett, D. R. "Anglo-Latin Literature to 1066." In *Medieval England: An Encyclopedia*, edited by P. E. Szarmach, M. T. Tavormina, and J. T. Rosenthal, 38–41. New York and London: Garland, 1998.

Lapidge, Michael. "The Anglo-Latin Background." In *A New Critical History of Old English Literature*, edited by S. B. Greenfield and D. G. Calder, 5–37. New York: New York University Press, 1986. Reprinted as "Anglo-Latin Literature," in *ALL 600–899*, 1–35. 1996.

——. "Anglo-Latin Studies: A Decennial Retrospective." *American Notes and Queries*, n.s., 3 (1990): 79–85.

——. *Anglo-Latin Literature 900–1066*. London and Rio Grande, OH: Hambledon Press, 1993.

——. *Anglo-Latin Literature 600–899*. London and Rio Grande, OH: Hambledon Press, 1996.

Love, Rosalind C. "Insular Latin Literature to 900." In *The Cambridge History of Early Medieval English Literature*, edited by Clare A. Lees, 120–57. Cambridge: CUP, 2013.

O'Brien O'Keeffe, K., and A. P. M. Orchard, eds. *Latin Learning and English Lore: Studies in Anglo-Saxon Literature for Michael Lapidge*. 2 vols. Toronto: University of Toronto Press, 2005.

Orchard, Andy. "Latin and the Vernacular Languages: The Creation of a Bilingual Textual Culture." In *After Rome*, edited by Thomas Charles-Edwards, 191–219. Oxford: Oxford University Press, 2003.

Sharpe, Richard. *A Handlist of the Latin Writers of Great Britain and Ireland Before 1540*. Turnhout: Brepols, 1997; with updates available from the author's website: http://www.history.ox.ac.uk/sharpe/index.htm.

The Character of Anglo-Latin

Howlett, D. R. "Early Insular Latin Poetry." *Peritia* 17–18 (2003–4): 61–109.

Lapidge, Michael. "Poeticism in Pre-Conquest Anglo-Latin Prose." In *Aspects of the Language of Latin Prose*, edited by T. Reinhardt, M. Lapidge, and J. N. Adams, 321–37. Proceedings of the British Academy 129. Oxford: OUP, 2005.

The Contents of the Anglo-Saxons' Libraries

Biggs, F. M., T. D. Hill, and P. E. Szarmach, eds. *Sources of Anglo-Saxon Literary Culture: A Trial Version*. Binghamton, NY: Center for Medieval and Early Renaissance Studies, SUNY Binghamton, 1990.

——. T. D. Hill, P. E. Szarmach, E. G. Whatley, and D. A. Oosterhouse. *Sources of Anglo-Saxon Literary Culture, Vol. 1: Abbo of Fleury, Abbo of Saint-Germain-Des-Pres, and Acta Sanctorum*. Kalamazoo, MN: Medieval Institute Publications, Western Michigan University, 2001. https://saslc.nd.edu/publications.html.

Fontes Anglo-Saxonici Project: A Register of Written Sources used by Anglo-Saxon Authors. English Faculty, University of Oxford. http://fontes.english.ox.ac.uk.

Gneuss, H., and M. Lapidge. *Anglo-Saxon Manuscripts: A Bibliographical Handlist of Manuscripts and Manuscript Fragments Written or Owned in England up to 1100*. Toronto: University of Toronto Press, 2014.

Lapidge, M. *The Anglo-Saxon Library*. Oxford: OUP, 2006.

Augustine and the Canterbury School

Brooks, N. *The Early History of the Church of Canterbury*. Leicester: Leicester University Press, 1984.

——. "The Anglo-Saxon Cathedral Community." In *A History of Canterbury Cathedral*, edited by P. Collinson, N. Ramsay, and M. Spark, 1–37. Oxford: OUP, 1995.

Gameson, R., ed. *St. Augustine and the Conversion of England*. Stroud: Sutton, 1999.

Meens, R. "A Background to Augustine's Mission to Anglo-Saxon England." *ASE* 23 (1994): 5–17.

Theodore and Hadrian at Canterbury

Lapidge, M. "The School of Theodore and Hadrian." *ASE* 15 (1986): 45–72. Reprinted in *ALL 600–899*, 141–68. 1996.

——. ed. *Archbishop Theodore: Commemorative Studies on His Life and Influence*. CSASE 11. 1995.

——. and Bernhard Bischoff, eds. *Biblical Commentaries from the Canterbury School of Theodore and Hadrian*. CSASE 10. 1994.

Hessels, J. H. *A Late Eighth-Century Latin-Anglo-Saxon Glossary Preserved in the Library of the Leiden University (Voss. lat. Q 69)*. Cambridge: CUP, 1906.

Pheifer, J. D. "Early Anglo-Saxon Glossaries and the School of Canterbury." *ASE* 16 (1987): 17–44.

Ireland, Iona, and the North of England

Charles-Edwards, Thomas M. *Early Christian Ireland.* Cambridge: CUP, 2000.

Herbert, M. *Iona, Kells, and Derry: The History and Hagiography of the Monastic Families of Columba.* Oxford: Clarendon, 1988.

——. "Latin and Vernacular Hagiography of Ireland from the Origins to the Sixteenth Century." In *Hagiographies: International History of the Latin and Vernacular Hagiographical Literature in the West from Its Origins to 1550.* Vol. 3, edited by Guy Philippart, 327–60. Turnhout: Brepols, 2001.

Sharpe, Richard, trans. *Adomnan of Iona: Life of St. Columba.* Harmondsworth: Penguin, 1995.

Whatley, E. G. "Late Old English Hagiography, ca. 950–1150." In *Hagiographies: International History of the Latin and Vernacular Hagiographical Literature in the West from its Origins to 1550.* Vol. 2, edited by G. Philippart, 429–99. Turnhout: Brepols, 1996.

Seventh-Century Irish Learned Culture: Exegesis and Grammar

Bischoff, Bernhard. "Wendepunkte in der Geschichte der lateinischen Exegese im Frühmittelalter." *Mittelalterliche Studien* I (1966): 205–73. Translated by C. O'Grady. "Turning-Points in the History of Latin Exegesis in the Early Middle Ages." In *Biblical Studies: The Medieval Irish Contribution*, edited by M. McNamara, 74–160. Dublin: Dominican Publications, 1976.

Gorman, Michael. "The Myth of Hiberno-Latin Exegesis." *Revue Bénédictine* 110 (2000): 42–95.

Law, Vivien. *Wisdom, Authority, and Grammar in the Seventh Century: Decoding Virgilius Maro Grammaticus.* Cambridge: CUP, 1995.

Smyth, Marina. *Understanding the Universe in Seventh-Century Ireland.* Woodbridge: Boydell Press, 1996.

The Hisperica Famina

Herren, Michael W., ed. and trans. *The Hisperica Famina I: The A-Text.* Toronto: Pontifical Institute of Mediaeval Studies, 1974.

Orchard, Andy. "The Hisperica Famina as Literature." *Journal of Medieval Latin* 10 (2000): 1–40.

Stevenson, J. B. "Bangor and the Hisperica Famina." *Peritia* 6–7 (1987–8): 202–16.

Northumbria: Laying the Groundwork

Brown, George H. "Bede the Educator." *Jarrow Lectures*. Jarrow: St. Paul's Church, 1996.

Hunter Blair, Peter. "Whitby as a Centre of Learning in the Seventh Century." In *Learning and Literature in Anglo-Saxon England: Studies Presented to Peter Clemoes*, edited by M. Lapidge and H. Gneuss, 3–32. Cambridge: CUP, 1985.

Fletcher, E. "Benedict Biscop." In *Bede and His World: The Collected Jarrow Lectures, 1979–1993*. Vol. 2, 539–54. Aldershot: Ashgate, 1994.

Wood, Ian. *The Most Holy Abbot Ceolfrid*. Jarrow Lectures. Jarrow: St. Paul's Church, 1995.

Aldhelm of Malmesbury (d. 709/10)

Texts and Translations

Aldhelm. *Aldhelmi Opera*. Edited by R. Ehwald. MGH, Auctores Antiquissimi 15. Berlin: Weidmann, 1919. http://www.dmgh.de/index.html.

Aldhelm. *Aldhelmi Malmesbiriensis Prosa de Virginitate: Cum Glosa Latina atque Anglosaxonica*. 2 vols. Edited by Scott Gwara and R. Ehwald. Corpus Christianorum Series Latina (CCSL) 124A. Turnhout: Brepols, 2001.

Lapidge, Michael, and Michael Herren, trans. *Aldhelm: The Prose Works*. Cambridge: Brewer, 1979.

——. and J. L. Rosier, trans. *Aldhelm: The Poetic Works*. Cambridge: Brewer, 1985.

Porter Stork, Nancy. *Through a Gloss Darkly: Aldhelm's Riddles in the British Library MS Royal 12.C.xxiii*. Toronto: PIMS, 1990.

Selected Secondary Reading

Barker, K., and N. Brooks, eds. *Aldhelm and Sherborne: Essays to Celebrate the Foundation of the Bishopric*. Oxford: Oxbow, 2007.

Lapidge, Michael. "The Career of Aldhelm." *ASE* 36 (2007): 15–69.

Orchard, Andy. *The Poetic Art of Aldhelm*. CSASE 8. 1993.

Remley, Paul. "Aldhelm as Old English Poet: Exodus, Asser, and the Dicta Ælfredi." In *Latin Learning and English Lore: Studies in Anglo-Saxon Literature for Michael Lapidge*. Vol. 1, edited by K. O'Brien O'Keeffe and A. Orchard, 90–108. Toronto: University of Toronto Press, 2005.

Thornbury, Emily. *Becoming A Poet in Anglo-Saxon England*. Cambridge: CUP, 2014.

Winterbottom, Michael. "Aldhelm's Prose Style and its Origins." *ASE* 6 (1977): 39–76.

Bede (673–735)

Didactic Works

Bede. *Opera Didascalica.* Edited by C. W. Jones, C. B. Kendall, and M. H. King. CCSL 123A. 1975.

Wallis, Faith, and Calvin B. Kendall, trans. *Bede: On the Nature of Things and On Times.* Liverpool: LUP, 2010.

Computistical Works

Bede. *Opera Didascalica.* Edited by C. W. Jones. CCSL 123B. 1977.

——. *Opera Didascalica.* Vol. 123A. Edited by C. W. Jones. CCSL 123C. 1980.

Wallis, F., trans. *Bede: The Reckoning of Time.* Liverpool: LUP, 1999.

Biblical Exegesis

Bede. *Opera Exegetica* 1 *Libri Quatuor in Principium Genesis.* Edited by C. W. Jones. CCSL 118A. 1967.

——. *Opera Exegetica* 2 *In primam partem Samuhelis.* Edited by D. Hurst. CCSL 119. 1962.

——. *Opera Exegetica* 2A *De Tabernaculo. De Templo. In Ezram et Neemiam.* Edited by D. Hurst. CCSL 119A. 1969.

——. *Opera Exegetica* 2B *In Tobiam. In Proverbia. In Cantica Canticorum.* Edited by D. Hurst, and *In Habacuc*, edited by J. E. Hudson. CCSL 119B. 1983.

——. *Opera Exegetica* 3 *In Lucae Evangelium Expositio. In Marci Evangelium Expositio.* Edited by D. Hurst. CCSL 120. 1960.

——. *Opera Exegetica* 4 *Expositio Actuum Apostolorum. Retractatio in Actus Apostolorum. Nomina Regionum atque Locorum de Actibus Apostolorum. In Epistolas VII Catholicas.* Edited by M. L. W. Laistner and D. Hurst. CCSL 121. 1983.

——. *Opera Exegetica* 5 *Expositio Apocalypseos.* Edited by R. Gryson. CCSL 121A. 2001.

Connolly, S. *Bede: On the Temple.* Liverpool: LUP, 1995.

Connolly, S. *On Tobit and the Canticle of Habakkuk.* Dublin: Four Courts Press, 1997.

DeGregorio, S. *Bede on Ezra and Nehemiah.* Liverpool: LUP, 2006.

Holder, A. *Bede: On the Tabernacle.* Liverpool: LUP, 1994.

——. *The Venerable Bede: On the Song of Songs and Selected Writings.* Mahway, NJ: Paulist Press, 2011.

Hurst, D. *Bede the Venerable: The Commentary on the Seven Catholic Epistles.* Kalamazoo, MI: Cistercian Publications, 1985.

Kendall, C. B. *On Genesis: Bede.* Liverpool: LUP, 2008.

Martin, L. T. *The Venerable Bede: Commentary on the Acts of the Apostles*. Kalamazoo, MI: Cistercian Publications, 1989.
Trent Foley, W., and A. Holder. *Bede: A Biblical Miscellany*. Liverpool: LUP, 1999.
Wallis, F. *Bede: Commentary on Revelation*. Liverpool: LUP, 2013.

Poetry

Bede. *Opera homiletica et Opera rhythmica*. Edited by D. Hurst and J. Fraipont. CCSL 122. 1955.

History

Bede. *Venerabilis Baedae Opera Historica*. Edited by C. Plummer. 2 vols. Oxford: Clarendon, 1896.
——. *Bede's Ecclesiastical History of the English People*. Edited and translated by B. Colgrave and R. A. B. Mynors. Oxford: Clarendon, 1969. Reprint, 1991.
——. *The Ecclesiastical History of the English People*. Edited and translated by J. McClure and R. Collins. Worlds Classics. Oxford: OUP, 1994. http://www.fordham.edu/halsall/sbook.html.
——. *Storia Degli Inglesi: Historia ecclesiastica gentis Anglorum*. 2 vols. Edited by M. Lapidge. Translated by P. Chiesa. Milan: Mondadori, 2008–10.
——. *The Abbots of Wearmouth and Jarrow*. Edited and translated by C. Grocock and I. Wood. OMT. Oxford: Clarendon Press, 2013.

Homilies

Bede. *Opera homiletica et Opera rhythmica*. Edited by D. Hurst and J. Fraipont. CCSL 122. 1955.
——. *Bede the Venerable: Homilies on the Gospels*. 2 vols. Edited and translated by L. T. Martin and D. Hurst. Kalamazoo, MI: Cistercian Publications, 1991.

Hagiography

Bede. "Vita S. Felicis." *Patrologia Latina* (PL) 94.789–98.
See also HAGIOGRAPHY on p. 51 of this volume.

Martyrology

Lifshitz, Felice, trans. "Bede, Martyrology." In *Medieval Hagiography: An Anthology*, edited by T. Head, 169–97. New York and London: Garland, 2000.
Quentin, Henri. *Les martyrologes historiques du Moyen Age*. Paris: J. Gabalda, 1908.

Selected Secondary Reading

Bonner, Gerald, ed. *Famulus Christi: Essays in Commemoration of the Thirteenth Centenary of the Birth of the Venerable Bede*. London: SPCK, 1976.

Brown, G. H. *A Companion to Bede*. Woodbridge: Boydell and Brewer, 2009.

DeGregorio, S., ed. *Innovation and Tradition in the Writings of the Venerable Bede*. Morgantown: West Virginia University Press, 2006.

——. ed. *The Cambridge Companion to Bede*. Cambridge: CUP, 2010.

Sharpe, Richard. "The Varieties of Bede's Prose." In *Aspects of the Language of Latin Prose*, edited by T. Reinhardt, M. Lapidge, and J. N. Adams, 339–55. Proceedings of the British Academy 129. Oxford: OUP, 2005.

Ward, Benedicta. *The Venerable Bede*. London: G. Chapman, 1990.

Wynfrith/Boniface (d. 754)

Letters

Boniface. *S. Bonifatii et Lullii Epistolae*. Edited by M. Tangl. MGH, Epistolae Selectae I. Berlin: Weidmann, 1916.

Boniface. *The Letters of Saint Boniface*. Translated by E. Emerton. New York: Columbia University Press, 1940; reprinted with an introduction and bibliography by T. F. X. Noble, 2000.

Didactic Works

Boniface. *Ars grammatica and Ars metrica*. Edited by G. Gebauer and B. Löfstedt, 1–99, 109–13. CCSL 133B. 1980.

Enigmata

See THE ANGLO-LATIN RIDDLE TRADITION on p. 45 of this volume.

Selected Secondary Reading

Clay, J. H. *In the Shadow of Death: Saint Boniface and the Conversion of Hessia, 721–54*. Turnhout: Brepols, 2010.

McKitterick, R. *Anglo-Saxon Missionaries in Germany: Personal Connections and Local Influences*. Brixworth Lecture. Leicester: University of Leicester, 1991.

Orchard, A. "Old Sources, New Resources: Finding the Right Formula for Boniface." *ASE* 30 (2001): 15–38.

Reuter, T., ed. *The Greatest Englishman: Essays on St. Boniface and the Church at Crediton*. Exeter: Paternoster Press, 1980.

Schaefer, U. "Two Women in Need of a Friend: A Comparison of The Wife's Lament and Eangyth's Letter to Boniface." In *Germanic Dialects: Linguistic and Philological Investigations*, edited by B. Brogyanyi and T. Krömmelbein, 491–524. Amsterdam and Philadelphia, PA: J. Benjamins, 1986.

Alcuin of York (d. 804)

Poetry

Alcuin. Edited by E. Dümmler, 206–7, 220–351. MGH. Poetae Latini Aevi Carolini 1. Berlin: Weidmann, 1881.
Godman, P., ed. and trans. *Alcuin: The Bishops, Kings, and Saints of York*. Oxford: Clarendon, 1982.
——. ed. and trans. *Poetry of the Carolingian Renaissance*. London: Duckworth, 1985.

Letters

Alcuin. *Epistolae*. Edited by E. Dümmler, 1–493. MGH. Epistolae IV: Epistolae Karolini Aevi 2. Berlin: Weidmann, 1895.
Allott, S., trans. *Alcuin of York: His Life and Letters*. York: Sessions, 1974.
Chase, C., ed. *Two Alcuin Letter Books Edited from the British Museum MS Cotton Vespasian A XIV*. Toronto: PIMS, 1975.

Scholastic Texts

Alcuin. *Opera omnia*. PL 101.

Biblical Exegesis

Alcuin. *Operum omnium pars secunda: Opuscula exegetica*. PL 100.515–1163.

Theological Works

Alcuin. *Opera Omnia*. PL 100–101.

Hagiography

See HAGIOGRAPHY on p. 51 of this volume.

Selected Secondary Reading

Bullough, Donald. *Alcuin: Achievement and Reputation*. Leiden: Brill, 2004.
Garrison, Mary. "The Emergence of Carolingian Latin Literature and the Court

of Charlemagne (780–814)." In *Carolingian Culture: Emulation and Innovation*, edited by R. McKitterick, 111–40. Cambridge: CUP, 1994.

——. "The Social World of Alcuin: Nicknames at York and at the Carolingian Court." In *Alcuin of York*, edited by L. A. J. R. Houwen and A. A. MacDonald, 59–79. Groningen: Egbert Forsten, 1998.

——. "The Bible and Alcuin's Interpretation of Current Events." *Peritia* 16 (2002): 68–84.

——. "An Aspect of Alcuin: 'Tuus Albinus' - Peevish Egotist or Parrhesiast?" In *Ego Trouble: Authors and their Identities in the Early Middle Ages*, edited by R. Corradini, R. McKitterick, M. Gillis, and I. van Renswoude, 137–51. Forschungen zur Geschichte des Mittelalters 15. Vienna: ÖAW, 2010.

Godman, P. "Alcuin's Poetic Style and the Authenticity of 'O mea cella'." *Studi Medievali*, 3e series, 20 (1979): 555–83.

——. *Poets and Emperors: Frankish Politics and Carolingian Poetry*. Oxford: Clarendon, 1987.

Kempshall, Matthew S. "The Virtues of Rhetoric: Alcuin's Disputatio de rhetorica et de uirtutibus." *ASE* 37 (2008): 7–30.

Newlands, C. E. "Alcuin's Poem of Exile: 'O mea cella'." *Mediaevalia* 11 (1985): 19–45.

Orchard, A. "Wish You Were Here: Alcuin's Courtly Poetry and the Boys Back Home." In *Courts and Regions in Medieval Europe*, edited by S. Rees Jones, R. Marks, and A. J. Minnis, 21–43. Woodbridge: Boydell and Brewer, 2000.

Pucci, J. "Alcuin's Cell Poem: A Vergilian Reappraisal." *Latomus* 49 (1990): 839–49.

The Anglo-Latin Riddle Tradition

Texts and Translations

Lapidge, M., and J. L. Rosier, eds. *Aldhelm: The Poetic Works*. Cambridge: Brewer, 1985.

de Marco, M., and F. Glorie, eds. *Collectiones Aenigmatum Merovingicae Aetatis*. CCSL 133–133A. 1968.

Pitman, J. H. *The Riddles of Aldhelm*. Yale Studies in English LXVII. New Haven, CT: Yale University Press, 1925.

Selected Secondary Reading

Howe, N. "Aldhelm's Enigmata and Isidorian Etymology." *ASE* 14 (1985): 37–59.

Lerer, S. *Literacy and Power in Anglo-Saxon Literature*. Lincoln: University of Nebraska Press, 1991.

Milovanovic-Barham, C. "Aldhelm's Enigmata and Byzantine Riddles." *ASE* 22 (1993): 51–64.

Orchard, A. "Enigma Variations: The Anglo-Saxon Riddle-Tradition." In *Latin Learning and English Lore: Studies in Anglo-Saxon Literature for Michael Lapidge*. Vol. 1, edited by K. O'Brien O'Keeffe and A. Orchard, 284–304. Toronto: University of Toronto Press, 2005.

Porter Stork, N. *Through a Gloss Darkly: Aldhelm's Riddles in the British Library MS Royal 12.C.xxiii*. Toronto: PIMS, 1990.

Salvador-Bello, M. *Isidorean Perceptions of Order: The Exeter Book Riddles and Medieval Latin Enigmata*. Morgantown, WV: West Virginia University Press: 2015.

Scott, P. D. "Rhetorical and Symbolic Ambiguity: The Riddles of Symphosius and Aldhelm." In *Saints, Scholars and Heroes: Studies in Honour of Charles W. Jones*. Vol. 1, edited by M. H. King and W. M. Stevens, 117–44. Collegeville, MN: Hill Monastic Manuscript Library, Saint John's Abbey and University, 1979.

Smith, D. K. "Humour in Hiding: Laughter Between the Sheets in the Exeter Book Riddles." In *Humour in Anglo-Saxon Literature*, edited by D. K. Smith, 79–98. Rochester, NY: D. S. Brewer, 2000.

Ædilvvlf

Campbell, A., ed. *Æthelwulf De Abbatibus*. Oxford: Clarendon Press, 1967.

Lapidge, M. "Aediluulf and the School of York." In *Lateinische Kultur im VIII. Jahrhundert: Traube-Gedenkschrift*, edited by A. Lehner and W. Berschin, 161–78. St. Ottilien: EOS Verlag, 1990. Reprinted in *ALL 600–899*, 381–98. 1996.

The Ninth-Century Decline in Literature Culture

Brooks, N. P. "Ninth-Century England: The Crucible of Defeat." *Transactions of the Royal Historical Society*, 5th series, 29 (1979): 1–20.

Lapidge, M. "Latin Learning in Ninth-Century England." In *ALL 600–899*, 409–54. 1996.

King Alfred and His Successors: Latin Learning Revives

Asser. *Life of King Alfred.* Edited by W. H. Stevenson. Oxford: Clarendon, 1959. Reprinted with an introductory article by D. Whitelock.

Keynes, Simon D., and Michael Lapidge, trans. *Alfred the Great.* Harmondsworth: Penguin, 1983.

Lapidge, M. "Some Latin Poems as Evidence for the Reign of Athelstan." *ASE* 9 (1981): 61–92. Reprinted in *ALL 900–1066*, 49–86. 1993.

Selected Secondary Reading

Dumville, David. N. *Wessex and England from Alfred to Edgar: Six Essays on Political, Cultural and Ecclesiastical Revival.* Woodbridge: Boydell and Brewer, 1992.

Keynes, Simon. "King Athelstan's Books." In *Learning and Literature in Anglo-Saxon England,* edited by M. Lapidge and H. Gneuss, 143–201. Cambridge: CUP, 1985.

Lapidge, Michael. "Schools, Learning and Literature in Tenth-Century England." In *ALL, 900–1066*, 1–48. 1993.

The Tenth-Century Hermeneutic Style: Pomp and Circumstance

[For Frithegod, Lantfred, Byrhtferth, and .B. see under HAGIOGRAPHY on p. 51 of this volume]

Baker, P. S., and M. Lapidge, eds. *Byrhtferth's Enchiridion.* Early English Texts Society, Supplementary Series 15. Oxford: Oxford University Press, 1995.

Campbell, A., ed. *The Chronicle of Æthelweard.* London and New York: Nelson, 1962.

Lapidge, M. "St Dunstan's Latin Poetry." *Anglia* 98 (1980): 101–6. Reprinted in *ALL 900–1066*, 151–56. 1993.

——. "Three Latin Poems from Æthelwold's School at Winchester." *ASE* 1 (1972): 85–137. Reprinted in *ALL 900–1066*, 225–77. 1993.

Selected Secondary Reading

Bullough, Donald. "The Educational Tradition in England from Alfred to Ælfric: Teaching 'utriusque linguae'." In *Carolingian Renewal: Sources and Heritage*, 297–334. Manchester: Manchester University Press, 1991.

Gretsch, Mechthild. *The Intellectual Foundations of the English Benedictine Reform*. CSASE 25. 1999.

Gwara, Scott. J. "Manuscripts of Aldhelm's Prosa de Virginitate and the Rise of Hermeneutic Literacy in Tenth-Century England." *Studi Medievali* 35 (1994): 101–59.

Kiff-Hooper, J. A. "Classbooks or Works of Art? Some Observations on the Tenth-Century Manuscripts of Aldhelm's De laude virginitatis." In *Church and Chronicle in the Middle Ages: Essays Presented to John Taylor*, edited by I. Wood and G. A. Loud, 15–26. London: Hambledon Press, 1991.

Lapidge, Michael. "A Frankish Scholar in Tenth-Century England: Frithegod of Canterbury / Fredegaud of Brioude." *ASE* 17 (1988): 45–65. Reprinted in *ALL 900–1066*, 157–81. 1993.

——. "The Hermeneutic Style in Tenth-Century Anglo-Latin Literature." ASE 4 (1975): 67–111. Reprinted in *ALL 900–1066*, 105–49. 1993.

Stevenson, Jane. "The Irish Contribution to Anglo-Latin Hermeneutic Prose." In *Ogma: Essays in Celtic Studies in Honour of Próinséas Ní Chatháin*, edited by M. Richter and J.-M. Picard, 268–82. Dublin: Four Courts, 2002.

Winterbottom, Michael. "The Style of Aethelweard." *Medium Aevum* 36 (1967): 109–18.

Ælfric and Wulfstan

Texts

Fehr, B., ed. *Die Hirtenbriefe Aelfrics in altenglischer und lateinischer Fassung*. Reprinted with a supplement to the introduction by P. Clemoes. Darmstadt: Wissenschaftliche Buchgesellschaft, 1966.

Hall, T. N. "Wulfstan's Latin Sermons." In *Wulfstan, Archbishop of York: The Proceedings of the Second Alcuin Conference*, edited by M. Townend, 93–109. Turnhout: Brepols, 2004.

Jones, C. A., ed. and trans. *Ælfric's Letter to the Monks of Eynsham*. CSASE 24. 1998.

Wilcox, J., ed. *Ælfric's Prefaces*. Durham: Durham Medieval Texts, 1994.

See also HAGIOGRAPHY on p. 51 of this volume.

The Anglo-Saxon Classroom

Texts and Translations

Garmonsway, G. N., ed. *Ælfric's Colloquy*. 2nd ed. London: Methuen, 1947. Reprint, 1961.

Gwara, Scott, ed. *Latin Colloquies from Pre-Conquest Britain*. Toronto: PIMS, 1996.

Porter, David W., and Scott Gwara, eds. and trans. *Anglo-Saxon Conversations: The Colloquies of Ælfric Bata*. Woodbridge: Boydell and Brewer, 1997.

Stevenson, W. H., ed. *Early Scholastic Colloquies*. Anecdota Oxoniensia, Medieval & Modern Series XV. Oxford: Clarendon Press, 1929.

Selected Secondary Reading

Anderson, E. R. "Social Idealism in Ælfric's Colloquy." *ASE* 3 (1974): 153–62.

Lapidge, Michael. "Latin Learning in Dark Age Wales: Some Prolegomena." In *Proceedings of the Seventh International Congress of Celtic Studies, Oxford, 1983*, edited by D. Ellis Evans, J. G. Griffiths, and E. M. Jope, 91–107. Oxford: D. E. Evans, 1986.

Lendinara, Patrizia. "The World of Anglo-Saxon Learning." In *The Cambridge Companion to Old English Literature*, edited by M. Godden and M. Lapidge, 264–81. Cambridge: CUP, 1986. Reprinted, 2000.

Porter, David W. "The Latin Syllabus in Anglo-Saxon Monastic Schools." *Neophilologus* 78 (1994): 1–20.

Anglo-Latin Poetics

Lapidge, Michael. "Aldhelm's Latin Poetry and Old English Verse." *Comparative Literature* 31 (1979): 209–31. Reprinted in *ALL 600–899*, 247–70. 1996.

Orchard, Andy. "After Aldhelm: The Teaching and Transmission of the Anglo-Latin Hexameter." *Journal of Medieval Latin* 2 (1992): 96–133.

——. *The Poetic Art of Aldhelm*. CSASE 8. 1993.

Ruff, Carin. "The Place of Metrics in Anglo-Saxon Latin Education: Aldhelm and Bede." *Journal of English and Germanic Philology* 104 (2005): 149–70.

Thornbury, Emily. *Becoming A Poet in Anglo-Saxon England*. Cambridge: CUP, 2014.

Genre Surveys

Charters

Sawyer, Peter H. *Anglo-Saxon Charters: An Annotated List and Bibliography*. London: Royal Historical Society, 1968. Revised version www.trin.cam.ac.uk/kemble.

Computistica

Baker, Peter S. "Computus." In *The Wiley-Blackwell Encyclopaedia of Anglo-Saxon England*, edited by M. Lapidge, J. Blair, S. Keynes, and D. Scragg, 121–22. Chichester: Wiley-Blackwell, 2014.

Grammar

Law, Vivien. *The Insular Grammarians*. Woodbridge: Boydell, 1982.

——. "Grammar, Latin (Study of)." In *The Wiley-Blackwell Encyclopaedia of Anglo-Saxon England*, edited by M. Lapidge, J. Blair, S. Keynes, and D. Scragg, 221–23. Chichester: Wiley-Blackwell, 2014.

Glosses and Glossaries

Lendinara, Patrizia. "Glossaries." In *The Wiley-Blackwell Encyclopaedia of Anglo-Saxon England*, edited by M. Lapidge, J. Blair, S. Keynes, and D. Scragg, 212–14. Chichester: Wiley-Blackwell, 2014.

——. *Anglo-Saxon Glosses and Glossaries*. Aldershot: Ashgate, 1999.

Lindsay, W. M. *Studies in Early Mediaeval Latin Glossaries*, edited by M. Lapidge. Collected Studies Series. Aldershot: Ashgate, 1996.

Legislation

Haddan, A. W., and W. Stubbs, eds. *Councils and Ecclesiastical Documents*. 3 vols. Oxford: Clarendon Press, 1869–78.

Whitelock, D., C. N. L. Brooke, and M. Brett, eds. *Councils and Synods*. 2 vols. Oxford: Clarendon Press, 1964–81.

Letters

Alcuin. *Epistolae I*. Edited by E. Dümmler. MGH. Epistolae Karolini Aevi 2. Berlin: Weidmann, 1895.

Aldhelm. *Aldhelmi Opera*. Edited by R. Ehwald. MGH. Auctores Antiquissimi 15. Berlin: Weidmann, 1919, pp. 475–503.

Boniface and Lull. *S. Bonifatii et Lulli Epistolae*. Edited by M. Tangl. MGH. Epistolae Selectae I. Berlin: Weidmann, 1916.

Garrison, Mary. "Letter Collections." In *The Wiley-Blackwell Encyclopaedia of Anglo-Saxon England*, edited by M. Lapidge, J. Blair, S. Keynes, and D. Scragg, 288–89. Chichester: Wiley-Blackwell, 2014.

MGH. Epistolae Merowingici et Karolini aevi I. Epistolae. Berlin: Weidmann, 1892.

Liturgy

Pfaff, Richard W., ed. *The Liturgical Books of Anglo-Saxon England*. Old English Newsletter Subsidia 23. Kalamazoo, MI: Medieval Institute, Western Michigan University, 1995.

——. *The Liturgy in Medieval England: A History*. Cambridge: CUP, 2009.

Medical, Scientific, and Pseudo-Scientific Texts

Cameron, L. "Medical Literature and Medicine." In *The Wiley-Blackwell Encyclopaedia of Anglo-Saxon England*, edited by M. Lapidge, J. Blair, S. Keynes, and D. Scragg, 309–11. Chichester: Wiley-Blackwell, 2014.

Hagiography

Berschin, Walther. *Biographie und Epochenstil im lateinischen Mittelalter.* 4 vols. Stuttgart: A. Hiersemann, 1986–2001.

Lapidge, Michael. "The Saintly Life in Anglo-Saxon England." In *The Cambridge Companion to Old English Literature,* edited by M. Godden and M. Lapidge, 243–63. Cambridge: CUP, 1991.

——. and R. C. Love. "The Latin Hagiography of England and Wales (600–1550)." In *Hagiographies: International History of the Latin and Vernacular Hagiographical Literature in the West from its Origins to 1550.* Vol. 3, edited by G. Philippart, 203–325. Turnhout: Brepols, 1996.

Ridyard, S. J. *The Royal Saints of Anglo-Saxon England.* Cambridge: CUP, 1988.

Rollason, David. *Saints and Relics in Anglo-Saxon England.* Oxford: Blackwell, 1989.

Anglo-Latin Hagiography: The Primary Sources

Seventh- and Eighth-Century Texts

Alcuin. "Homilia de natale S. Willibrordi." PL 101.710–14.

——. "De Vita Sancti Willibrordi Episcopi." In *Poetae Latini Aevi Carolini I,* edited by E. Dümmler, 207–20. MGH. Antiquitates. Berlin: Weidmann, 1881.

——. "Vita S. Willibrordi" [prose]. In *Passiones Vitaeque Sanctorum,* edited by B. Krusch and W. Levison, 113–41. MGH. Scriptores Rerum Merovingicarum 7. Hannover: Hahn, 1920.

Bede. "Vita S. Cuthberti." In *Bedas metrische Vita S. Cuthberti,* edited by W. Jaager. Palaestra 198. Leipzig: Mayer and Muller, 1935.

Colgrave, Bertram, ed. and trans. *The Life of Bishop Wilfrid by Eddius Stephanus.* Cambridge: CUP, 1927.

——. ed. and trans. *Two Lives of St. Cuthbert.* Cambridge: CUP, 1940. Reprinted 1985.

——. ed. and trans. *The Earliest Life of Gregory the Great.* Lawrence, KA: University of Kansas Press, 1968. Reprinted, Cambridge: CUP, 1985.

Felix. *Vita S. Guthlaci.* Edited and translated by Bertram Colgrave. Cambridge: CUP, 1956.

Hygeburc. "Vitae Willibaldi et Wynnebaldi." In *Supplementa tomorum I–XII, pars III,* edited by O. Holder-Egger, 80–117. MGH. Scriptores 15.1. Hannover: Hahn, 1887–88; partly translated in C. H. Talbot. *The Anglo-Saxon Missionaries in Germany.* London and New York: Sheed and Ward, 1954.

Plummer, C., ed. "Vita S. Ceolfridi." In *Venerabilis Baedae Opera Historica.* Vol. 1, 388–404. Oxford: Clarendon, 1896.

Stephen of Ripon (Eddius Stephanus). "Vita S. Wilfridi I episcope Eboracensis." In *Passiones vitaeque sanctorum aevi Merovingici,* edited by W. Levison, 163–263. Scriptores Rerum Merovingicarum 6. MGH. Hannover: Hahn, 1913.

Willibald of Mainz. *Vitae Sancti Bonifatii Archiepiscopal Moguntini*. Edited by W. Levison, 1–58. MGH. Scriptores Rerum Germanicarum in usum scholarium 57. Hannover: Hahn, 1905.

Tenth-Century Texts

Abbo of Fleury. "Passio S. Edmundi." In *Three Lives of English Saints*, edited by M. Winterbottom, 67–87. Toronto: PIMS, 1972.

Adelard. "Vita S. Dunstani." In *The Early Lives of St. Dunstan*, edited by M. Lapidge and M. Winterbottom, 112–45. OMT. Oxford: Clarendon Press, 2011.

Ælfric of Eynsham. "Vita S. Æthelwoldi." In *Wulfstan of Winchester's Life of St. Æthelwold*, edited by M. Lapidge and M. Winterbottom, 71–80. OMT. 1991.

Arnold, T., ed. *Historia de S. Cuthberto*. Symeonis Monachi Opera Omnia. Vol. 2, 196–214. London: Longman, 1882–85.

.B. "Vita S. Dunstani." In *The Early Lives of St Dunstan*, edited and translated by M. Lapidge and M. Winterbottom, 2–109. OMT. 2011.

Byrhtferth of Ramsey. "Vita S. Ecgwini." In *Byrhtferth of Ramsey: The Lives of St. Oswald and St. Ecgwine*, edited and translated by M. Lapidge, 206–303. OMT. 2009.

——. "Vita S. Oswaldi." In *Byrhtferth of Ramsey: The Lives of St. Oswald and St. Ecgwine*, edited and translated by M. Lapidge, 2–201. OMT. 2009.

Frithegod. "Breuiloquium de S. Wilfrido." In *Frithegodi Monachi et Wulfstani Cantoris Narratio Metrica de Sancto Swithuno*, edited by A. Campbell, 1–62. Zurich: Thesaurus Mundi, 1950.

Johnson South, T. *Historia de Sancto Cuthberto: A History of Saint Cuthbert and a Record of His Patrimony*. D. S. Brewer: Cambridge, 2002.

Lantfred of Winchester. "Translatio et miracula S. Swithuni." In *The Cult of St. Swithun*, edited and translated by M. Lapidge, 217–32. Winchester Studies 4.ii. Oxford: Clarendon, 2003.

Lapidge, M. and M. Winterbottom, eds. and trans. *Wulfstan of Winchester's Life of St. Æthelwold*. OMT. 1991.

Wulfstan. "Narratio Metrica de Sancto Swithuno." In *Frithegodi Monachi et Wulfstani Cantoris Narratio Metrica de Sancto Swithuno*, edited by A. Campbell, 63–177. Zurich: Thesaurus Mundi, 1950.

The Eleventh Century: Anonymous Texts

Barlow, F., ed. and trans. *The Life of King Edward Who Rests at Westminster*. 2nd ed. OMT. 1992.

Dumville, D. N., S. Keynes, and M. Lapidge, eds. "The Annals of St. Neots with Vita prima S. Neoti." in *The Anglo-Saxon Chronicle: A Collaborative Edition* 17. Woodbridge: Boydell and Brewer, 1985.

Fell, C. E., ed. "Passio S. Edwardi martyris." In *Edward King and Martyr.* Leeds

Texts and Monographs, n.s. Leeds: University of Leeds, 1971.
James, M. R. "Two Lives of St. Ethelbert, King and Martyr." *English Historical Review* 32, no 2. (April 1917): 214–44.
Lapidge, M., ed. "Vita S. Swithuni." In *The Cult of St. Swithun*, 611–97. Winchester Studies 4.ii. Oxford: Clarendon, 2003.
Love, R. C., ed. and trans. *Three Eleventh-Century Anglo-Latin Saints' Lives: Vita S. Birini, Vita et miracula S. Kenelmi, and Vita S. Rumwoldi*. OMT. 1995.
Rollason, D. W., ed. "Passio SS Ethelberti et Ethelredi." In *The Mildrith Legend: A Study in Early Medieval Hagiography in England*, 90–104. Leicester: Leicester University Press, 1982.
Whatley, E. G., ed. "Vita S. Erkenwaldi." In *The Saint of London: The Life and Miracles of St. Erkenwald*, 86–97. Binghamton, NY: Medieval & Renaissance Texts & Studies, 1989.

Goscelin of St. Bertin

Wulfsige

Love, R. C., trans. "The Life of St. Wulfsige of Sherborne by Goscelin of Saint-Bertin." In *St. Wulfsige and Sherborne: Essays to Celebrate the Millennium of the Benedictine Abbey, 998–1998*, edited by K. Barker, D. A. Hinton, and A. Hunt, 98–123. Oxford: Oxbow, 2005.
Talbot, C. H., ed. "The Life of St Wulsin of Sherborne by Goscelin." *Revue Bénédictine* 49 (1959): 68–85.

Edith of Wilton

Wilmart, A., ed. "La légende de Ste Édithe en prose et vers par le moine Goscelin." *Analecta Bollandiana* 56 (1938): 5–101, 265–307; translated in S. Hollis, ed., *Writing the Wilton Women: Goscelin's Legend of Edith and Liber Confortatorius*, 23–93. Turnhout: Brepols, 2004.

Ivo of Persia

Vita et miracula S. Yuonis, ed. PL 155.79–90 [*Vita*].
Macray, W. D., ed., *Chronicon Abbatiae Rameseiensis*, lix–lxxxiv. Rerum Britannicarum medii aevi scriptores 83. London: Longman, 1886. [*Miracula*]

Ely Ladies

Love, R. C., ed. and trans. *Goscelin of Saint-Bertin. The Lives of the Female Saints of Ely*. OMT. 2004. [Lives of Seaxburh, Eormenhild, Wihtburh, Wærburh and Miracles of Æthelthryth]

Barking Ladies

Colker, M. L., ed. "Texts of Jocelyn of Canterbury which Relate to the History of Barking Abbey." *Studia Monastica* 7 (1965): 383–460. [Lives of Æthelburh, Hildelith, and Wulfhild]

Hagiography of St. Augustine

Historia maior de aduentu S. Augustini. ActaS May VI.375–95 and PL 80, cols. 43–94.

Historia maior de miraculis S. Augustini. ActaS May VI.397–411.

Historia minor de uita S. Augustini. PL 150, cols. 743–64.

Historia minor de miraculis S. Augustini. In London, BL, Cotton Vespasian B.xx, fols. 18v–23v.

Historia translationis S. Augustini et aliorum sanctorum. ActaS May VI.411–43 and excerpts in PL 155, cols. 13–46.

Lives of Augustine's Colleagues and Successors (Laurence, Mellitus, Justus, Honorius, Deusdedit, Theodore, Hadrian)

London, BL, Cotton Vespasian B.xx, fols. 197r–248v and Harley 105, fols. 205r–250v. (unprinted)

Mildreth

Colker, M. L., ed. "A Hagiographic Polemic." *Mediaeval Studies* 39 (1977): 60–108. (on *Libellus contra inanes S. uirginis Mildrethe usurpatores*)

Rollason, D. W., ed. "Vita S. Mildrethe uirginis." In *The Mildrith Legend: A Study in Early Medieval Hagiography in England*, 108–43. Leicester: Leicester University Press, 1982.

——. ed. "Goscelin of Canterbury's Account of the Translation and Miracles of St. Mildrith (BHL 5961/4): An Edition with Notes." *Mediaeval Studies*, 48 (1986): 139–210.

Mildburh

Vita et miracula S. Milburge, unprinted; ed. and trans. R. C. Love. (in progress)

Eadwold the Hermit of Cerne

Licence, T., ed., "Goscelin of Saint-Bertin and the Hagiography of St. Eadwold of Cerne." *Journal of Medieval Latin* 16 (2006): 182–207. (hitherto unprinted lections)

Folcard of Saint-Bertin

Botwulf

Vita S. Botolphi. ActaS June III.402–3; IV.327–8.

Birch, W. de Gray, ed. *Translatio S. Botolphi.* In *Liber Vitae: Register and Martyrology of New Minster and Hyde Abbey, Winchester*, 286–90. London: Simpkin & Co., 1892.

John of Beverley

Raine, J., ed. "Vita S. Iohannis." In *Historians of the Church of York and its Archbishops.* Vol. 1, 239–60. Rolls Series (3 vols.). London: Longman & Co., 1879.

Wilson, S., trans. *The Life and After-life of St. John of Beverley: The Evolution of the Cult of an Anglo-Saxon Saint.* Aldershot: Ashgate, 2006. (esp. pp. 143–56)

Tancred, Torhtred and Tova

Birch, W. de Gray, ed. *Liber Vitae*, 284–86.

Osbern of Canterbury

Ælfheah

Wharton, H., ed. "Vita et translatio S. Elphegi." In *Anglia Sacra.* Vol. 2, 122–47. London: Impensis Richardi Chiswel, ad insigne Rosae Coronatae in coemeterio S. Pauli, 1691.

Shaw, F., trans. *Osbern's Life of Alfege.* London: St. Paul's, 1999.

Dunstan

Stubbs, W., ed. "Vita et miracula S. Dunstani." In *Memorials of St. Dunstan*, 69–191. London: Longman, 1874.

Eadmer of Canterbury

Dunstan

Stubbs, W., ed. "Vita et miracula S. Dunstani." In *Memorials of St. Dunstan*, 162–249. London: Longman, 1874.

Muir, B. J., and A. J. Turner, eds. and trans. "Vita S. Dustani." In *Eadmer of Canterbury: Lives and Miracles of Saints Oda, Dunstan, and Oswald*, 44–211. OMT. Oxford: Clarendon Press, 2006.

Oswald

Raine, J., ed. "Vita et miracula S. Oswaldi." In *Historians of the Church of York and Its Archbishops*. Vol. 2, 1–59. Rolls Series (3 vols.). London: Longman & Co., 1886.

Muir, B. J., and A. J. Turner, eds. and trans. "Vita S. Oswaldi." In *Eadmer of Canterbury: Lives and Miracles of Saints Oda, Dunstan, and Oswald*, 216–89. OMT. Oxford: Clarendon Press, 2006.

Odo

Wharton, H., ed. "Vita S. Odonis Cantuariensis." In *Anglia Sacra*. Vol. 2, 78–87. London: Impensis Richardi Chiswel, ad insigne Rosae Coronatae in coemeterio S. Pauli, 1691.

Muir, B. J., and A. J. Turner, eds. and trans. "Vita S. Odonis." In *Eadmer of Canterbury: Lives and Miracles of Saints Oda, Dunstan, and Oswald*, 4–39. OMT. Oxford: Clarendon Press, 2006.

Wilfrid

Raine, J., ed. "Vita S. Wilfridi Eboracensis." *Historians of the Church of York*. Vol. 1, 163–226. Rolls Series (3 vols.). London: Longman & Co., 1879.

Muir, B. J., and A. J. Turner, eds. and trans. *Vita Sancti Wilfridi Auctore Edmero*. Exeter: University of Exeter Press, 1998.

Later Medieval Compilations of Hagiography (Containing Abbreviated Versions of Possibly Much Earlier Texts)

[for contents lists, see Lapidge and Love, "The Latin Hagiography of England and Wales"]

John of Tynemouth. *Sanctilogium Angliae, Walliae, Scotiae et Hiberniae*. Edited by C. Horstman. Nova Legenda Angliae. 2 vols. Oxford: Clarendon Press, 1901.

Gotha, Forschungsbibliothek I.81. (The Gotha compilation, 14th century); contents listed in P. Grosjean. "De codice hagiographico Gothano." *Analecta Bollandiana* 58 (1940): 90–103.

London, BL, Lansdowne 436. (The Romsey legendary, 14th century); contents listed in P. Grosjean. "Vita S. Roberti Novi Monasterii in Anglia abbatis." *Analecta Bollandiana* 61 (1938): 334–60.

Anglo-Latin Hagiography: Selected Secondary Reading

Seventh- and Eighth-Century Hagiography

Bonner, G., D. W. Rollason, and C. Stancliffe, eds. *St. Cuthbert, His Cult and His Community to AD 1200.* Woodbridge: Boydell and Brewer, 1989.

Ciccarese, M. P. "Osservazioni sulle fonti e modelli della 'Vita Guthlaci' di Felice." *Studi Storico-Religiosi* 5 (1981): 135–42.

Coates, S. "The Bishop as Pastor and Solitary: Bede and the Spiritual Authority of the Monk Bishop." *Journal of Ecclesiastical History* 47 (1996): 601–19.

Damon, J. *Soldier Saints and Holy Warriors: Warfare and Sanctity in the Literature of Early England.* Aldershot: Ashgate, 2003.

Jones, C. W. *Saints' Lives and Chronicles in Early England.* Ithaca, NY: Cornell University Press, 1947.

Kirby, D. P. "Bede, Eddius Stephanus and the Life of Wilfrid." *English Historical Review* 98 (1983): 101–14.

——. "The Genesis of a Cult: Cuthbert of Farne and Ecclesiastical Politics in Northumbria in the Late Seventh and Early Eighth Centuries." *Journal of Ecclesiastical History* 46 (1995): 383–97.

Lapidge, M. "Bede's Metrical Vita S. Cuthberti." In *St. Cuthbert, His Cult and His Community to AD 1200,* edited by G. Bonner, D.W. Rollason, and C. Stancliffe, 77–93. Woodbridge: Boydell and Brewer, 1989.

Limone, O. "La vita di Gregorio Magno dell'Anonimo di Whitby." *Studi Medievali* 3.1 (1978): 37–67.

McClure, J. "Bede and the Life of Ceolfrid." *Peritia* 3 (1984): 71–84.

Stancliffe, C., and E. Cambridge, eds. *Oswald: Northumbrian King to European Saint.* Stamford: Paul Watkins, 1995.

Foley, W. T. "Suffering and Sanctity in Bede's Prose Life of St. Cuthbert." *Journal of Theological Studies* 50 (1999): 102–16.

Tenth-Century Texts

Gransden, A. "Abbo of Fleury's Passio Sancti Edmundi." *Revue Bénédictine* 105 (1995): 20–78.

Lapidge, M. "B. and the Vita S. Dunstani." In *ALL, 900–1066,* 279–91. 1993.

——. "Byrhtferth and Oswald." In *St. Oswald of Worcester: Life and Influence,* edited by N. Brooks and C. Cubitt, 64–83. London and New York: Leicester University Press, 1996.

——. "Byrhtferth and the Vita S. Ecgwini." *Mediaeval Studies* 41 (1979): 331–53. Reprinted in *ALL, 900–1066,* 293–315. 1993.

The Eleventh Century

Fell, C. E. "Edward King and Martyr and the Anglo-Saxon Hagiographic Tradition." In *Ethelred the Unready: Papers from the Millenary Conference*, edited by D. Hill, 1–14. British Series 59. Oxford: British Archaeological Reports, 1978.

Hayward, P. A. "Translation-Narratives in Post-Conquest Hagiography and English Resistance to the Norman Conquest." *Anglo-Norman Studies* 21 (1999): 67–93.

Love, R. C. "'Torture Me, Rend Me, Burn Me, Kill Me!' Goscelin of Saint-Bertin and the Depiction of Female Sanctity." In *Writing Women Saints in Anglo-Saxon England*, edited by P. E. Szarmach, 274–306. Toronto: UTP, 2013.

Ridyard, S. J. "Condigna Veneratio: Norman Attitudes to Anglo-Saxon Saints." *Anglo-Norman Studies* 9 (1987): 179–206.

Rollason, D. W. "The Cults of Murdered Royal Saints in Anglo-Saxon England." *ASE* 11 (1982): 1–22.

Sharpe, R. "Goscelin's St. Augustine and St. Mildreth: Hagiography and Liturgy in Context." *Journal of Theological Studies* 41 (1990): 502–16.

Online Resources for the Study of Anglo-Latin

Anglo-Latin Texts Online

Camden, D., ed. *Corpus Scriptorum Latinorum*. http://www.forumromanum.org/literature/index.html.

David Camden's Corpus Scriptorum Latinorum – sketchy Latin author list, with some links to texts and translations, including Abbo of Fleury, Alcuin, Asser, Bede.

Halsall, P., ed. *Internet Medieval Sourcebook*. http://www.fordham.edu/halsall/sbook.html.

For Anglo-Latin, the IMS includes translations (and links for translations) of the following: Bede's *HE*, Willibald's Life of Boniface, the Correspondence of Boniface (48 letters); Ælfric's Old English version of Abbo's Life of Edmund; Asser's Life of Alfred; excerpts from the Whitby Life of Gregory the Great; Bede's Prose Life of Cuthbert; the *Historia Abbatum* of Lives of the Abbots of Wearmouth-Jarrow; Hygeburc's *Hodoeporicon of Willibald*; Willibald's Life of Boniface; Alcuin's Life of Willibrord.

Harsch, U., ed. *Bibliotheca Augustanta*. http://www.fh-augsburg.de/~harsch/augustana.html.

Ulrich Harsch's *Blbliotheca Augustana* (all in Latin!), includes e-texts (Latin) or facsimiles and pictures of Bede's *HE* (text of preface, facsimile from books 1 & 2), the whole of the metrical Life of Cuthbert, the *Historia Abbatum*, the *Letter to Ecgbert*, and the *De Orthographia*.

The Latin Library. http://www.thelatinlibrary.com/.

Under 'Christian' includes a small selection of Alcuin's poems; under 'medieval' includes Abbo of Fleury's *Passio S. Eadmundi*, and Asser's *Life of Alfred*.

Monumenta Germaniae Historica. http://www.dmgh.de.

MGH contains all the Bonifatian correspondence, Aldhelm's works, Alcuin's Letters, poems and hagiography, Hugeburc.

Hagiography

BHLMS Index analytique des Catalogues de manuscrits hagiographiques latins publiés par les Bollandistes. http://bhlms.fltr.ucl.ac.be/.

Provides access to the BHLMS *Index analytique des Catalogues de manuscrits hagiographiques latins publiés par les Bollandistes*, which allows you to find out which manuscripts a given hagiographical text is preserved in (but only the manuscripts catalogued by the Bollandists)

North Sea Currents: Old English and Old Norse in Comparison and in Contact

Richard Dance[1]

IT HARDLY NEEDS SAYING that Old Norse language and literature are of enormous relevance for the student of Old English, at a whole range of levels.[2] The delineation of the relationships between the words, sounds, grammar, and other features of the early English and Scandinavian languages has been a central concern since the beginnings of comparative Germanic linguistics. The close kinship of their medieval literatures, variously understood and interpreted, has also been a consistent emphasis in the scholarship, such that few if any surveys of the Old English literary canon fail to draw comparisons with the components of Old Norse textual culture. My aims in this essay are rather more modest. I shall not attempt to offer an introduction to the Old Norse language or its literature; guides to the primary materials and to scholarly discussions of them are plentiful and easily accessible in a range of handbooks and other synoptic treatments.[3] I shall instead focus on one particular, and particularly provocative, aspect of the comparative study of Old English and Old Norse: namely, the linguistic and literary-cultural exchanges which took place when speakers of the two languages met in Viking Age England. This field is in itself, of course, a very large one, and I shall provide no more than a short review of the main elements in recent scholarly discussion, divided loosely into the "literary" and the "linguistic."[4]

Literary Connections

Hunting for analogues between the surviving literary, especially poetic, corpora of the two languages is a pursuit of long standing.[5] It has been conducted at all levels and scales of analysis, from the big game of stories, characters, and narrative structure, as well as the larger generic and thematic foci, to the *lepidoptera* of individual motifs, vocabulary items, and phraseology.[6] Some of these analogues are old friends in the critical literature, and would seem unchallengeable as evidence of a genuine connection, of whatever antiquity, between English and Norse traditions. For example, there is the shared legendary material whose investigation is the bread and butter of scholarship on texts like *Beowulf*, *Widsith*, and *Deor* on the one hand, and the Norse *fornaldarsögur* and Eddic verse like *Völundarkviða* on the other; or the fundamental generic similarities which underpin work on wisdom/gnomic literature in both languages, stretching to correspondences of style and wording such as the touchstone of *The Wanderer*, lines 108–9, and *Hávamál*, stanzas 76–77. Other likenesses are more tenuous, and the question of whether the supposed similarities constitute evidence of actual connection or simple coincidence is a recurrent preoccupation. Controversy may come to beset cases where a relationship had at one time seemed demonstrable; emblematic is the debate over the source of similarities between *Beowulf* and *Grettis saga*.[7]

If one does suppose a genuine "link" in any case, then in tandem with this comes the (if anything more tendentious) matter of explaining its origin. The conventional stance is to assume shared inheritance from common Germanic stock, encouraged by the fact that some of the most visible correspondences between English and Norse traditions consist in these literatures' common cast of legendary, heroic figures from the Migration Age itself. But there has been an increased tendency over the last few decades, championed especially by Frank (in a series of pieces beginning in 1979),[8] to query the default invocation of this inheritance as opposed to more recent Anglo-Norse contacts in the Viking Age. Advocates of this position continue to accept that some features are most likely to reflect shared transmission from a common past (e.g., fundamental aspects of the meter of alliterative poetry);[9] but many other elements have now come up for grabs as potentially indicative of contemporary Norse influence upon Old English literary endeavors, or of a shared North Sea cultural milieu. In this way, Frank would explain the common interest in heroic legendary material;[10] the same holds for the generic shades of *erfidrápur* that have been descried in *Beowulf*,[11] and those of skaldic eulogy in the Anglo-Saxon Chronicle verse,[12] and much else besides. This opening up of possible explanations has done much to refresh scholarship on the subject, and to solicit useful re-engagement with old orthodoxies.[13] It stems from the belief that our perspective on Anglo-Saxon literary production can only be broadened and enriched if it takes into account those subjects, modes, and devices (especially those having to do with the panegyric and mythological) which survive most clearly expressed in Norse tradition, but which must have been brought to Viking Age England, and which it is plausible to assume interacted with native literary culture on the ground. This conjunction, if it happened, would have occurred largely on the fringes, in the wings as it were, of the activity sanctioned by the monastic centers of Anglo-Saxon book production; but perhaps we might still spot its effects peeping from behind the curtain occasionally, if we knew how to recognize them. After all, the evidence for Norse influence upon English culture is manifest in a variety of other spheres at this period (language, graphic art, and hairstyles, to name but the most often cited),[14] and so it seems only fair that it should be detectable in literary cross-fertilization to boot.

The problem remains, however, that contemporary borrowing of this sort has proven very difficult to demonstrate convincingly in any one given instance. The close examination of English and Norse appropriations of even very similar-seeming material often serves to remind one of their fundamental differences as much as their overlaps, and has a tendency to muddy the waters (see for instance Jesch's reassessment of the "beasts of battle" motif).[15] If this is so when the comparison between the contents of traditions seems well-founded, then these caveats apply all the more when it comes to (inevitably more tenuous) claims for artistic influence at the level of verbal style, and suggestions of "a distinctive viking-age fashion in imagery."[16] Individual studies of this type, it should be stressed, can have much to offer, suggesting as they do aesthetically enlightening, eye-opening ways of elucidating specific poetic imagery or rehabilitating textual cruces by imaginative close-reading.[17] Easy though it is to see the merit in exploring connections at this level, and to sympathize with the impatient belief that they are indeed there to be demonstrated, it is also very hard to counter the skepticism that has and, perhaps, must be expressed as to the intractable difficulties of proof, even in the most alluring of cases.[18] All too often, scholars are wont to find themselves pinioned between these two conflicting positions (despite their optimism, Frank and Bjork both foreground the potentially crippling problems of methodology).[19] Even when the linguistic footprint of contact is apparent in a given text in the form of loanwords, it must be remembered that this is not necessarily evidence of *literary* borrowing (a distinction too often neglected when dealing with e.g., *Brunanburh*).[20] We should, arguably, be still more cautious about making claims for such borrowing in poems where this footprint is not discernible. In this light, the total absence of verifiable Norse-derived words in Old English poems the length of *Exodus* and *Beowulf*, which could well be pre-Viking Age compositions, is far from a trivial concern.[21]

It may be noted that arguments for the transfer of literary material have tended to concentrate on the influence of Norse on English, hardly surprising when it was the Scandinavians who were the most visibly active travelers in our Viking Age context. Assessments of literary/linguistic traffic do not, however, have to imply a one-way street: English linguistic influence upon Norse poetry has long been mooted,[22] and in recent years there has been increased interest, on this and other grounds (including peculiarities of diction, meter, and narrative content), in the claim that particular Eddic poems originated in or were very strongly influenced by Viking Age England (notably the Helgi lays, *Völuspá*, *Völundarkviða*, and *Þrymskviða*).[23] Nevertheless, most of the same difficulties apply here as those which hamstring arguments for Norse influence on English texts: the case for any single point is rarely compelling, and the weight of their combination is chiefly a matter of faith (the most convincing, and a current favorite bone of this particular contention, is perhaps *Völundarkviða*).[24]

Many of these issues are, however, pointedly obviated by some recent studies which have taken a somewhat different tack, and which open up prospects for future research. These studies eschew the piecemeal focus on the exchange of particular features between literary traditions, in whatever direction, in favor of a more broadly comparative interpretation of their roles in the context of Viking Age English culture. A detailed consideration of this context, and the multifaceted expectations of authors and audiences which it implies within much the same period and place, represents a means of approaching a more fully-rounded impression of "Anglo-Saxon England's literary history."[25] Furthermore, it promises to unlock aspects of the meaning of both English and Norse texts often overlooked in the search for specific and direct influence.[26] The lion's share of scholarship in this vein has centered upon the Old Norse verse (especially in skaldic meters) known to have been composed in England, or for Scandinavian patrons connected with England, during the Viking Age.[27] Townend's work on the *Knútsdrápur* is nicely demonstrative of the efficacy of this method. The image he paints of Winchester as the focus of complementary but entirely contemporary traditions, both equally representative of Cnut's public face(s) and attitudes to artistic patronage, is eye-opening.[28] The historical contextualization of the "eulogistic" verse in the Anglo-Saxon Chronicle can also be used to broaden the inquiry into its relationship with skaldic poetry.[29] Perhaps one of the most startling contexts which has been invoked, and emblematic of the fruitfulness of this particular perspective on the literary traditions of the period, belongs to the skaldic verse in memory of the Anglo-Danish Earl

Waltheof. This verse was apparently composed in post-Conquest England, and its mythological kennings and traditional *dróttkvætt* meter must (presumably) have been delivered in an Anglo-Norman court setting.[30]

Linguistic Influences

Scholarship dedicated to the linguistic outcomes of Anglo-Norse relations in the Viking Age has also been directed primarily at traffic *from* rather than *towards* Scandinavia (though there are some exceptions).[31] Given the evident scale and range of effects that contact with Old Norse speakers had upon the English language in the early medieval period, this is scarcely to be wondered at. Recent attempts at the elucidation of this contact will be my focus in the brief survey that follows.[32]

Some comment on the consequences of Anglo-Scandinavian interactions for the vocabulary of English, often accompanied by speculations as to the penetration of Norse influence into other linguistic domains (phonological, morphological, syntactic), is a staple of handbooks and histories of the English language. Those which focus in detail on the Old and/or Middle English periods, or on borrowings in English, usually contain the most useful introductory remarks.[33] Research dedicated to this topic in recent decades has been characterized by an attempt to reconstruct and codify more precisely the linguistic relationship of speakers of Norse and English when they came into contact in Viking Age England; and by the quest to understand, with the benefit of increasingly sophisticated theoretical models, the means by which Norse-derived material might have entered English. The "creolization" hypotheses which came into the limelight in the 1970s and 1980s,[34] while serving to draw attention to much useful material, ought probably to be noticed more for their enthusiasm than their success in pursuing what is now regarded as a less than completely congruent (or at any rate unsubtly applied) contact model. These earlier studies have been succeeded by discussions which, as well as arguably being better grounded in their knowledge of the historical and textual evidence, offer more nuanced and discriminating readings of the possible processes at work. A series of accounts have now reassessed (and in some cases redefined) what may usefully be meant by the term "creole" in describing the Anglo-Norse situation, and/or have sought to show that the transfer of Scandinavian linguistic material into English may be better understood in relation to other, less radical contact-based phenomena.[35] The biggest strides have been made by Townend, whose monograph offers a uniquely detailed consideration of the evidence for intercultural contact (including onomastic data). His identification of adequate mutual intelligibility between speakers of Norse and English has allowed for the more precise framing of the processes involved, in terms of a combination of borrowing and shift-based interference.[36]

As has become clear, a firm grip on robust, properly-focussed (and theoretically-sensitive) explanations for the outcome of language contact is essential when one tries to elucidate the specifics of the Anglo-Norse situation. However, such an approach will only provide partial answers if it is not married to a serious consideration both of the linguistic forms which provide much of the evidence for this particular instance of contact, and of the textual traditions in which those forms are recorded. There is still some fundamental work to do on the lexical items which scholars have claimed as loans from Norse, on their etymologies, forms, and semantic and stylistic nuances, if we hope to identify the extent to which Norse-derived material was appropriated by English and to understand the factors that underlie its acceptance, use, and spread.[37] The Old English period has now been treated in an exemplary way in a series of works by Pons-Sanz, culminating in a major book that identifies, catalogues, and interprets the distribution and usage of Norse-derived lexis in the entire Old English corpus.[38] The essential groundwork has long since been laid for studies of the far more numerous Norse derivations in Middle English and later (see in particular the monographs by Björkman and Rynell),[39] and general remarks and summations continue to provide useful orientation.[40] Some trends in loan-word attestation in Middle English texts are observable from an analysis of samples available to students of corpus linguistics, but the level of detail accessible by broad sweeps is inevitably limited.[41] As long ago as 1978, Angus McIntosh pointed out the potential value in a concerted effort to assemble a complete list of the Norse-derived lexis in Middle English texts;[42] his call-to-arms, however, remains in large measure unanswered. The need for both the coal-face collection of data (including fundamental etymological work) and for thoroughgoing, context-specific analyses remains massive. There have been a number of recent studies which have continued to open up this territory to exploration, focusing in-depth on particular texts or groups of words from one or more of these perspectives (etymology, distribution, semantics, style), including work by Kries (medieval Scots), Skaffari (early Middle English), and Bator (words in Middle English since obsolete),[43] as well as my own forays into this area;[44] but vast tracts remain to be mapped.

NOTES

[1] This is a revised and updated version of an article which appeared in the online journal *Literature Compass* (issue 1 (2004): 1–10) under the title "North Sea Currents: Old English-Old Norse Relations, Literary and Linguistic." I am grateful to the editors of *Literature Compass* for permission to reuse material here; and to Jayne Carroll, Sara Pons-Sanz, Judy Quinn, Paul Szarmach, Matthew Townend and Elaine Treharne for their valuable comments on various incarnations of this piece.

[2] The term "Old Norse" is retained here in its broad (and what still seems to me its most readily understood) philological sense, i.e., to refer (collectively or non-specifically) to the Scandinavian languages in the period approximately 700–1500 AD. But since "Norse" has been and can be taken to denote things Norwegian in particular, and because of the centrality of Iceland in medieval textual production, readers should note that it has become common practice in recent decades to refer to the literary corpus as "Old Norse-Icelandic" (see the remarks in O'Donoghue, *Old Norse-Icelandic Literature*, pp. 6–7). On the other hand the practice in Bandle (et al.), eds., *The Nordic Languages*, indicates a relatively novel preference amongst some historical linguists for the term "Old Nordic."

[3] For introductions to the corpus of Old Norse literature and study of it, consult, e.g., O'Donoghue, *Old Norse-Icelandic Literature*; Clunies-Ross, *Cambridge Introduction*; and the essays in McTurk, ed., *Companion*; Clover and Lindow, eds., *Old Norse-Icelandic Literature*; and Clunies Ross, ed., *Old Icelandic*. Handy summaries are also provided by Andersson, "Old Norse-Icelandic Literature"; Szokody, "Types of Texts I"; Jörgensen, "Types of Texts II"; and by a wide range of entries in Pulsiano, ed., *Medieval Scandinavia*. For skaldic verse, see the website of the ongoing project to re-edit the entire skaldic corpus (http://abdn.ac.uk/skaldic/db.php). Other indispensable resources on the internet include *BONIS* (searchable Bibliography of Old Norse-Icelandic Studies; https://alvis-bib.sdu.dk/uhtbin/cgisirsi/?ps=2rNb60sij9/BONIS/130140011/60/81/X); and *EGIL* (Electronic Gateway for Icelandic Literature, including electronic texts, http://www.egil.nottingham.ac.uk/). For the Scandinavian languages, the first port of call is now the monumental Bandle (et al.), eds., *The Nordic Languages* (the main material on the origins of Norse and its history up to the end of the "Old" period is in chapters 62–118). For good, shorter surveys of the early history of Scandinavian languages, see also the excellent accounts in Barnes, "Language" and "Languages and Ethnic Groups"; and Gordon's *Introduction* remains a useful starting-point for grammar. The most easily accessible dictionaries are the ongoing *Ordbog over det norrøne prosasprog* (online at http://onp.ku.dk/, with access to slips for unpublished entries); Fritzner's *Ordbog* (searchable online at http://www.edd.uio.no/perl/search/search.cgi?appid=86&tabid=1275); Zoëga, *Concise Dictionary* (online at http://www.ling.upenn.edu/~kurisuto/germanic/oi_zoega_about.html and http://norse.ulver.com/dct/zoega/index.html); and

the Cleasby-Vigfusson, *Icelandic-English Dictionary* (online at http://www.ling.upenn.edu/~kurisuto/germanic/oi_cleasbyvigfusson_about.html). For a recent, brief overview of the evidence for the Old Norse language as spoken outside Scandinavia, see Barnes, "History and Development." For the Scandinavian runic inscriptions in the British Isles, see the summary in Barnes, "Runic Evidence"; the surveys in Holman, *Runic Inscriptions*; and Barnes and Page, *Runic Inscriptions*.

[4] For some recent guides to the historical background of Anglo-Norse contacts in the Viking Age, which I shall not go into further here, see e.g., Keynes, "Vikings in England"; Richards, *Viking Age England*; Dumville, "Vikings in the British Isles"; Hadley, *Vikings in England*; Carroll, Harrison, and Williams, *Vikings in Britain and Ireland*; and the essays in Graham-Campbell (et al.), eds., *Vikings and the Danelaw*, and Hadley and Richards, eds., *Cultures in Contact*; and for a model study of Scandinavian influence in a major English region see Townend, *Viking Age Yorkshire*. On the representation of the Anglo-Saxons in later Icelandic literary sources, note also Fjalldal, *Anglo-Saxon England*.

[5] Note e.g., Bjork, "Scandinavian Relations," p. 388.

[6] For overviews, discussions, and fuller examples, see especially Frank, "Anglo-Scandinavian Poetic Relations"; and Bjork, "Scandinavian Relations." See also Townend, "Pre-Cnut Praise-Poetry," pp. 357–59; Carroll, "Poetic Discourse," pp. 34–60; Bibire, "North Sea Language Contacts," pp. 101–5; and O'Donoghue, *Old Norse-Icelandic Literature*, pp. 136–48.

[7] On this matter see especially Orchard, *Pride and Prodigies*, pp. 140–68 and Fjalldal, *Long Arm*. For guides to discussion of the Norse analogues to Beowulf, in particular, see especially Andersson, "Sources and Analogues," pp. 129–34 and 146–48; Orchard, *Critical Companion*, pp. 98–129; Fulk, Bjork, and Niles, eds., *Klaeber's Beowulf*, esp. pp. xxxvii–xliii, clxxxiii–v; and Niles, ed., *Beowulf and Lejre*, esp. pp. 169–254, 287–93. North (*Origins of Beowulf*, pp. 194–224) has recently discussed parallels in *Beowulf* to some Norse mythological motifs. For further reflections on some semantic comparanda and putative narrative connections between Old (and Middle) English and Old Norse, see also Taylor, *Sharing Story*.

[8] See Frank, "Old Norse Memorial Eulogies"; "Skaldic Verse"; "Anglo-Saxon Audience"; "What Kind of Poetry"; "Anglo-Scandinavian Poetic Relations"; and "North Sea Soundings."

[9] For comparative work on Old English and Old Norse meter, consult Fulk and Gade, "Bibliography."

[10] Frank, "Anglo-Scandinavian Poetic Relations," pp. 76–77. See also Poole, "Crossing the Language Divide," esp. pp. 603–5; and further Niles, "Danish Origins," esp. pp. 45–50.

[11] Frank, "Old Norse Memorial Eulogies."

[12] Harris, "*Brunanburh* 12b–13a"; and Niles, "Skaldic Technique."

[13] O'Donoghue usefully reads this recent willingness to invoke contact and cultural exchange as a reaction against earlier scholarship's preferred appropriation

of a common Germanic prehistoric identity, "as contemporary myths of origins become more inclined to value racial diversity than to insist on racial purity" (*Old Norse-Icelandic Literature*, p. 136); and cf. also Frank, "Anglo-Saxon Audiences," pp. 350–51.

[14] See e.g., Frank, "Anglo-Scandinavian Poetic Relations," pp. 74–75.

[15] Jesch, "Eagles, Ravens and Wolves."

[16] Frank, "Anglo-Scandinavian Poetic Relations," p. 78.

[17] On particular texts see notably Frank, "Skaldic Verse" (*Beowulf*); Harris, "*Brunanburh* 12b–13a," and Niles, "Skaldic Technique" (both on *Brunanburh*); Frank, "Anglo-Saxon Audiences" (*Exodus* and *Beowulf*), "What Kind of Poetry" (*Exodus*), and "North Sea Soundings" (*Andreas*); and Poole, "Crossing the Language Divide" (various, including *Brunanburh*, *Maldon*, *Judith*).

[18] See especially Townend, "Pre-Cnut Praise-Poetry," pp. 357–59; and Carroll, "Poetic Discourse," pp. 34–60. As a pithy reflection on the intransigence of the methodological difficulties, noteworthy is Page's remark that the tools available for work of this sort, "are too blunt to attack the problems of a pair of literatures surviving in random sample and with a complete absence of chronology" (Page, Review of *The Vikings*, p. 309; cited in Frank, "Anglo-Scandinavian Poetic Relations," p. 75).

[19] See Frank, "Anglo-Scandinavian Poetic Relations," p. 75; and Bjork, "Scandinavian Relations," p. 397.

[20] On this point see Townend, "Pre-Cnut Praise Poetry," p. 359; and Carroll, "Poetic Discourse," esp. pp. 34 and 47–60.

[21] For the (especially linguistic/metrical) evidence in favor of an early dating of these poems, see Fulk, *Old English Meter*, esp. pp. 348–92 for conclusions, and the essays in Neidorf, ed., *Dating of Beowulf*. For other recent summaries of work on the dating of Beowulf, see Orchard, *Critical Companion*, pp. 5–6; Fulk, Bjork, and Niles, eds., Klaeber's Beowulf, pp. clxiii–clxxx; and also Frank, "A Scandal in Toronto."

[22] See Hofmann, *Nordisch-Englische*, pp. 21–148, though his conclusions are in need of detailed reassessment. For some recent discussion see Poole, "Crossing the Language Divide"; and O'Donnell, Townend, and Tyler, "European Literature," pp. 611–12.

[23] For references, see Bjork, "Scandinavian Relations," p. 389; McKinnell, "Eddic Poetry"; Gunnell, "Eddic Poetry," p. 94; and Schulte, "Language Contact," p. 770.

[24] See e.g., McKinnell, "The Context of *Völundarkviða*" and "Eddic Poetry," pp. 331–33; and also Poole, "Crossing the Language Divide," p. 603. It should be stressed that the situation is quite different when it comes to early Scandinavian Christian literature, especially homiletic prose, some of which is demonstrably influenced by material (in both Latin and the vernacular) imported from England; see Abram, "Anglo-Saxon Influence," and work cited therein; and O'Donnell, Townend, and Tyler, "European Literature," pp. 609–16. For the intriguing case

of the Old English and Old Norse versions of the *Prose Phoenix*, and their possible contexts, see Pons-Sanz, "Two Compounds."

[25] Townend, "Contextualizing the *Knútsdrápur*," pp. 178–79.

[26] For the principles involved, see also Carroll, "Poetic Discourse," pp. 6–7.

[27] For a corpus of the skaldic poems see Jesch, "Skaldic Verse." For major studies, see Hines, "Egill's *Höfuðlausn*"; Carroll, "Poetic Discourse," pp. 148–240; Townend, "Pre-Cnut Praise Poetry," "Contextualizing the *Knútsdrápur*," and "Cnut's Poets"; and Poole, "Crossing the Language Divide," pp. 582–602. Of related interest are Townend, "Norse Poets and English Kings" and "Whatever Happened."

[28] Townend, "Contextualizing the *Knútsdrápur*," esp. pp. 168–78; and see also Jesch, "Cultural Paganism," esp. pp. 58–63. On the presentation of Cnut in skaldic verse, see also the important study in Frank, "King Cnut." For a stimulating discussion of the literature of Cnut's reign in the broader cultural contexts of eleventh-century Europe, see O'Donnell, Townend, and Tyler, "European Literature," esp. pp. 609–16.

[29] Townend argues that any generic similarities between the two may be better assigned to the "heroic age" conditions in Viking Age England which allowed panegyric verse in both languages to flourish, rather than to the results of direct borrowing ("Pre-Cnut Praise-Poetry," pp. 359–70).

[30] See Jesch, "Skaldic Verse," pp. 321–23; Parsons, "How Long," p. 307; and O'Donoghue, *Old Norse-Icelandic Literature*, pp. 144–48.

[31] See notably Hofmann, *Nordisch-Englische*, pp. 21–148; and now Gammeltoft and Holck, "*Gemstēn* and Other Old English Pearls," together with the attempts discussed above to localize the composition of certain Norse poems to England or otherwise to find English influence on their diction. The identification of certainly English (as opposed to other West Germanic) borrowings in Scandinavian sources is fraught with difficulty; for some brief assessments and guides to further reading see Schulte, "Language Contact," pp. 769–70; Braunmüller, "Language Contact," p. 1034; and Fellows-Jensen, "From Scandinavia to the British Isles," pp. 257–58.

[32] On place-names (which I shall not cover here), see in particular the excellent surveys in Abrams and Parsons, "Place-Names," and Townend, "Scandinavian Place-Names in England"; and recent reviews of the subject such as Fellows-Jensen, "Scandinavian Settlement" and "Scandinavian Background"; Sandred, "Language Contact," esp. pp. 2065–71. On the range of onomastic and other linguistic traffic in both directions, and with regard to all the languages of Britain and Ireland, see also the useful overview in Fellows-Jensen, "From Scandinavia to the British Isles." On the rather more vexing question of contact between speakers of North Germanic languages and (the precursors of) Old English *before* the Viking Age, which is bound up with the broader (and complex) matter of genetic filiation among the Germanic languages, see for instance the useful accounts and references in Nielsen, *Germanic Languages*; Townend, *Language and History*,

pp. 25–26, 29; Bandle (et al.), eds., *Nordic Languages*, chapters 62–65; and notably the work of Hines, "Philology, Archaeology" and "Archaeology and Language," as well as the remarks in Schulte, "Language Contact," pp. 770–71.

[33] Of the (relatively) modest number of loan-words usually identified in Old English texts, most often cited are words connected to legislation, social rights, and responsibilities, such as *lagu* (law), *grið* (protection), *husting* (assembly), *saht* (agreement), *þræll* (slave), *utlaga* (outlaw); but a range of others expressing very commonplace concepts are already to be found too (e.g., *loft* (sky), *hyttan* (meet), *scinn* (skin), *tacan* (take)). In Middle English and later periods, the lexical influence from Norse is far more varied and more apparent; the most familiar examples cited in the handbooks include *anger, call, cast, die, give, guest, ill, leg, loan, loose, meek, nay, skirt, sky, though, till, ugly, want, window, wing,* and the pronouns *they, their,* and *them.* Amongst the fuller recent surveys and summaries may be listed the discussions in Kastovsky, "Semantics and Vocabulary," pp. 320–36; Burnley, "Lexis and Semantics," pp. 415–23; Nielsen, *Continental Backgrounds*, pp. 165–88; Braunmüller, "Language Contact," pp. 1029–34; Sandred, "Language Contact," esp. pp. 2063–65; Townend, "Contacts and Conflicts"; and the extensive accounts in Miller, *External Influences*, pp. 91–147; and Durkin, *Borrowed Words*, pp. 171–221. See also my discussion in Dance, "English in Contact: Norse."

[34] Typified by Domingue, "Middle English"; and Poussa, "Evolution of Early Standard English."

[35] A considered account, and a good place to start, is Görlach, "Middle English." Other notable discussions, with varying adherence to the idea of "creole" or "creoloid" stages in the development of English, include: Wallmannsberger, "Creole Hypothesis"; Hansen, "Historical Implications"; Thomason and Kaufman, *Language Contact*, esp. pp. 275–304; Hines, "Creole in Context"; Danchev, "ME Creolization Hypothesis"; McWhorter, "What Happened to English?"; Braunmüller, "Language Contact," pp. 1032–33. And see further the reviews of some of the arguments in Barnes, "Norse in the British Isles," pp. 67–74; Mitchell, "Englishness," pp. 163–70; Townend, "Viking Age England," pp. 91–92; Townend, *Language and History*, pp. 196–99; and Dance, *Words Derived from Old Norse*, pp. 295–98. Among recent, noteworthy studies of specific phenomena or features of English which bear on these issues, especially as regarding morphological and syntactic developments (and useful as sources of further reading) are Dalton-Puffer, "Middle English is a Creole"; Allen, "Middle English Case Loss"; and Miller, "Origin and Diffusion" and "Morphosyntactic Legacy." The work by Emonds and Faarlund (see especially their provocatively titled book, *English: The Language of the Vikings*) also focuses on the Scandinavian influence on English syntax, and mounts the argument that, when looked at syntactically, Modern English must be the direct descendent not of Old English but of a (massively relexified) "Anglicized Norse" spoken in Viking Age England. This is in many ways an unexpected throwback to the polemical claims of catastrophic breaks in the transmission of English typified by the heavier-handed creolization theories

(although it seems to have been written without awareness of the more recent scholarship cited in this section).

[36] Townend, *Language and History*. The main issues are flagged in Townend, "Viking Age England," and examined in the context of other contacts with English in the early medieval period in his "Contacts and Conflicts"; and see also Townend, *English Place-Names*, esp. pp. 96–98. For the latest thinking on the survival of Norse as a separate language in England, see Parsons, "How Long." For some remarks on the anecdotal evidence in Norse sources for communication between speakers of the two languages, see also Fjalldal, *Anglo-Saxon England*, pp. 3–21.

[37] On this fundamental point see the remarks in Townend, "Viking Age England," pp. 92–93.

[38] Pons-Sanz, *Lexical Effects*. See also her earlier, in-depth analysis of the Norse-derived vocabulary in the works of Wulfstan (*Norse-Derived Vocabulary in Late Old English Texts*), and (among others) her studies of the Northumbrian glosses (*Scandinavian Loanwords* and "A Sociolinguistic Approach"), *The Battle of Maldon* ("Norse-Derived Terms and Structures"), and the Anglo-Saxon Chronicle ("Norse-Derived Vocabulary in the Anglo-Saxon Chronicle"). Among earlier scholarship, there is good coverage of the Old English period in the work of Peters ("Zum skandinavischen Lehngut," and "Onomasiologische Untersuchungen"), and the survey by Hofmann (*Nordisch-Englische*, pp. 149–252); and see also Wollmann, "Scandinavian Loanwords." Certain accounts in the handbooks and general histories are also illuminating; among the most useful summaries is Kastovsky, "Semantics and Vocabulary," pp. 320–36. Other notable remarks include those in Bibire, "North Sea Language Contacts"; and the short account of Wulfstan's oeuvre in Kubouchi, "Wulfstan's Scandinavian Loanword Usage."

[39] Björkman, *Scandinavian Loan-Words*; Rynell, *Rivalry of Scandinavian*. Hug, *Scandinavian Loanwords*, analyzes the place of Norse-derived words in a limited set of conceptual fields (relating to landscape and the air). With respect to dialectal distribution (medieval and/or Modern English and Scots) important contributions include Flom, "Scandinavian Influence"; Thorson, "Anglo-Norse Studies"; McGee, "Geographical Distribution"; Kolb, "Skandinavisches in den nordenglischen Dialekten"; Samuels, "Scandinavian Belt"; and Kries, *Skandinavisch-schottische*.

[40] Of note is Burnley, "Lexis and Semantics," pp. 415–23; see also Smith, "Norse in Scotland." Other fairly recent work on the contact situation and the history of Norse-derived material in English includes that by Rot (e.g., *Language Contact*, pp. 279–309); Moskowich (-Spiegel Fandiño) (e.g., *Los escandinavos en Inglaterra*; *Language Contact and Vocabulary Enrichment*); and Bator (*Obsolete Scandinavian Loanwords*). Notice also the recent collection of vocabulary by Ó Muirithe, *Viking Word-Hoard* and its *Supplement*.

[41] See e.g., Skaffari, "Touched by an Alien Tongue" (and *Early Middle English Loanwords*, which goes beyond the analysis of corpus data); and Moskowich,

Language Contact and Vocabulary Enrichment. Skaffari admirably surveys the principles and usefulness of the corpus method, and also touches upon its limitations, at least for the early Middle English period: "In studies of lexicon, quantified information serves to illustrate developments but cannot shed light on all issues that are relevant. Since the early texts only have a limited range of accessible external characteristics, it is the internal linguistic and textual context in which loanwords are used that is likely to provide more material for in-depth explorations of loanwords in Early Middle English." ("Touched by an Alien Tongue," p. 519).

[42] McIntosh, "Middle English Word Geography." For some recent experiments in the etymological tagging of electronic copies of medieval English texts, see Bianchi, "Towards an Electronic *LALME*" and Cuesta, García, and Carredano, "Electronic Corpus"; and for a more ambitious etymological treatment of words in a large electronic text corpus (of early Middle English) see *A Corpus of Narrative Etymologies*.

[43] See Kries, *Skandinavisch-schottische*, summarized (in English) in "Scottish-Scandinavian Relations"; Skaffari, *Early Middle English Loanwords* (including a case-study of *Vices and Virtues*); Bator, *Obsolete Scandinavian Loanwords*. The semantic contexts of all medieval English words, including Norse derivations, can now be pursued in unprecedented depth thanks to the publication of the *Historical Thesaurus of the OED* (available online at http://historicalthesaurus.arts.gla.ac.uk and (in revised form) at http://www.oed.com/thesaurus).

[44] See Dance, *Words Derived from Old Norse* and "Tomarȝan hit is awane" (early Middle English, especially the South-West Midlands); "Ealde æ" (the "transition" from Old to Middle English texts); and "Tor for to telle" (*Sir Gawain and the Green Knight*); I am currently writing a full etymological study of the Norse-derived words in the latter text. My *Gawain* data will, in turn, form part of "The *Gersum* Project," a collaborative investigation (with Sara Pons-Sanz and Brittany Schorn) of the Scandinavian influence on the vocabulary of late Middle English alliterative poetry, which began in January 2016 (see http://www.gersum.org).

Bibliography

Abram, C. "Anglo-Saxon Influence in the Old Norwegian Homily Book." *Mediaeval Scandinavia* 14 (2004): 1–35.

Abrams, L., and D. N. Parsons. "Place-Names and the History of Scandinavian Settlement in England." In *Land, Sea and Home*, edited by J. Hines, A. Lane, and M. Redknap, 379–431. The Society for Medieval Archaeology Monograph 20. Leeds: Maney, 2004.

Allen, C. "Middle English Case Loss and the 'Creolization' Hypothesis." *English Language and Linguistics* 1 (1997): 63–89.

Andersson, T. M. "Sources and Analogues." In *A Beowulf Handbook*, edited by R. E. Bjork and J. D. Niles, 125–48. Exeter: Exeter University Press, 1997.

——. "Old Norse-Icelandic Literature." In *Early Germanic Literature and Culture*, edited by B. Murdoch and M. Read, 171–203. Rochester, NY and Woodbridge: Camden House, 2004.

Bandle, O., K. Braunmüller, E. H. Jahr, A. Karker, H.-P. Naumann, and U. Teleman, eds. *The Nordic Languages: An International Handbook of the History of the North Germanic Languages.* 2 vols. Handbücher zur Sprach- und Kommunikationswissenschaft 22. Berlin and New York: de Gruyter, 2002–5.

Barnes, M. P. "Norse in the British Isles." In *Viking Revaluations: Viking Society Centenary Symposium, 14–15 May, 1992*, edited by A. Faulkes and R. Perkins, 65–84. London: Viking Society for Northern Research, 1993.

——. "History and Development of Old Nordic Outside the Scandinavia of Today." In *The Nordic Languages: An International Handbook of the History of the North Germanic Languages.* Vol. 1, edited by O. Bandle, et al., 1053–57. Handbücher zur Sprach- und Kommunikationswissenschaft 22. Berlin and New York: de Gruyter, 2002.

——. "Languages and Ethnic Groups." In *The Cambridge History of Scandinavia, I: Prehistory to 1520*, edited by K. Helle, 94–102. Cambridge: Cambridge University Press, 2003.

——. "The Scandinavian Languages in the British Isles: The Runic Evidence." In *Scandinavia and Europe 800–1350: Contact, Conflict, and Coexistence*, edited by J. Adams and K. Holman, 121–36. Medieval Texts and Cultures of Northern Europe 4. Turnhout: Brepols, 2004.

——. "Language." In *A Companion to Old Norse-Icelandic Literature and Culture*, edited by R. McTurk, 173–89. Oxford: Blackwell Publishing, 2005.

Barnes, M. P., and R. I. Page. *The Scandinavian Runic Inscriptions of Britain*. Runrön 19. Uppsala: Uppsala Universitet, 2006.

Bator, M. *Obsolete Scandinavian Loanwords in English*. Studies in English Medieval Language and Literature 26. Frankfurt am Main: P. Lang, 2010.

Bianchi, B. "Towards an Electronic *LALME*: Scandinavian and French Influence in some Late Middle English Texts from Cheshire." In *Studies in Middle

English Forms and Meanings, edited by G. Mazzon, 73–84. Studies in English Medieval Language and Literature 19. Frankfurt am Main: P. Lang, 2007.

Bibire, P. "North Sea Language Contacts in the Early Middle Ages: English and Norse." In *The North Sea World in the Middle Ages: Studies in the Cultural History of North-Western Europe*, edited by T. R. Liszka and L. E. M. Walker, 88–107. Dublin: Four Courts Press, 2001.

Bjork, R. E. "Scandinavian Relations." In *A Companion to Anglo-Saxon Literature*, edited by P. Pulsiano and E. Treharne, 388–99. Oxford: Blackwell Publishing, 2001.

Björkman, E. *Scandinavian Loan-Words in Middle English*. 2 vols. Studien zur englischen Philologie 7, 11. Halle: Max Niemeyer, 1900–1902.

Braunmüller, K. "Language Contact during the Old Nordic Period I: With the British Isles, Frisia and the Hanseatic League." In *The Nordic Languages: An International Handbook of the History of the North Germanic Languages*. Vol. 1, edited by O. Bandle et al., 1028–39. Handbücher zur Sprach- und Kommunikationswissenschaft 22. Berlin and New York: de Gruyter, 2002.

Burnley, D. "Lexis and Semantics." In *The Cambridge History of the English Language II, 1066–1476*, edited by N. Blake, 409–99. Cambridge: Cambridge University Press, 1992.

Carroll, J. "Poetic Discourse in Viking Age England: Texts and Contexts." PhD diss., University of Nottingham, 2001.

Carroll, J., S. H. Harrison, and G. Williams. *The Vikings in Britain and Ireland*. London: British Museum Press, 2014.

Cleasby, R., and G. Vigfusson. *An Icelandic-English Dictionary*. 2nd ed., with a supplement by Sir W. A. Craigie. Oxford: Clarendon Press, 1957.

Clover, C. J., and J. Lindow, eds. *Old Norse-Icelandic Literature: A Critical Guide*. Medieval Academy Reprints for Teaching 42. Toronto: University of Toronto Press, 2005. First published 1985 by Cornell University Press.

Clunies Ross, M., ed. *Old Icelandic Literature and Society*. Cambridge Studies in Medieval Literature 42. Cambridge: Cambridge University Press, 2000.

——. *The Cambridge Introduction to the Old Norse-Icelandic Saga*. Cambridge: Cambridge University Press, 2010.

A Corpus of Narrative Etymologies from Proto-Old English to Early Middle English and accompanying Corpus of Changes. Compiled by R. Lass, M. Laing, R. Alcorn, and K. Williamson. Edinburgh: University of Edinburgh, 2013– . http://www.lel.ed.ac.uk/ihd/CoNE/CoNE.html.

Cuesta, J. Fernández, L. García García, and J. G. Amores Carredano. "Compilation of an Electronic Corpus of Northern English Texts from Old to Early Modern English." In *The Use and Development of Middle English: Proceedings of the Sixth International Conference on Middle English, Cambridge 2008*, edited by R. Dance and L. Wright, 35–59. Studies in English Medieval Language and Literature 38. Frankfurt am Main: P. Lang, 2012.

Dalton-Puffer, C. "Middle English is a Creole and Its Opposite: On the Value of Plausible Speculation." In *Linguistic Change Under Contact Conditions*, edited by J. Fisiak, 35–50. Trends in Linguistics, Studies and Monographs 81. Berlin and New York: de Gruyter, 1995.

Dance, R. *Words Derived from Old Norse in Early Middle English: Studies in the Vocabulary of the South-West Midland Texts*. Medieval and Renaissance Texts and Studies 246. Tempe, AZ: Center for Medieval and Renaissance Studies, 2003.

——. "'Tomarȝan hit is awane': Words Derived from Old Norse in Four Lambeth Homilies." In *Foreign Influences in Medieval English*, edited by J. Fisiak and M. Bator, 77–127. Studies in English Medieval Language and Literature 28. Frankfurt am Main: P. Lang, 2011.

——. "English in Contact: Norse." In *English Historical Linguistics: An International Handbook*. Vol. 2, edited by A. Bergs and L. J. Brinton, 1724–37. Handbooks of Linguistics and Communication Science 34.2. Berlin and New York: de Gruyter, 2012.

——. "*Ealde æ, niwæ laȝe*: Two Words for 'Law' in the Twelfth Century," with an appendix by R. Dance and A. Conti. *New Medieval Literatures* 13 (2012): 149–82. (Special issue: *Producing and Using English Manuscripts in the Post-Conquest Period*, edited by E. Treharne, O. Da Rold, and M. Swan.)

——. "'Tor for to telle:' Words Derived from Old Norse in *Sir Gawain and the Green Knight*." In *Multilingualism in Medieval Britain (c. 1066–1520)*, edited by J. A. Jefferson and A. Putter (with the assistance of A. Hopkins), 41–58. Medieval Texts and Cultures of Northern Europe 15. Turnhout: Brepols, 2013.

Danchev, A. "The Middle English Creolization Hypothesis Revisited." In *Studies in Middle English Linguistics*, edited by J. Fisiak, 79–108. Trends in Linguistics, Studies and Monographs 103. Berlin and New York: de Gruyter, 1997.

Degnbol, H., *et al*, eds. *Ordbog over det norrøne prosasprog / A Dictionary of Old Norse Prose*. Copenhagen: Arnamagnaean Commission, 1989–.

Domingue, N. Z. "Middle English: Another Creole?" *Journal of Creole Studies* 1 (1977): 89–100.

Dumville, D. N. "Vikings in the British Isles: A Question of Sources." In *The Scandinavians from the Vendel Period to the Tenth Century: An Ethnographic Perspective*, 209–40. Woodbridge: Boydell and Brewer, 2002.

Durkin, P. *Borrowed Words: A History of Loanwords in English*. Oxford: Oxford University Press, 2014.

Emonds, J. E., and J. T. Faarlund. *English: The Language of the Vikings*. Olomouc Modern Language Monographs 3. Olomouc, Czech Republic: Palacký University, 2014.

Fellows-Jensen, G. "From Scandinavia to the British Isles and Back Again. Linguistic Give-and-Take in the Viking Period." In *The Twelfth Viking Congress*, edited by B. Ambrosiani and H. Clarke, 253–68. Stockholm: Birka Project, 1994.

——. "Scandinavian Settlement in the British Isles and Normandy: What the Place-Names Reveal." In *Scandinavia and Europe 800–1350: Contact, Conflict, and Coexistence*, edited by J. Adams and K. Holman, 137–47. Medieval Texts and Cultures of Northern Europe 4. Turnhout: Brepols, 2004.

——. "The Scandinavian Background to English Place-Names." In *Perceptions of Place: Twenty-First-Century Reassessments of English Place-Name Studies*, edited by J. Carroll and D. N. Parsons, 75–101. Studies in the Early History of Britain: Makers of England. Nottingham: English Place-Name Society, 2013.

Fjalldal, M. *The Long Arm of Coincidence: The Frustrated Connection between Beowulf and Grettis Saga*. Toronto, Buffalo, London: University of Toronto Press, 1998.

——. *Anglo-Saxon England in Icelandic Medieval Texts*. Toronto, Buffalo, London: University of Toronto Press, 2005.

Flom, G. T. *Scandinavian Influence on Southern Lowland Scotch, a Contribution to the Study of the Linguistic Relations of English and Scandinavian*. New York: Columbia University Press, 1900.

Frank, R. "Old Norse Memorial Eulogies and the Ending of *Beowulf*." *Acta* 6 (1979): 1–19.

——. "Skaldic Verse and the Date of *Beowulf*." In *The Dating of Beowulf*, edited by C. Chase, 123–39. Toronto, Buffalo, London: Boydell and Brewer, 1981.

——. "Did Anglo-Saxon Audiences Have a Skaldic Tooth?" *Scandinavian Studies* 59 (1987): 338–55.

——. "What Kind of Poetry is *Exodus*?" In *Germania: Comparative Studies in the Old Germanic Languages and Literatures*, edited by D. G. Calder and T. C. Christy, 191–205. Wolfeboro and Woodbridge: Boydell and Brewer, 1988.

——. "Anglo-Scandinavian Poetic Relations." *ANQ*, n.s., 3 (1990): 74–9.

——. "King Cnut in the Verse of His Skalds." In *The Reign of Cnut, King of England, Denmark and Norway*, edited by A. R. Rumble, 106–24. Studies in the Early History of Britain: Makers of England. London: Leicester University Press, 1994.

——. "North-Sea Soundings in *Andreas*." In *Early Medieval English Texts and Interpretations: Studies Presented to Donald G. Scragg*, edited by E. Treharne and S. Rosser, 1–11. Medieval and Renaissance Texts and Studies 252. Tempe, AZ: Arizona Center for Medieval and Renaissance Studies, 2002.

——. "A Scandal in Toronto: *The Dating of 'Beowulf'* a Quarter Century on." *Speculum* 82 (2007): 843–64.

Fritzner, J., ed. *Ordbog over det gamle norske sprog*. 3 vols. Oslo: T.J. Møller, 1867.

Fulk, R. D. *A History of Old English Meter*. Middle Ages Series. Philadelphia: University of Pennsylvania Press, 1992.

Fulk, R. D., and K. E. Gade. "A Bibliography of Germanic Alliterative Meters." *Jahrbuch für Internationale Germanistik* 34 (2002): 87–186.

Fulk, R. D., R. E. Bjork, and J. D. Niles, eds. *Klaeber's Beowulf.* 4th ed. Toronto: University of Toronto Press, 2008.

Gammeltoft, P., and J. P. Holck. "*Gemstēn* and Other Old English Pearls — A Survey of Early Old English Loanwords in Scandinavian." *NOWELE* 50–51 (2007): 131–61.

Gordon, E. V. *An Introduction to Old Norse.* 2nd ed. Oxford: Oxford University Press, 1957.

Görlach, M. "Middle English: A Creole?" In *Linguistics Across Historical and Geographical Boundaries, in Honour of Jacek Fisiak: Part I, Linguistic Theory and Historical Linguistics*, edited by D. Kastovsky and A. Szwedek, 329–44. Trends in Linguistics, Studies and Monographs 32. Berlin: de Gruyter, 1986.

Graham-Campbell, J., R. Hall, J. Jesch, and D. N. Parsons, eds. *Vikings and the Danelaw: Select Papers from the Proceedings of the Thirteenth Viking Congress, Nottingham and York, 21–30 August 1997.* Oxford: Oxbow Books, 2001.

Gunnell, T. "Eddic Poetry." In *A Companion to Old Norse-Icelandic Literature and Culture*, edited by R. McTurk, 82–100. Oxford: Blackwell Publishing, 2005.

Hadley, D. M. *The Vikings in England: Settlement, Society and Culture.* Manchester: Manchester University Press, 2006.

Hadley, D. M., and J. D. Richards, eds. *Cultures in Contact: Scandinavian Settlement in England in the Ninth and Tenth Centuries.* Studies in the Early Middle Ages 2. Turnhout: Brepols, 2000.

Hansen, B. H. "The Historical Implications of the Scandinavian Element in English: A Theoretical Evaluation." *NOWELE* 9 (1984): 53–95.

Harris, J. "*Brunanburh* 12b–13a and Some Skaldic Passages." In *Magister Regis: Studies in Honor of Robert Earl Kaske*, edited by A. Groos, 61–68. New York: Fordham University Press, 1986.

Hines, J. "Philology, Archaeology and the *Adventus Saxonum vel Anglorum.*" In *Britain 400–600: Language and History*, edited by A. Bammesberger and A. Wollmann, 17–36. Anglistische Forschungen 205. Heidelberg: Universitätsverlag, 1990.

——. "Scandinavian English: A Creole in Context." In *Language Contact in the British Isles: Proceedings of the Eighth International Symposium on Language Contact in Europe, Douglas, Isle of Man, 1988*, edited by P. Sture Ureland and G. Broderick, 403–27. Tübingen: M. Niemeyer, 1991.

——. "Egill's *Höfuðlausn* in Time and Place." *Saga-Book of the Viking Society* 24 (1995): 83–104.

——. "Archaeology and Language in a Historical Context: The Creation of English." In *Archaeology and Language II: Archaeological Data and Linguistic Hypotheses*, edited by R. Blench and M. Spriggs, 283–94. One World Archaeology 29. London and New York: Routledge, 1998.

Hofmann, D. *Nordisch-Englische Lehnbeziehungen der Wikingerzeit.* Bibliotheca

Arnamagnæana 14. Copenhagen: E. Munksgaard, 1955.

Holman, K. *Scandinavian Runic Inscriptions in the British Isles: Their Historical Context.* Senter for middelalderstudier, Skrifter 4. Trondheim: Tapir, 1996.

Hug, S. *Scandinavian Loanwords and Their Equivalents in Middle English.* European University Studies: Linguistics 62. Bern, Frankfurt am Main, New York, and Paris: P. Lang, 1987.

Jesch, J. "Skaldic Verse in Scandinavian England." In *Vikings and the Danelaw: Select Papers from the Proceedings of the Thirteenth Viking Congress, Nottingham and York, 21–30 August 1997,* edited by J. Graham-Campbell, R. Hall, J. Jesch, and D. N. Parsons, 313–25. Oxford: Oxbow Books, 2001.

——. "Eagles, Ravens and Wolves: Beasts of Battle, Symbols of Victory and Death." In *The Scandinavians from the Vendel Period to the Tenth Century: An Ethnographic Perspective,* edited by J. Jesch, 251–71. Woodbridge: Boydell and Brewer, 2002.

——. ed. *The Scandinavians from the Vendel Period to the Tenth Century: An Ethnographic Perspective.* Woodbridge: Boydell and Brewer, 2002.

——. "Scandinavians and 'Cultural Paganism' in Late Anglo-Saxon England." In *The Christian Tradition in Anglo-Saxon England: Approaches to Current Scholarship and Teaching,* edited by P. Cavill, 55–68. Cambridge: D. S. Brewer, 2004.

Jörgensen, N. "Old Nordic Types of Texts II: Old Swedish and Old Danish." In *The Nordic Languages: An International Handbook of the History of the North Germanic Languages.* Vol. 1, edited by O. Bandle, et al., 990–99. Handbücher zur Sprach- und Kommunikationswissenschaft 22. Berlin and New York: de Gruyter, 2002.

Kastovsky, D. "Semantics and Vocabulary." In *The English Language: The Beginnings to 1066.* Vol. 1, edited by R. M. Hogg, 290–408. The Cambridge History of the English Language. Cambridge: Cambridge University Press, 1992.

Kay, C., J. Roberts, M. Samuels, and I. Wotherspoon. *The Historical Thesaurus of the Oxford English Dictionary.* 2 vols. Oxford: Oxford University Press, 2009.

Keynes, S. "The Vikings in England, *c.* 790–1016." In *The Oxford Illustrated History of the Vikings,* edited by P. Sawyer, 48–82. Oxford and New York: Oxford University Press, 1997.

Kolb, E. "Skandinavisches in den nordenglischen Dialekten." *Anglia* 83 (1965): 127–53.

Kries, S. *Skandinavisch-schottische Sprachbeziehungen im Mittelalter: Der altnordische Lehneinfluss.* NOWELE Supplement Series 20. Odense: University Press of Southern Denmark, 2003.

——. "Scottish-Scandinavian Relations in the Middle Ages: The Linguistic Evidence." *NOWELE* 50–51 (2007): 109–30.

Kubouchi, T. "Wulfstan's Scandinavian Loanword Usage: An Aspect of the Linguistic Situation in the Late Old English Danelaw." In *Inside Old English: Essays in Honour of Bruce Mitchell*, edited by J. Walmsley, 134–52. Oxford: Blackwell Publishing, 2006.

McGee, A. van K. "The Geographical Distribution of Scandinavian Loan-Words in Middle English, with Special Reference to the Alliterative Poetry." PhD diss., Yale University, 1940.

McIntosh, A. "Middle English Word Geography: Its Potential Rôle in the Study of the Long-term Impact of the Scandinavian Settlements upon English." In *The Vikings, Proceedings of the Symposium of the Faculty of Arts of Uppsala University, June 6–9, 1977*, edited by T. Andersen and K. I. Sandred, 124–30. Symposia Universitatis Upsaliensis annum quingentesimum celebrantis 8. Uppsala and Stockholm: Almqvist & Wiksell, 1978.

McKinnell, J. "The Context of *Völundarkviða*." *Saga-Book of the Viking Society* 23 (1990): 1–27.

——. "Eddic Poetry in Anglo-Scandinavian Northern England." In *Vikings and the Danelaw: Select Papers from the Proceedings of the Thirteenth Viking Congress, Nottingham and York, 21–30 August 1997*, edited by J. Graham-Campbell, R. Hall, J. Jesch, and D. N. Parsons, 327–44. Oxford: Oxbow Books, 2001.

McTurk, R., ed. *A Companion to Old Norse-Icelandic Literature and Culture*. Oxford: Blackwell Publishing, 2005.

McWhorter, J. H. "What Happened to English?" *Diachronica* 19 (2002): 217–72.

Miller, D. G. "The Origin and Diffusion of English 3 sg *-s*." *Studia Anglica Posnaniensia* 38 (2002): 353–61.

——. "The Morphosyntactic Legacy of Scand-English Contact." In *For the Loue of Inglis Lede*. Medieval English Mirror 1, edited by M. Krygier and L. Sikorska, 9–39. Frankfurt am Main: P. Lang, 2004.

——. *External Influences on English, from Its Beginnings to the Renaissance*. Oxford: Oxford University Press, 2012.

Mitchell, B. "The Englishness of Old English." In *From Anglo-Saxon to Early Middle English, Studies Presented to E. G. Stanley*, edited by M. Godden, D. Gray and T. Hoad, 163–81. Oxford: Clarendon Press, 1994.

Moskowich, I. *Language Contact and Vocabulary Enrichment: Scandinavian Elements in Middle English*. Studies in English Medieval Language and Literature 34. Frankfurt am Main: P. Lang, 2012.

Moskowich-Spiegel Fandiño, I. *Los Escandinavos en Inglaterra y el cambio léxico en Inglés medieval*. Monografias (Universidade da Coruña) 28. A Coruña: Universidade da Coruña, Servicio de Publicacións, 1995.

Neidorf, L., ed. *The Dating of Beowulf: A Reassessment*. Cambridge: D. S. Brewer, 2014.

Nielsen, H. F. *The Germanic Languages: Origins and Early Dialectal Interrelations*. Tuscaloosa, AL: University of Alabama Press, 1989.

——. *The Continental Backgrounds of English and its Insular Development until 1154*. NOWELE Supplement Series 19. Odense: Odense University Press, 1998.

Niles, J. D. "Skaldic Technique in *Brunanburh*." *Scandinavian Studies* 59 (1987): 256–66.

——. ed. *Beowulf and Lejre*. Medieval and Renaissance Texts and Studies 323. Tempe, AZ: Arizona Center for Medieval and Renaissance Studies, 2007.

——. "On the Danish Origins of the *Beowulf* Story." In *Anglo-Saxon England and the Continent*, edited by H. Sauer and J. Story, with the assistance of G. Waxenberger, 41–62. Medieval and Renaissance Texts and Studies 394. Tempe, AZ: Arizona Center for Medieval and Renaissance Studies, 2011.

North, R. *The Origins of Beowulf: From Vergil to Wiglaf*. Oxford: Oxford University Press, 2006.

O'Donnell, T., M. Townend, and E. M. Tyler. "European Literature and Eleventh-Century England." In *The Cambridge History of Early Medieval English Literature*, edited by C. Lees, 607–36. Cambridge: Cambridge University Press, 2013.

O'Donoghue, H. *Old Norse-Icelandic Literature: A Short Introduction*. Oxford: Blackwell Publishing, 2004.

Ó Muirithe, D. *From the Viking Word-Hoard: A Dictionary of Scandinavian Words in the Languages of Britain and Ireland*. Dublin: Four Courts Press, 2010.

——. *A Supplement to the Dictionary of Scandinavian Words in the Languages of Britain and Ireland*. Dublin: Four Courts Press, 2013.

Orchard, A. *Pride and Prodigies: Studies in the Monsters of the Beowulf-Manuscript*. Cambridge: D. S. Brewer, 1995.

——. *A Critical Companion to Beowulf*. Cambridge: D. S. Brewer, 2003.

Page, R. I. Review of *The Vikings*, edited by R. T. Farrell. *Saga-Book of the Viking Society* 21, no. 4 (1985): 308–11.

Parsons, D. N. "How Long Did the Scandinavian Language Survive in England? Again." In *Vikings and the Danelaw: Select Papers from the Proceedings of the Thirteenth Viking Congress, Nottingham and York, 21–30 August 1997*, edited by J. Graham-Campbell, R. Hall, J. Jesch, and D. N. Parsons, 299–312. Oxford: Oxbow Books, 2001.

Peters, H. "Zum skandinavischen Lehngut im Altenglischen." *Sprachwissenschaft* 6 (1981): 85–124.

——. "Onomasiologische Untersuchungen zum skandinavischen Lehngut im Altenglischen." *Sprachwissenschaft* 6 (1981): 169–85.

Pons-Sanz, S. M. *Analysis of the Scandinavian Loanwords in the Aldredian Glosses to the Lindisfarne Gospels*. Vol. 9, Studies in English Language and Linguistics, Monographs. Valencia: Lengua Inglesa, Universitat de València, 2000.

——. "A Sociolinguistic Approach to the Norse-Derived Words in the Glosses to the Lindisfarne and Rushworth Gospels." In *New Perspectives on English Historical Linguistics: Selected Papers from 12 ICEHL, Glasgow, 21–26 August 2002: Lexis and Transmission*. Vol. 2, edited by C. Kay, C. Hough, and I. Wotherspoon, 177–92. Current Issues in Linguistic Theory 252. Amsterdam and Philadelphia: John Benjamins Publishing Co., 2004.

——. *Norse-Derived Vocabulary in Late Old English Texts: Wulfstan's Works, a Case Study*. NOWELE Supplement Series 22. Odense: University Press of Southern Denmark, 2007.

——. "Two Compounds in the Old English and Old Norse Versions of the *Prose Phoenix*." *Arkiv för nordisk filologi* 122 (2007): 137–56.

——. "Norse-Derived Terms and Structures in *The Battle of Maldon*." *Journal of English and Germanic Philology* 107 (2008): 421–44.

——. "Norse-Derived Vocabulary in the Anglo-Saxon Chronicle." In *Reading the Anglo-Saxon Chronicle: Language, Literature, History*, edited by A. Jorgensen, 275–304. Studies in the Early Middle Ages 23. Turnhout: Brepols, 2010.

——. *The Lexical Effects of Anglo-Scandinavian Linguistic Contact on Old English*. Studies in the Early Middle Ages 1. Turnhout: Brepols, 2013.

Poole, R. "Crossing the Language Divide: Anglo-Scandinavian Language and Literature." In *The Cambridge History of Early Medieval English Literature*, edited by C. Lees, 579–606. Cambridge: Cambridge University Press, 2013.

Poussa, P. "The Evolution of Early Standard English: The Creolization Hypothesis." *Studia Anglica Posnaniensia* 14 (1982): 69–85.

Pulsiano, P. *Medieval Scandinavia: An Encyclopedia*. New York and London: Garland, 1993.

Richards, J. D. *Viking Age England*, rev. ed. Stroud: Tempus, 2000.

Rot, S. *Language Contact*. Bamberger Beiträge zur englischen Sprachwissenschaft 29. Frankfurt am Main, Bern, New York, Paris: P. Lang, 1991.

Rynell, A. *The Rivalry of Scandinavian and Native Synonyms in Middle English, Especially Taken and Nimen (with an excursus on Nema and Taka in Old Scandinavian)*. Lund Studies in English 13. Lund: C. W. K. Gleerup, 1948.

Samuels, M. L. "The Great Scandinavian Belt." *Current Issues in Linguistic Theory* 41 (1985): 269–81.

Sandred, K. I. "Language Contact Outside Scandinavia III: With England and Scotland." In *The Nordic Languages: An International Handbook of the History of the North Germanic Languages*. Vol. 2, edited by O. Bandle, et al., 2062–73. Handbücher zur Sprach- und Kommunikationswissenschaft 22. Berlin and New York: de Gruyter, 2005.

Schulte, M. "Language contact in the period between Ancient Nordic and Old Nordic', in *The Nordic Languages: An International Handbook of the History of the North Germanic Languages*. Vol. 1, edited O. Bandle, et al., 769–77. Handbücher zur Sprach- und Kommunikationswissenschaft 22. Berlin and New York: de Gruyter, 2002.

Skaffari, J. "Touched by an Alien Tongue: Studying Lexical Borrowings in the Earliest Middle English." In *A Changing World of Words: Studies in English Historical Lexicography, Lexicology and Semantics*, edited by J. E. Díaz

Vera, 500–21. Amsterdam and New York: Editions Rodopi, 2001.

——. *Studies in Early Middle English Loanwords: Norse and French Influences.* Anglicana Turkuensia 26. Turku: University of Turku, 2009.

Smith, J. J. "Norse in Scotland." *Scottish Language* 13 (1994): 18–33.

Szokody, O. "Old Nordic Types of Texts I: Old Icelandic and Old Norwegian." In *The Nordic Languages: An International Handbook of the History of the North Germanic Languages.* Vol 1, edited by O. Bandle, et al., 981–9. Handbücher zur Sprach- und Kommunikationswissenschaft 22. Berlin and New York: de Gruyter, 2002.

Taylor, P. B. *Sharing Story: Medieval Norse-English Literary Relationships.* AMS Studies in the Middle Ages 25. New York: AMS Press, 1998.

Thomason, S. G., and T. Kaufman. *Language Contact, Creolization and Genetic Linguistics.* Berkeley, Los Angeles, Oxford: University of California Press, 1988.

Thorson, P. *Anglo-Norse Studies: An Inquiry into the Scandinavian Elements in the Modern English Dialects, Part I.* Amsterdam: Swets en Zeitlinger, 1936.

Townend, M. *English Place-Names in Skaldic Verse.* EPNS Extra Series 1. Nottingham: English Place-Name Society, 1998.

——. "Viking Age England as a Bilingual Society." In *Cultures in Contact: Scandinavian Settlement in England in the Ninth and Tenth Centuries*, edited by D. M. Hadley and J. D. Richards, 89–105. Studies in the Early Middle Ages 2. Turnhout: Brepols, 2000.

——. "Pre-Cnut Praise-Poetry in Viking Age England." *Review of English Studies* n.s. 203 (2000): 349–70.

——. "Contextualizing the *Knútsdrápur*: Skaldic Praise-Poetry at the Court of Cnut." *Anglo-Saxon England* 30 (2001): 145–79.

——. "Norse Poets and English Kings: Skaldic Performance in Anglo-Saxon England." *Offa* 58 (2001): 269–75.

——. *Language and History in Viking Age England: Linguistic Relations Between Speakers of Old Norse and Old English.* Studies in the Early Middle Ages 6. Turnhout: Brepols, 2002.

——. "Whatever Happened to York Viking Poetry? Memory, Tradition and the Transmission of Skaldic Verse." *Saga-Book of the Viking Society* 27 (2003): 48–90.

——. "Contacts and Conflicts: Latin, Norse, and French." In *The Oxford History of English*, edited by L. Mugglestone, 61–85. Oxford: Oxford University Press, 2006.

——. "Cnut's Poets: An Old Norse Literary Community in Eleventh-Century England." In *Conceptualizing Multilingualism in England, c. 800 – c. 1250*, edited by E. M. Tyler, 197–215. Studies in the Early Middle Ages 27. Turnhout: Brepols, 2011.

——. "Scandinavian Place-Names in England." In *Perceptions of Place: Twenty-First-Century Reassessments of English Place-Name Studies*, edited by J.

Carroll and D. N. Parsons, 103–26. English Place-Name Society. Nottingham: English Place-Name Society, 2013.

——. *Viking Age Yorkshire*. Pickering: Blackthorn Press, 2014.

Wallmannsberger, J. "The 'Creole Hypothesis" in the History of English." In *Historical English: On the Occasion of Karl Brunner's 100th Birthday*, edited by M. Markus, 19–36. Innsbrucker Beiträge zur Kulturwissenschaft, Anglistische Reihe 1. Innsbruck: Institut für Anglistik, Universität Innsbruck, 1988.

Wollmann, A. "Scandinavian Loanwords in Old English." In *The Origins and Development of Emigrant Languages. Proceedings from the Second Rasmus Rask Colloquium, Odense University, November 1994*, edited by H. F. Nielsen and L. Schøsler, 215–42. Odense: Odense University Press, 1996.

Zoëga, G. T. *A Concise Dictionary of Old Icelandic*. Oxford: Clarendon Press, 1926.

Légend hÉrenn: "The Learning of Ireland" in the Early Medieval Period

Máire Ní Mhaonaigh

Introduction

That the various cultures of Britain and Ireland were in continuous contact with one another down through the medieval period (and beyond) scarcely needs reiterating, nor does the fact that this constant interaction occasioned much opportunity for mutual influence and exchange of ideas in a wide variety of areas. Early evidence for contact between Ireland and England is of an ecclesiastical nature; the role played by the Irish mission in seventh-century Northumbria in the conversion of numerous Englishmen being particularly significant in this regard.[1] The English were also moved to journey to Ireland, Bede remarking that many of them travelled to study there.[2] Among those educated among the Irish, possibly at Iona,[3] was King Aldfrith of Northumbria (d. 704) who may even have been accorded an Irish name, Flann Fína.[4] A contemporary and correspondent of his, Aldhelm of Malmesbury (d. 709/710), has also been linked with that most famous of Irish monastic outposts;[5] although elsewhere in his writing he seeks to dissuade colleagues from crossing the Irish Sea.[6]

Yet journey westwards many of them did, some settling in Ireland in the process. Bede refers to two English communities there:[7] Rathmelsigi, which has been identified by Kenneth Nicholls as Cluain Melsige (Clonmelsh, Co. Carlow),[8] and the more significant monastery of Mayo (Mag nÉo *na Saxan*, "of the Saxons").[9] The land for that establishment was provided by an unidentified *comes*[10] and the intimate association between church and secular powers implied by this and other such acts ensured that cross-cultural connections were not confined to the religious sphere. Indeed Adomnán, abbot of Iona and a key figure in the English conversion process, first went to Northumbria on political business, visiting King Aldfrith to plead for the release of Irish hostages who had been captured in a Saxon raid on Brega in 685.[11] As Hermann Moisl has demonstrated, this represents but a single episode in a long, complex relationship between

Bernician royalty and the northern Irish dynasty of Uí Néill, indicating political contact at the highest level.[12]

That such interaction should have been reflected in intellectual endeavors is only to be expected since the learned classes of both Ireland and Anglo-Saxon England were based in ecclesiastical establishments, which comprised the countries' social elite.[13] Their common features are seen most clearly in the manuscript productions of this early period, as witnessed in the scholarly debates concerning the precise place of origin of such illuminated gospel books as the late seventh-century Book of Durrow, the Lindisfarne Gospels, from about 700, and the eighth-century masterpiece, the Book of Kells.[14] While discussion has often focused on script and manuscript illumination, the contents of the earliest Latin manuscripts from Britain and Ireland also bear comparison, liturgical texts in both areas having pride of place. Grammar is also a concern,[15] as is hagiography,[16] and law;[17] Insular Latin culture manifests itself in Ireland and England in similar ways. Contact lines have frequently left their marks, as is evident from glosses in both Latin and Old Irish on Bede's *De rerum natura* and *De temporum ratione*, in what may be ninth-century Irish manuscripts now preserved in Karlsruhe and Vienna.[18] The Rushworth Gospels, ascribed to one who bore the Irish name Mac Riaguil, and containing tenth-century Old English glosses, constitutes another vibrant witness to the positive results of a cultural confluence.[19] The perpetrators of that continuing exchange are shadowy figures, remaining nameless apart from a few well-known exceptions. These include Josephus Scottus, a student of Alcuin of York (d. 804), whom the latter praised in a letter to Joseph's Irish teacher, Colcu.[20] Also well-known are a trio of Irishmen, Dub Sláine, Mac Bethad and Máel Inmain, of whom the *Anglo-Saxon Chronicle* relates that they set to sea without oar or rudder in 891, landing on the English coast, and made straight for the court of Alfred the Great.[21]

Given the focus of that king's intellectual program, they would have encountered vernacular learning alongside its Latin counterpart at his court, in a bilingual situation like the one with which they were familiar. Contemporary annalistic records in Old Irish and Old English survive from Alfred's time and earlier, as do vernacular martyrologies[22] and a number of prose compositions, the subject-matter of which is, in the case of the Irish material in particular, remarkably diverse.[23] Early poetry has also survived in the two languages: an Irish equivalent of the book of vernacular verse, which Asser claims was given to Alfred by his mother, would have been a copy of *Audacht Morainn*, a metrical *speculum principum* with a composition date of *circa* 700.[24] The rich corpus of Old Irish law tracts contains poetry, as well as prose, dating somewhere between the law-code of the sixth-century Kentish King Æthelberht and the ninth-century laws of Alfred the Great.[25]

In the century or so after Alfred's birth, *Beowulf*, as it survives, may have been composed. Comparable heroic Irish material is also difficult to date; what is clear, however, is that on two adjacent islands, pre-Christian heroes were embraced by churchmen and commemorated in the vernacular at roughly the same time. Poetry was the chosen medium of Anglo-Saxon authors, whereas their Irish counterparts preferred a prosimetric form with a predominance of prose. Notwithstanding this difference, the two literatures bear comparison. Patrick Wormald was tempted "to connect the major Irish role in Anglo-Saxon evangelization with the fact that Ireland and England were the only two parts of the West to celebrate ancestral heroes in their own tongue."[26] Literary rather than cultural considerations have informed the recurrent attempts to link *Beowulf* specifically with Old Irish narratives; *Fled Bricrend* (Bricriu's Feast), *Táin Bó Fraích* (The Cattle-Raid of Fráech), and *Sex aetates mundi* being commonly cited as sources or analogues in this regard.[27] David Dumville has sought to set such putative connections in their historical and literary context. In so doing, he stresses the common concerns of the two cultures, "as well as the clear possibility of direct influence by one on the other."[28] Illumination of the latter cannot proceed properly without an exposition of the former. In addition, even where no connection can be shown to have existed, the parallel elucidation of two corpora born of similar social circumstances and subsequently sharing many comparable developments, can shed new light on each of the literatures in turn.

"Alfredian" Ireland

Comúaim n-ecalsa fri túaith

Alfred's reign has frequently been cited as a convenient starting point from which to survey Old English material;[29] its productivity and specific focus on the production of vernacular texts ensured that the literary landscape was transformed by its end. Notwithstanding the substantial evidence for the cultivation of a wide range of compositions in Irish in Ireland's equivalent of the pre-Alfredian era,[30] the ninth and tenth centuries also marked a perceptible shift in the use of the vernacular in the western-most island.[31]

This is evidenced most clearly in annalistic writing in which extensive use of Irish can be dated to around this time.[32] Vernacular hagiography also dates from the ninth century, the earliest extant example being a Life of Brigit which, significantly, is a bilingual text of which roughly one quarter is in Latin.[33] Saints were also commemorated in Irish in martyrologies, the earliest of which, a metrical "Calendar of Óengus" (*Félire Óengusso*) was composed in the early years of the same century.[34] The author of this work, Óengus mac Óengobann, describes himself as *céle Dé* (a companion of God), associating himself with a group of eighth-century ecclesiastics who sought to promote a purer, ascetic, more spiritual way of life. Their desire to communicate with the laity, as well as fellow clerics, has been linked with the growth in the production of devotional texts in the vernacular.[35] Somewhat earlier than Alfred and, for broadly similar reasons, *céli Dé* in Ireland were concerned with access to that which is "most needful to know."

Alfred took the matter into his own hands, learning to read and write and gathering around him clerics who could establish his ambitious program of educational reform. By contrast, there is no evidence for court schools and very little for lay literacy in Ireland at this time;[36] textual production was firmly ensconced in an ecclesiastical embrace. Máel Muru of Othain (the monastery of Fahan, Co. Donegal), for example, is accorded the title *rígfili Érenn* (chief/royal-poet of Ireland) in his annalistic obit for the year 887.[37] Among the compositions of this monastic scholar is a lengthy pseudo-historical poem, *Can a mbunadas na nGáedel* (What are the origins of the Irish?), in which the wanderings of the Irish and their eventual conquest of Ireland are set out.[38] As a foundation-legend for Ireland's noble families, the work was obviously of primary interest to the representatives of those groups ruling in Máel Muru's own day. Thus, church personnel provided relevant texts for a secular elite, acquiring all-important political patronage in return. However, the precise mechanics of this mutually beneficial working relationship remain to some extent obscure.[39] Of key importance may well have been scholars who straddled both religious and royal spheres. These included Cormac mac Cuilennáin, king-bishop of Munster, who was killed in battle fighting Leinster and Connacht opponents in 908. His literary fame was such that numerous works were anachronistically attributed to him;[40] notwithstanding this he may indeed have written some extant metrical compositions.[41] A genuine association with one of two versions of a Glossary bearing his name, *Sanas Cormaic* (Cormac's Glossary), is also possible,[42] indicating an interest in diverse branches of learning.[43] We know less of his intellectual activities than we do of those of his English contemporary, Alfred; nonetheless, the surviving evidence suggests that the Irish king also actively pursued scholarly research.

In both his royal-episcopal persona and his learned compositions, which may include a saint's eulogy as well as a list of Munster kings,[44] Cormac mac Cuilennáin embodies the spirit of close cooperation between Church and secular authorities. This was the defining feature of early medieval Ireland's literary life. Its significance was highlighted by contemporary authors who sought to explicate the nature of this intellectual interdependency. An elaborate attempt is found in the eighth-century, so-called pseudo-historical prologue to the great collection of legal texts known as the *Senchas Már* (Great Lore).[45] In the tale that, according to John Carey, "symbolically portrays the creation of a Christian Irish culture,"[46] a consortium of nine men was chosen to arrange the laws, made up of three bishops, three kings, and three men of learning.[47] The textual basis of this arrangement is made clear in the comment that "*Nó-fis*, then, is the name of the book they arranged, i.e., the knowledge of nine men" (Nófis didiu anim in liubair-se ro ordaigset, .i. fis nónbuir).[48] The explanation found favor among the learned classes; it occurs in the ninth-century Glossary associated with Cormac in a form obviously dependent on the earlier prologue.[49]

In the tradition of his predecessors, therefore, Cormac mac Cuilennáin (or a contemporary of his) sought to sanction the close cerebral connections between ecclesiastical and political powers operating in his own time by endorsing what had been earlier described as *comúaim n-ecalsa fri túaith* (the sewing together of Church and secular authority).[50] The case is made again in a later, well-crafted etiology concerning another aristocratic figure, Cenn Fáelad mac Ailella of the Northern Uí Néill, whose death as *sapiens*, an ecclesiastical scholar, is recorded in chronicle entries for 679.[51] Of the historical figure nothing is known; his fame lies in the fact that he came to personify how Ireland's literary heritage came into being. Wounded in the battle of Mag Rath in 637, according to an eleventh- or twelfth-century preface to the law tract *Bretha Étgid* (Judgments Concerning an Offense), Cenn Fáelad's injury involved the removal of his *incinn dermait*, that part of his brain inclining him to forget.[52] Thus unencumbered, he was in a unique position to profit from the learning to which he was exposed in his convalescent home, Tech Bricín Drecain, within whose monastic confines was housed "a school of Latin learning, a school of law and a school of poetry" (scol leigind 7 scol feinechais 7 scol filed).[53] Having memorized all that he heard "he cast them into poetic form and wrote them on slabs and on tablets" (docuir-sium glonsnaithi filed fuithib 7 doscrib-sum iat a lecaib 7 i taiblib).[54] Cenn Fáelad's significance was deemed such that part of "one of the central texts of early Irish learning,"[55] *Auraicept na nÉces* (The Poets' Primer), was attributed to him; a version of the tale of his remarkable recovery was later prefaced to this work.[56]

"Pre-Alfredian" Ireland

A mba ferr do cach bérlu

As a founding father of Irish literature, Cenn Fáelad has his English counterpart in Cædmon, another shadowy seventh-century figure, whose story "has in effect been taken as the foundation-legend of the Old English Christian poetic tradition."[57] David Dumville has astutely compared the narratives concerning the two exemplary poets, despite the considerable chronological gap between them.[58] Doubts have been expressed about the authorship of much of the verse allegedly written by Cædmon. It is also far from clear whether the metrical compositions ascribed to Cenn Fáelad in the eighth-century law tracts, *Míadslechta* (Sections concerning Rank) and *Bretha Nemed* (Judgments concerning Privileged Persons), are indeed by him.[59] Nonetheless, as Kim McCone has noted, their existence indicates that his association with learning is certainly earlier than the Middle Irish legend celebrating his literary prowess.[60]

Cædmon's poems display a familiarity with the Bible, specifically Exodus and Genesis; the first book of the Bible also inspired the author of the eighth-century poets' manual, *Auraicept na nÉces*, with which Cenn Fáelad's name was later associated.[61] However, the story of the Tower of Babel with which the canonical part of the text begins was probably mediated through well-known sources, such as Orosius and Isidore of Seville.[62] The starting point for the author of the *Auraicept* was the widespread doctrine of the three sacred languages, Hebrew, Latin and Greek; nonetheless, he skillfully placed his own tongue among them by describing how it was invented ten years after the dispersal at the Tower by Fénius Farrsaid who was asked to create a language out of many languages.[63] This he did: "a mba ferr íarum do cach bérlu ocus a mba lethu ocus a mba caímiu, is ed doreped isin nGoídilc" (what was best then of every language and what was widest and finest was cut out into Irish).[64] His cultural confidence is further reflected in the Greek derivation he assigns to this master-language: "Goídelc ... ó Goídiul mac Angin ... do Grécaib" (Goídelc [Irish] ... named after Goídel son of Angen ... of the Greeks).[65] Moreover, it permeates his sustained comparison between Latin and Irish in which the vernacular is seen to be of equal status with its classical counterpart.[66]

This scholarly sophistication bespeaks an intense engagement with Irish as a literary language, as well as an intimate acquaintance with Latin. Contact between them more than three hundred years previously had brought the earliest form of Irish writing, Ogam, into being, the inventors of which were familiar not merely with the Latin alphabet but with the works of fourth-century Latin grammarians as well.[67] While undoubtedly indebted to Latin, these earlier creators of what was an epigraphic script display something of the attitude of the *Auraicept* author. Damian McManus has underlined their "independence of mind" which ensured that Ogam was the perfect vehicle for the phonemic inventory of their own tongue.[68]

That language developed from the Primitive Irish of the framers of the Ogam alphabet into Archaic Irish (600–700), Old Irish (700–900), and Middle Irish (900–1200), all three linguistic stages being reflected in manuscript sources. Those drafting the later Ogam inscriptions and the early manuscript scribes "must have been one and the same people";[69] it is not surprising, therefore, that reverence for Ogam is evident in a variety of texts.[70] Chief among these is *Auraicept na nÉces*, since it is with the *beithe-luis-nin* or alphabet of Ogam that Latin is frequently compared.[71] Yet by the time this text was composed Ogam was no longer being used in inscriptions, though the script was occasionally employed in manuscripts to provide an illustration of how it appeared, as well as in authorial inscriptions[72] and in short functional texts on other kinds of material.[73] However, neither these scholastic Ogams, as they are termed, nor the Ogam inscriptions themselves record anything comparable with the section of the *Dream of the Rood*, carved in eighth-century runes on the Ruthwell Cross. Poetic compositions in Ireland, as in England for the most part, belonged on the manuscript page.

Slicht Libair ... inso

The pages that have survived from the two regions differ somewhat in date. The tenth-century Vercelli Book in which the *Dream of the Rood* survives in its entirety, along with its three companion codices of roughly the same date, predate the earliest extant Irish manuscript in the vernacular, *Lebor na hUidre* (The Book of the Dun Cow), perhaps by some one hundred years.[74] In form it differs significantly from the four English poetic books since it contains a predominance of prose encompassing pseudo-historical literature,[75] as well as some religious material, including two homilies after which the scribe who inserted them was labelled by later scholars H (= Homilist).[76] Since only about half of the volume has survived[77] any attempt at ascertaining its original function must remain speculative; nonetheless, an interest in "the two legendary spheres of influence of Emain [Navan Fort] and Temair [Tara]" is clearly evident.[78] Máire Herbert has shown how many of the texts contained in *Lebor na hUidre* were carefully mediated to their audience in a manner revealing the very real contemporary concerns of their authors.[79] As living history, the book had an immediate resonance in its own time.[80]

Part of its authority derived from the fact that it drew on pre-existing sources, the expression, *Slicht Libair ... inso* (an extract from the Book of ... here) being a common refrain.[81] Our manuscript, therefore, provides important evidence for scribal activity, in the vernacular, at an earlier date. Among the works drawn on was *Cín Dromma Snechtai* (The Book of Druimm Snechtai), a codex named after the monastery of Drumsnat (Co. Monaghan),[82] which is specifically referred to on five occasions in *Lebor na hUidre*.[83] Other references to this now lost manuscript, the most significant being in a sixteenth-century compilation of legal and literary material in London, British Library manuscript, Egerton 88, ensure that we can compile a putative table of contents for "The Book of Drumsnat."[84] On the basis of the seventeen or so textual items assigned to it, each with different degrees of certainty, the codex constituted a varied collection of both prose and poetic narratives, many of which have a northern or midland bias. Encompassing some material which has been dated to the seventh century, it also contained other tales dating from the eighth.[85] Whether *Cín Dromma Snechtai* itself was written in the eighth century or whether it was a tenth-century "Book" copied from an earlier archetype continues to be debated.[86] Its significance as a "witness," either directly or at one remove, to mature and confident writing in Irish at a remarkably early period, cannot be overstated.

In its preference for the vernacular, as well as in subject-matter, *Cín Dromma Snechtai* resembles *Lebor na hUidre*, not least because ten texts may have been common to both works.[87] By contrast, early Irish manuscripts are predominantly in Latin and, like the earliest English manuscripts, are for the most part religious in tone.[88] Alongside their copious vernacular glosses, some of these sources also preserve longer vernacular passages in prose and verse. Thus, we can still view traces of a vibrant literary tradition in contemporary dress. Bilingualism is its hallmark, as indicated by the alternating sections in Latin and Irish in a seventh-century Homily preserved in an eighth-century manuscript now in Cambrai.[89] Moreover, Latin retained primacy, as is evident from the interface between Irish and Latin texts on a manuscript page; the vernacular frequently occupied a marginal position, taking as its starting point the higher-status language of Scriptures.[90] Notwithstanding this, the creative manipulation by the scribes of their own tongue is demonstrable in the scattering of vernacular poems surviving in the eighth- or ninth-century manuscript, *Codex Sancti Pauli*, which include an artistic homage to a cat.[91] Irony has also been mastered, a ninth-century weary pilgrim suggesting that a journey to Rome amounts to "a lot of work [for] little profit" (mór saido, becc torbai), continuing: "the King you seek here – if you don't bring him with you, you won't find him" (in Rí chondaigi hi foss/ mani mbera latt ní fogbai).[92]

Without such journeys overseas, however, much of the earliest writing in Irish would have been lost, for it is in manuscripts which found homes in continental monasteries and libraries that it has, for the most part, been preserved.[93] Since a religious or grammatical codex was more likely to have been accorded space in the satchel of a scholar-traveller than *Cín Dromma Snechtai* or its ilk, the dichotomy between the nature of the surviving literary traces and allusions in later sources to a wealth of diverse material *in aliis libris* is easily explained.[94] Despite also being ecclesiastical products, these *araile libair* (other books)[95] were lost in an Irish context, taken to be read aloud at the more precarious setting of a king's court perhaps, never to be returned.[96] Survival of some such codices into the eleventh and twelfth centuries, and beyond has ensured that some of their literary contents have survived, committed to parchment afresh by reverent learned successors. Yet, we can rarely determine with certainty the exact effect of the intervening hand(s).

Dúle feda

Notwithstanding this, the variety of material to which those hands had access is obvious, even if its survival in non-contemporary manuscripts means that the precise date of some of the texts in question is far from clear.[97] A chronological list of poems in Irish, containing thirty-three items apparently composed before 900, has been challenged at various points;[98] nonetheless, its core of unquestionably Old Irish compositions bears witness to an early vernacular poetic tradition of remarkable vitality. Religious verse is prevalent, including hymns to saints Brigit and Columba,[99] as well as portraits of Christ in partial Irish dress.[100] One of these is a skillful reworking of a Latin version of the apocryphal Gospel of Thomas, perhaps late seventh-century in date.[101] Another composition consists of a pair of interlinked poems addressed to Mary and attributed to a northern scholar, Blathmac, whose father, Cú Brettan was active in the middle of the eighth century.[102] Such ascriptions need not be genuine; however, when compared linguistically with eighth-century glosses in contemporary manuscripts, Blathmac's poetry does appear to have been composed about this time. More problematic is the dating of early poetic fragments said to be the work of Colmán mac Lénéni, who died *circa* 606,[103] and of Dallán Forgaill's *Amra Coluim Cille*, an elegy to the Irish founder of Iona who died in 597.[104]

Irrespective of whether the earliest extant poem in Irish was written before the end of the sixth century, Ireland boasts a corpus of devotional poetry, some of which was certainly composed as Theodore and Hadrian's famous school was flourishing in Canterbury. Credited with nourishing the development of religious verse in Old English,[105] the quality of this school was soon celebrated, at the expense of Irish centers of learning, in the case of Aldhelm of Malmesbury, as Rosalind Love remarks.[106] That the cultural climate in Ireland was conducive to such literary production explains why "thronging students by the fleet-load" assembled there, much to the disdain of the Anglo-Saxon bishop.[107] Aldhelm knew as much, of course, having received some training in Ireland's northern outpost, Iona;[108] whether prostitutes or pagan stories repelled him, he turned his back dramatically on an erstwhile intellectual haven, seeking perhaps through his anti-Irish rhetoric to settle old scholarly scores.[109]

Of seventh-century Irish prostitutes nothing further is recorded and purely pagan stories have simply not survived. Had Aldhelm maintained his contacts with Ireland he might conceivably have experienced its narrative literature, a number of vernacular tales having been dated to the century of his death. These include a pair of interlinked compositions, *Echtrae Chonnlai* (The Expedition of Connlae) and *Immram Brain* (The Voyage of Bran), both of which feature supernatural women who lure unsuspecting men to an Otherworld of unparalleled pleasures.[110] Its general tenor is Christian in tone, being a place "in which there is neither death nor sin nor transgression" (i-nna-bí bás na peccad na imarmus).[111] Indeed, as John Carey has noted, the description in the earlier of the two narratives, *Echtrae Chonnlai*, whence the woman has come (*Do-dechad-sa a tírib béo*, "I have come from the lands of the living")[112] is used elsewhere of Heaven and is reminiscent of the biblical *terra uiuentium*.[113] As the woman herself is the harbinger of Christianity, Heaven is her natural home.[114] Nonetheless, her appearance as a mysterious woman, "in unfamiliar clothing" (i n-étuch anetargnad),[115] deliberately echoes that of goddesses in other tales.[116] Thus, the author is seeking to synthesize the competing Otherworlds that formed part of his early eighth-century world view.[117] What may be Ireland's earliest extant vernacular story set the artistic stakes remarkably high.

Skill and sophistication are similarly the hallmarks of other early productions, as is a synthesis of old and new. A rich, substantial corpus of legal material has survived, the earliest datable text of which, *Cáin Fhuithirbe* (The Law of Fuithirbe), is roughly contemporary with the seventh-century law codes of Kentish kings.[118] As Anglo-Saxon legal sources reveal close cooperation between Church and "State," so too do their Irish counterparts point to intensive ecclesiastical involvement in the production of this legal material.[119] Where they differ is in the extensive range of subjects covered by the Irish texts, amounting to a blueprint for society of the most detailed kind.[120] About fifty texts dating from the seventh and eighth centuries form a collection of law texts, the *Senchas Már*, which includes material on clientship, marriage and kinship, as well as bees, cats and dogs.[121] Neighborly relations are regulated for,[122] as is sick-maintenance of all kinds;[123] arrangements for the proper conduct of society are also pursued.[124] Having northern associations, the *Senchas Már* is complemented by a smaller group of texts emanating from Munster which appear to have been more restricted in range.[125] The southern sources are also distinguishable stylistically from the *Senchas Már* material, containing a greater proportion of *rosc(ad)* (an alliterative, stress-counting poetic form). Thus, they are often deemed the products of a poetico-legal school.

In its alternation of stressed and unstressed syllables, as well as in its stylized syntax, *rosc* bears some resemblance to Old English metrical forms.[126] Irish poets employed syllabic rhyming quatrains alongside it, often in the same text.[127] Furthermore, both types of meter continued to be composed for a considerable period,[128] syllabic verse being the dominant unmarked type. By contrast, it did not become prevalent in England before the twelfth century, despite the occasional rhyming couplet which found its way into earlier works. The two regions have been deemed to have had a different approach to poetry in other ways too, since verse is the primary medium for Old English heroic lore. Warrior literature in Irish may be predominantly in prose, yet what may be its earliest witness, *Verba Scáthaige*, which shares thematic concerns with Ireland's premier "epic," *Táin Bó Cúailnge* (The Cattle-Raid of Cúailnge [Cooley]), is a poetic text.[129] Furthermore, its companion pieces in *Cín Dromma Snechtai*, whose pages it once most likely adorned, are for the most part metrical or at least prosimetric in form. Thus, the Irish evidence scarcely suggests a strict dichotomy between prose and verse. *Baile Chuinn Chétchathaig* (The Vision of Conn Cétchathach [of the hundred battles]) is a prophetic king-list also contained in the lost *Cín* which is plausibly dated to the late seventh century when the last ruler mentioned in the text, Fínnechta Fledach, reigned.[130] It is written in an elaborate, alliterative style. Moreover, such stylized language is not confined to works like *Baile Chuinn,* which are somewhat riddling in tone.[131] A didactic religious text, *Apgitir Chrábaid* (The Alphabet of Piety), which is ascribed to the abbot Colmán moccu Beognae (d. 611), but which may have been written a century or so after his time, is an ornate rhythmical primer which in its polished manner effectively gets its moral message across.[132]

Whatever its precise date, the literary refinement of *Apgitir Chrábaid*, and of many of the other texts we have encountered, bears witness to a vibrant intellectual culture in the vernacular which produced complex, sophisticated compositions in considerable quantity from a very early date. Their thematic diversity is remarkable, ranging from devotional literature to legal texts and encompassing chronicles and narrative material as well; "books of lore" (*dúle feda*) were produced in very many forms.[133] The documentation was of a social elite, written in ecclesiastical establishments and reveals close ties between political rulers and the Church. It also demonstrates the engagement of its authors with ideas and sources current elsewhere in their day.[134] For much of this early period, the involvement of the Irish in England was also intense, as Irish-led missions dominated the developing English Church. Literary exchanges undoubtedly formed part of that contact and it may be that their eastern neighbors learned much from the confident control the Irish had of their own written tongue. If so, they gave much in return and the cultural benefits were shared in both directions. The Irish Sea was to remain a crucial conduit in the centuries to come.

"Post-Alfredian" Ireland

The extent to which Vikings disrupted this cultural flow is debatable, as is their precise influence on the cultivation of literature on both sides of the Irish Sea. In the case of the western-most region, Máire Herbert has suggested that there was some interruption in scholarly activities in the tenth century, arguing that a variety of factors, including a more stable political situation, led to their resumption from the 980s or so onwards.[135] If the production rate of learned material in Ireland dipped somewhat, England appears to have entered a particularly active period propelled by Benedictine Reform. What Herbert sees as Ireland's rejuvenation phase reveals concerns similar to those of the English reformists.[136] Hagiographical material is abundant, some of it cast in homiletic form. One such text, *Betha Adomnáin*, the vernacular *Life of Adomnán*, biographer of Iona's founder, Columba, has been dated to the middle of the tenth century.[137] The eleventh and twelfth centuries witnessed a flowering of this genre, though many of the hagiographies in question have not yet been precisely dated.[138] As in England, apocryphal texts are prevalent; indeed the occurrence of the same apocrypha in both cultural regions has been cited as evidence for "mutual relationships ... between Irish and Anglo-Saxon."[139] Close textual analysis is necessary to define the direction of any borrowing; notwithstanding this, the use of common works points to, at the very least, exposure to similar sources and influences. The Apocalypse of Thomas, for example, was employed liberally in both regions; among the Irish authors who drew upon it were those who penned the perhaps tenth-century religious works, *In Tenga Bithnua* (The Evernew Tongue), described by John Carey as, "an account of the mysteries of the universe,"[140] and a poetic psalter, *Saltair na Rann* (The Psalter of the Quatrains).[141]

Coimgne cinte cóem-cheneóil

As the extensive creation history versified in *Saltair na Rann* attests, the Bible continued to be a major source of inspiration for medieval Irish literati, as it was for their learned counterparts in England and elsewhere. It provided them with a framework for their own recorded history: *Lebor Gabála Érenn* (The Book of the Taking of Ireland),[142] an elaborate prosimetric account of the origin of Ireland and her peoples. Drawing on biblical models, it alludes to the Exodus of the Israelites, with which the wandering Irish (*Gaídil*) are identified, as well as to the story of Noah and, in particular, of his son, Japheth, from whom all the invaders of Ireland are said to descend. In his provision of "the certain historical knowledge [*coimgne*] of a fair race" (coimgne cinte cóem-cheneóil),[143] the perhaps late eleventh-century author of this enterprising composition had access to historical poems by previous scholars, primarily the tenth-century Armagh ecclesiastic, Éochaid ua Flainn (936–1004); the eleventh-century *fer légind* (learned official) of Monasterboice, Flann Mainistrech mac Echthigirn (d. 1056); and the latter's contemporaries, Gilla Coemáin mac Gilla Shamthainne (d. 1072) and Tanaide (d. *ca.* 1075), about whom little is known.[144] The author's own creative input was considerable, however, and the resulting monumental "history" immediately found favor with the scholarly community, being revised and copied repeatedly in the twelfth century.[145]

Unlike Byrhtferth of Ramsey, whose *Historia regum* is, like *Lebor Gabála*, an overarching history of a territory and its people,[146] the author of the more elaborate and expansive Irish work does not appear to have drawn significantly on contemporary chronicles. This despite the fact that annalistic writing continued to form a major part of the activities of the learned Irish.[147] As the *Anglo-Saxon Chronicle* was continued in various places at different times by authors with specific biases, so too may the rich vein of Irish chronicling have as its starting point a common source, the now lost "Chronicle of Ireland," which appears to have come to an end in the year 911.[148] Identifiable strands thereafter include one from Clonmacnoise, which comprises the *Annals of Tigernach*, *Chronicum Scottorum*, as well as a seventeenth-century English translation, the *Annals of Clonmacnoise*.[149] A Munster collection, the *Annals of Inisfallen*, also drew on this western material down to the middle of the eleventh century, as David Dumville and Kathryn Grabowski have shown.[150] Several southern monastic centers also contributed to this source, including Emly, Killaloe, and Lismore. A compilation of similar provenance, *Miscellaneous Irish Annals* (the first part of which is also known as Mac Carthaigh's Book), which in its fragmentary extant form begins in 1114, represents for the most part a different southern strand.[151] The *Annals of Ulster*, by contrast, is a northern work. It and the *Annals of Loch Cé*, which begin in 1014, initially have a common core that comes from Armagh. An input from Derry into these interrelated texts has been detected from the late twelfth century.[152] Many of these compilations were employed in the seventeenth century, together with others now lost, by the so-called Four Masters whose *Annála Ríoghachta Éireann* (The Annals of the Kingdom of Ireland) forms a comprehensive history of Ireland, most of it based on earlier work.[153] Identifying the early layers incorporated by the four ecclesiastical scholars, however, is a difficult task.

Yet even if not always retrievable in its contemporary form, the wealth and variety of the extant annalistic collections indicate that creating and maintaining a record of events remained a major intellectual activity in many centers of learning in the tenth and eleventh centuries, and beyond. Moreover, notwithstanding their ecclesiastical provenance, the breadth of subject matter contained in these chronicles reveals continued close cooperation between king and cleric: these were social documents of interest to all. To take a random example, in 1012, the year in which the *Anglo-Saxon Chronicle* relates that Ealdorman Eadric and his counsellors went to London, the *Annals of Ulste*r remarks upon "an outbreak of colic ... in Armagh" (teidm tregait ... i nArd Macha) as a result of which three prominent ecclesiastics died. Two further entries deal directly with church matters, the deaths of two *airchinnig* (church officials) of Daiminis and Roscrea being noted in one; the slaying of the *airchinnech* of Slane by his rival, the *airchinnech* of nearby Dowth, in another. A third bears witness to the dependency of the Church on political patronage: on a march northwards, Brian Bórama, a Munster man and the most powerful king of Ireland in his day, "granted complete immunity to Patrick's churches" (tuc ogshoere do chellaib Patraicc), the most important of which was Armagh. The remaining three accounts concern secular matters: notices of the murder of the king of Conaille Muirthemne and a battle among Uí Echach are preserved, while a more prolonged campaign by the king of the northern territory of Cenél nÉogain against his long-standing enemies and near neighbors, Cenél Conaill, is set out in more detail. On the final leg of his expedition, the ruler in question, Flaithbertach son of Muirchertach, "took the greatest spoils both in captives and cattle that a king ever took" (tuc gabhala is moamh tuc ri riam eter brait ocus innile) – "though they are not counted" (ce nach n-airmter).[154]

The literary flavor evident in the latter remark is characteristic of numerous entries. The defeat of the troops of Máel Sechnaill mac Domnaill the following year is attributed to the fact that "a small number of nobles" (*uathad degdaine*) among them were drunk and hence foolishly gave battle "out of pride" (*tre diumus*). Poetic matter is interspersed;[155] narrative material is incorporated. The tone of the account of the battle of Clontarf in 1014, for example, between Brian Bórama and an assembled host of Leinster and Norse allies, is not always that of a dispassionate annalist: "Gnithir cath crodha etorra dona frith inntsamail" (A valiant battle was fought between them, the like of which was never [before] encountered). It also contains an augmented roll-call of the dead.[156]

Caraid tairisi

If annal writers had recourse to embellished retellings of the events they were recording, authors of those elaborate narratives made use of annalistic material in turn. *Cogadh Gáedhel re Gallaibh* (The War between Irish and Vikings), an early twelfth-century prose tale detailing Scandinavian attacks on Ireland, culminating in a highly subjective story about the encounter at Clontarf, is based in part on earlier collections of annals, some of them no longer available.[157] An eleventh-century text, the *Fragmentary Annals of Ireland*, similarly dealing with relations between Irish and Norse, also preserves much annalistic material as part of its narrative account.[158] Anglo-Saxon matters are occasionally included: as in the *Annals of Ulster*, the slaying of Ælle, king of the northern Saxons, by Danes in York is recorded, while the *Fragmentary Annals* augment the information concerning the sacking of the city.[159] Greater detail still is provided concerning the banishment from Ireland and subsequent flight of Ingimund to King Alfred's daughter, Æthelflæd, wife of the ailing Æethelfred.[160] Not satisfied with the lands near Chester he was granted by the queen, the Norse leader led an army to Chester itself. The Saxons were victorious with the aid of the Irish among the Scandinavian forces, who turned upon their leaders having been reminded that the Saxons in the past "did not give greater honor to any Saxon warrior or cleric than they have given to every Irish warrior and cleric who came to them" (gach oglach ocus gach cleireach Gaoidhealach tainig cuca-somh a hEirinn, ní tugsat a iomarcraidh onora d'óglach nó cleireach Saxan). Persuaded by the argument that the pagan foes should be as much the enemies of the Irish as of the Saxons, as "faithful friends" (caraid tairisi) of the English, the Irish turned sides.[161]

F. T. Wainwright accepted this incident in broad terms as historical, noting the record of Ingimund's presence in Anglesey in 902 in *Annales Cambriae* and linking it with the notice in the *Anglo-Saxon Chronicle* under the year 907 of the rebuilding of Chester by Æthelflæd.[162] While it may reflect an actual event, the Irish author feels the need to justify the story's inclusion ("níorbh áil dhamh a fhagbhail gan a scribheann na ndearnsad Lochlannaig ar ndul a hEirinn," "I did not wish to leave unwritten what the Scandinavians did having left Ireland")[163] and manipulates the information he has received. The treachery of the Irish is said to have been directed primarily at the *Danair* (Danes), "because they were less friends to them than the Norwegians" (úair ba lúgh ba caraid doibh iad ionáid na Lochlannaig).[164] The Norwegians fared no better, however, and elsewhere in the text it is in fact the Danes who are preferred.[165] Furthermore, while memories of Irish missions may conceivably inform the comment that foreign clerics were treated honorably by the Saxons, the call to common cause against the heathen has a shrill literary ring.[166]

Notwithstanding this, at the very least the author of the *Fragmentary Annals* displays some knowledge of historical rulers in the neighboring island, his portrayal of Æthelflæd as a skillful battle commander echoing the depiction of this "lady of the Mercians" in Anglo-Saxon sources.[167] References to Saxons in other literary works are not always as well anchored. They are mentioned in *Togail Bruidne Da Derga* (The Destruction of Da Derga's Hostel), for example, in an elaborate section of the tale in which Ingcél, a professional British reaver, describes from afar the arrangement of the troops in Da Derga's hostel which he and his Irish allies are about to attack. The establishment is said to contain *imda na Saxanach* (the chamber of the Saxons), alongside the chambers of named heroes and of specific professions.[168] As in many other of the chambers, nine men are said to be present there with "cropped hair" (*monga forbaidi*), wearing "purple garments" (*lennae corcri*) and carrying "nine spears" [and] "nine crimson red shields" (*noí manaise .ix. cromsceith deirg*).[169] Following the pattern in this section of the narrative, they are identified by a watchman, Fer Rogain, an Irish plunderer, and one of three foster-brothers of King Conaire Már, who is also present in the hostel. Having named the foreigners as Ósalt, Osbrit and Lindas, each with two companions, he describes them as three Saxon heirs-in-waiting in Conaire's retinue ("tri rigdomna do Saxanaib sin filet ocond ríg") and prophesies that they will share in the victory ("conrainfet in lucht sin búaid ngníma").[170] Two of the trio have Anglo-Saxon names, what may be Irish approximations of Oswald and Osfrith; the latter is given an Irish epithet, *lámfota* (long-armed). The origin of the third name is uncertain; one manuscript substitutes the alliterating "Oult" for "Lindas."[171] Nor can any of the three be identified; indeed it is highly unlikely that they represent historical personages. Notwithstanding this, it is significant that an Irish author, most likely in the twelfth century,[172] incorporated Saxon noble warriors into the army of a prehistoric Irish king.

Literary depictions of contemporary rulers occasionally accord them sway over neighboring islands; thus Brian Bórama is said to have levied "royal tribute" (*cíos rioghda*) upon the Saxons and Britons, as well as on various groups in Scotland.[173] While the tenth-/eleventh-century Munster king is not known to have extended his political activities outside Ireland, his great-grandson, Muirchertach Ua Briain, who commissioned a biography of his glorious ancestor in the early twelfth century, certainly did so. Brian's triumphant international campaign, therefore, is a wishful portrayal of what his descendant would like to achieve.[174] Other literary encounters were less forceful: *Tochmarc Emire* (The Wooing of Emer) suggests that the mighty hero Cú Chulainn was fostered with a Saxon, Ulbecán.[175] Saxon ancestry was also considered desirable. Niall "of the nine hostages" (*noígiallach*), progenitor of the great dynastic conglomeration Uí Néill is portrayed as the son of Cairenn, the daughter of a Saxon king.[176]

An eleventh-century composition, *Echtra mac nEchach Mugmedóin* (The Adventure of the Sons of Éochaid Mugmedón) presents Niall's biography in its fullest form.[177] Its author had access to earlier traditions about the northern king; his death-tale appears to date from the Old Irish period.[178] In the case of *Tochmarc Emire*, two versions of the narrative exist, an older one dating from the eighth century and a much expanded recension based on it, put together in perhaps the eleventh century.[179] An earlier form of *Togail Bruidne Da Derga* has also been preserved; a summary version of the more elaborate, much longer Middle Irish narrative is found in *Lebor na hUidre* where its source is specified as *Cín Dromma Snechtai*.[180] Preservation of early texts was considered important, though not for its own sake. As Máire Herbert has eloquently demonstrated, these works "provided access to a past which needed to be recovered ... because of its necessity for present and future."[181] Frequently serving a political need,[182] reworking might be repeated. A companion text of *Echtra mac nEchach Muigmedóin*, *Aided Crimthainn meic Fhidaig* (The Death-Tale of Crimthann mac Fidaig), focuses on the Connacht cousins of Uí Néill, descendants of Niall's three brothers, Brian, Fiachra and Ailill.[183] It justifies the dominance of Brian's seed, one of whom, Tairdelbach Ua Conchobair (d. 1156) was probably in power when the text was composed.[184] *Cath Almaine* (The Battle of Allen), a perhaps tenth-century composition that may have drawn on eighth-century material, was rewritten completely in the twelfth century and Cathal mac Finguine was incorporated into the tale. By rehabilitating their politically astute ancestor, the Éoganacht descendants of this historical Munster ruler, who died in 742, sought to highlight their own distinguished past.[185] Their Uí Briain neighbors looked to Brian Bórama; the Éoganachta had an even earlier model monarch through whom they too could promote their own long-established greatness.

Na dindgnai-sa turmim

Purposeful pride in one's ancestors was coupled with an identification with one's own place, the two being combined frequently in *dindshenchas* (lore of famous places), narratives in which the deeds of past heroes were mapped tangibly onto their territories, captured in a place-name commemorating the man. Such naming of the landscape is a feature of myriad compositions: thus, the different recensions of *Táin Bó Cúailnge* encompass stories of how various landmarks acquired their names. Occasionally, the name in question is alluded to in passing, the implied association with a particular warrior being deemed sufficient to explain its origin.[186] On other occasions, the connection is made explicit: when Finnabair, daughter of the king and queen of Connacht, Ailill and Medb, realized that she had been used as a sexual pawn in her mother's campaign, she died of shame (*atbail ar fhéili and sin*): "hence the place-name Finnabair Sléibe [Mountain-Finnabair]" (*is de atá Findabair Slébe*).[187] Indeed at times the author engages in his own etymologizing, spelling out why Focherd is the name of a place: "Combad de sin dano rod lil a n-ainm as Focherd dond inud .i. fó cerd .i. maith in cherd gascid donecmaic do Choin Culaind and sin" (So it was from that exploit that Focherd remained as the name of the place, that is *fó cerd* [good feat], good was the feat of arms which Cú Chulainn performed there).[188]

As in the case of Focherd (Faughart, Co. Louth), some of the dramatized places correspond to points on a modern map;[189] more presumably had medieval equivalents of which traces no longer remain.[190] It is unlikely, however, that all represent topographical reality; in a culture in which names had such resonance and in which a poet boasted of "these places I enumerate" (*na dindgnai-sa turmim*),[191] geography and literature need not always be perfectly aligned. Imagination was paramount in the comparable depictions of personal names, the majority of which relate to personages who did not exist.[192] Nonetheless, they continued to have relevance, part of the social patchwork in which contemporary occurrences also found a place, illuminated immeasurably by that which had gone before. The significance of these onomastic stories is indicated by their prominence in the corpus of eleventh- and twelfth-century material which has survived. Drawing on pre-existing matter, as well as employing considerable creative input themselves, learned scholars produced various compendia of names, veritable handbooks in which commentary on key individuals, dynasties and places were to be found. *Cóir Anmann* (The Fitness of Names), in its different Middle Irish recensions, focuses on the *dramatis personae* of the literary stage.[193] Prosimetric compilations of *dindshenchas* dating from the same period underline how medieval Irish historical writing was also driven by a sense of place.[194]

Fíanna bátar i ...

While Anglo-Saxon England has nothing quite comparable with these comprehensive compositions, the source material employed therein by the Irish authors would have been familiar to scholars across the Irish Sea. Specifically, the use of glossaries in *Cóir Anmann*, in particular,[195] points to the fact that in Ireland, as in post-Alfredian England, such texts formed part of the curriculum of schools.[196] Isidorean psychology is dominant, his *Etymologiae* was intimately embraced.[197] Referred to as "the summit of learning" (*in culmen*), it was procured in exchange for the last surviving copy of *Táin Bó Cúailnge*, according to a narrative linked to the latter, *De Fhaillsiugud Tána Bó Cúailnge* (The Finding of *Táin Bó Cúailnge*).[198] The tale bears witness to Isidore's standing, but also provides a significant insight into the value Irish scholars accorded their own cultural tradition; the equivalent of the "Etymologies," the *Táin* was not, surprisingly, considered to be in international demand.

Whether the *Táin* journeyed to England is a moot question, yet the heroic literature of the neighboring territories bears comparison in many ways, *fíanna bátar i* (the champions who were in ...) Ireland and in England being celebrated in their respective cultures.[199] The circumstances of the survival of this literary genre is also comparable in the two regions, since whatever their original date of composition, the texts come down to us in later forms. Continuous engagement with them ensured their recreation: the recension of the *Táin* preserved in the late twelfth-century manuscript, the Book of Leinster, differs markedly from the version in *Lebor na hUidre* both in content and in tone.[200] Heroic values are questioned; an evolving society directed its audience to issues of its own. To this end, new texts came into being, clearly linked to preceding compositions but signaling changing directions, both thematically and stylistically. *Cath Ruis na Ríg* (The Battle of Ros na Ríg), preserved alongside the *Táin* in the Book of Leinster, is one such text. Taking as its starting point the defeat (as it is presented) of Conchobar mac Nessa and his Ulaid kinsmen on the cattle-raid of Cúailnge (*Táin Bó Cúailnge*), the tale recounts how the Ulster king sought his revenge.[201] His allies on this occasion, however, are *carait écmaisse* (absent friends), summoned "throughout foreign lands" (*fo iathaib Gallecda*).[202] Moreover, the king is sidelined somewhat, overshadowed by Conall Cernach, his military commander – a Cú Chulainn of a different kind. While *Cath Ruis na Ríg* deals reverentially with its literary forebear, in a late-eleventh-century satire, *Aislinge Meic Conglinne* (The Vision of Mac Conglinne), *Táin Bó Cúailnge* and other compositions are unambiguously mocked.[203] A vibrant, thriving culture has scant need for sacred cows.

Scríbthar na scéla sin

That culture's cradle, the Church, was also not beyond ridicule. The eponymous hero of the *Aislinge*, Aniér mac Con Glinne,[204] "a famous scholar" (*scolaigi amru*) from Armagh "with an abundance of knowledge" (*co n-immad eolais*),[205] is sent to be crucified for reviling – with some justification[206] – the monastery of Cork.[207] A vision he experienced and subsequently related to the king of Munster, Cathal mac Finguine, thereby cured him of his insatiability and proved his salvation, the abbot's treasured "cowl" (*cochall*) being bestowed upon him as a reward.[208] Religious parody of the most delicious kind, *Aislinge meic Con Glinne* is comparable with satirical texts being composed elsewhere in Europe about the same time.[209] Its appearance in Ireland coincides, not unexpectedly, with a shift in the Church's intellectual role. Long the home of all kinds of learning, the Church gradually relinquished control of the cultivation of secular material to professional families, though it was not until the twelfth and thirteenth centuries that these came truly to the fore. The transitional period may have been lengthy, but that at least some of these professional families had their origins in hereditary ecclesiastical dynasties ensured that a certain degree of continuity prevailed.[210] Nonetheless, tensions undoubtedly surfaced. The unambiguous vote of the author of the late twelfth-century narrative, *Acallam na Senórach* (The Colloquy of the Ancients), was for continued clerical participation in the cultivation of literature; no less a saint than Patrick was made to endorse the engaging "pagan" tales of *fian*-[warrior-band] members, Caílte and Oisín, his guardian angels proclaiming, "let those stories be written" (*scríbthar na scéla sin*).[211] Yet that he felt the need to do so meant that change was inevitable. The twelfth-century codices, Rawlinson B502 and the Book of Leinster, may be ecclesiastical products but later manuscripts were produced in a secular milieu.[212]

Ireland's counterpart to the world of Anglo-Saxon learning, however, is one with a deep ecclesiastical hue.[213] Royal figures such as Cormac mac Cuilennáin may have been authors, but these held clerical office and were the exception rather than the rule. Like the Anglo-Saxons, the Irish had their learned abbots;[214] bishops too had a scholarly role.[215] *Fir légind* (learned men) are attested with a church affiliation;[216] it was in ecclesiastical centers that texts continued to be written and that precious books were stored.[217] Yet royal patronage was paramount, a tenth-century "chief poet of Ireland" (*primecess Erenn*),[218] Cináed ua hArtacáin, offering his compositions, among others, to Amlaíb Cuarán, Norse king of Dublin.[219] His slightly later, fellow-*príméces*, Cúán ua Lothcháin, served the midland ruler, Máel Sechnaill mac Domnaill. His involvement in internal politics was such that he was killed in neighboring Tethba. Cúán's slayers were to rue the day, however, since "the party that killed him became putrid within the hour" (*brenait a n-aenuair in lucht ro marb*), the annalist describing the incident as a poet's miracle (*firt filed innsein*).[220]

Engagement with local affairs, on the one hand, was coupled with familiarity with a wider world. Cúán and Cináed were "chief poets of Ireland" and whatever the reality behind this eloquent title, a scholar's circuit extended far beyond the remit of his own immediate territory (*túath*). Travel was sometimes international bringing with it exposure to new literary themes and forms. Foreign matter was adapted, none as enthusiastically as classical compositions, of which the Irish in many instances produced the first vernacular forms. Their version of the Alexander saga may be roughly contemporary with its Old English counterpart;[221] one recension of Dares Phrygius's *De excidio Troiae historia* may also be based on a tenth-century Irish exemplar.[222] Such material remained popular; the twelfth century saw the transposition of Lucan's *Pharsalia* and Statius's *Thebaid*, among other such texts, into an Irish literary milieu.[223] Latin learning was evidently sufficiently strong to furnish skillful "translators," though the trend towards adaptation in itself may indicate a greater need for assistance with Latin texts. The potential audience was considerable, the primarily heroic matter appealing to a people who could readily draw comparison with the deeds of their own literary warriors; all the more so since classical events were also afforded room in the overarching historical framework which came into being about the same time.[224] Moreover, clerical creators did not eschew the pagan nature of their material; as stated explicitly in *Acallam na Senórach*, pre-Christian material should also be embraced. These texts had significant influence on literary development in diverse ways.[225]

Conclusion

Ultimately, its predominantly "secular" feel may constitute the most perceptible difference between Old English and Medieval Irish literatures. The religious texts which form a prominent part of the Anglo-Saxon corpus were composed in Ireland also, but adorning the same manuscript pages are the exploits of kings and heroes; the lore of women (*banshenchas*)[226] and that of saints (*náemshenchas*)[227] are afforded the same creative space. Issues of transmission provide part of the explanation, *Beowulf* owing its precarious survival to its fortunate thematic connection with a group of other "more acceptable" texts. Yet this in itself is significant as an indicator of a markedly different cultural approach. The ninth-century author of *Félire Oengusso* may exult in the triumph of monasteries over pagan citadels;[228] within the cloisters of the former, however, the imagined activities of the latter were given shape.

In a number of narratives, the role of the Church as intermediary is given expression: it is through St. Patrick's power, for example, that Cú Chulainn and the fifth-century pseudo-historic king, Láegaire mac Néill, are brought together in *Siaburcharpat Con Culainn* (The Magical Chariot of Cú Chulainn), a tenth- or eleventh-century tale.[229] Cú Chulainn may urge Láegaire repeatedly to believe in God,[230] yet his heroic exploits are related sympathetically and Scribe H adds his genealogy to the end of the tale.[231] The Ulaid leader, Conchobar mac Nessa, is said to have been spared hell,[232] the reason for which is provided in that king's death-tale, a number of versions of which have survived. One of two men in Ireland who believed before the coming of Christianity, Conchobar died of grief on hearing of the crucifixion of Christ.[233] Finn mac Cumaill too was a precocious Christian, understanding through his formidable mantic powers "that there was indeed a true and glorious God, someone who had direction and power over us all" (go raibi in fírDhia forórdha ann .i. in nech aca raibe comus ocus comachta orainn uili).[234] As mediating forger of this rich, diverse material the Church assumed some measure of control.

As literary director, it could afford to be broadminded; indeed social circumstances demanded it must be so. The Book of Leinster may not be a patron's codex; nonetheless, the involvement of King Diarmait mac Murchada in its creation is tangible.[235] Royal approval, therefore, was a dominant concern. This interdependency of ecclesiastical and political rulers ensured that a broad literary palette was preserved. Whether their cooperation was closer than in Anglo-Saxon England is a moot question;

the results of their working relationship, however, were different in the two regions, the complex reasons for which have yet to be addressed. This requires scholars with an intimate knowledge of each of the two cultures and an appreciation of the literary gems which both territories possessed. To those engaged in the teaching and study of Old English, this brief and, of necessity, eclectic introduction to "the learning of Ireland" (*légend hÉrenn*)[236] can provide no more than a glimpse of the extraordinarily diverse material of that territory in the early medieval period. The richness and vitality of that literature bear witness to what was a remarkably inclusive definition on the part of the Irish of that which is "most needful to know."[237]

NOTES

[1] For an overview of ecclesiastical contacts between Ireland and England in the seventh and eighth centuries, see Hughes, "Evidence for Contacts between the Churches of the Irish and the English," pp. 49–67. See also Smith, "Writing in Britain and Ireland, *c.* 400 to *c.* 800," pp. 14–49; and Ní Mhaonaigh, "Of Bede's 'Five Languages and Four Nations,'" pp. 99–119.

[2] Bede, *Historia Ecclesiastica Gentis Anglorum* (henceforth HE), III.7, 25, 27.

[3] Bertram Colgrave, ed. and trans., *Two Lives of St. Cuthbert* (Cambridge, 1940) pp. 140, 236, 238.

[4] See Ireland, ed. and trans., *Old Irish Wisdom Texts Attributed to Aldfrith of Northumbria*.

[5] See Michael Lapidge, "Aldhelm and the 'Epinal-Erfurt Glossary,'" in *Aldhelm and Sherborne: Essays to Celebrate the Foundation of the Bishopric*, eds Katharine Barker and Nicholas Brooks (Oxford, 2010), pp. 129–63. On Aldhelm's Irish connections, see also Yorke, "Aldhelm's Irish and British Connections," pp. 164–80.

[6] The passages in question are discussed by Rosalind Love above, pp. 10–12.

[7] HE III.27.

[8] Ó Cróinín, "Rath Melsigi, Willibrord, and the Earliest Echternach Manuscripts," pp. 17–49, esp. p. 23. A destroyed *rath* on the site lends support to the identification: see Fanning, "Appendix: Some Field Monuments in the Townlands of Clonmelsh and Garryhundan, Co. Carlow," pp. 43–49.

[9] It is described as such in an annalistic entry recording its burning in 783: Mac Airt and Mac Niocaill, eds. and trans., *The Annals of Ulster (to A.D. 1131)* (henceforth AU), 738.3. On the history of the monastery, see Orschel, "Mag nEó na Sacsan: An English Colony in Ireland in the Seventh and Eighth Centuries," pp. 81–107.

[10] See Ní Mhaonaigh, "Of Saxons, a Viking and Normans," pp. 411–26.

[11] AU 685.2 and 687.5. On Adomnán's visit, see HE III.26; and Anderson and Anderson, eds. and trans., *Adomnán's Life of Columba*, II.46.

[12] Moisl, "The Bernician Royal Dynasty and the Irish in the Seventh Century," pp. 103–26, esp. pp. 120–24. See also, Charles-Edwards, *Early Christian Ireland*, pp. 429–38; and Wadden, "The First English Invasion," pp. 1–33.

[13] For a lucid analysis of the difficulties involved in isolating the "Irish strand in the English cultural weave," see Wright, *The Irish Tradition in Old English Literature*, pp. 3–5, 10–11, 15–20, 30–1, 34–5.

[14] For a brief summary of some of the contributions to the debate, see O'Sullivan, "Manuscripts and Palaeography," pp. 511–15 and references therein.

[15] See Law, *The Insular Latin Grammarians*; and a review-article of Law's book by Holtz, "Les Grammairiens Hiberno-Latins," pp. 170–84.

[16] The earliest Latin Life from Ireland is Cogitosus' *Life of Brigit of Kildare*, on which see Sharpe, "Vitae S. Brigitae: The Oldest Texts," pp. 81–106; and McCone, "Brigit in the Seventh Century," pp. 107–45. Patrick has been served by two seventh-century biographers, Muirchú and Tírechán: see Bieler, ed. and trans., *The Patrician Texts in the Book of Armagh*, pp. 61–167; Columba's Life was written by Adomnán (d. 704), a successor of his as abbot of Iona: see Anderson and Anderson, *Adomnán's Life*. Richard Sharpe has argued that a group of up to ten Lives preserved in a fourteenth-century manuscript, the *Codex Salmanticensis*, derive from an exemplar composed between ca. 740x850: Sharpe, *Medieval Irish Saints' Lives*, pp. 297–339. For a critical consideration of aspects of Sharpe's methodology, see Breatnach, "The Significance of the Orthography of Irish Proper Names in the *Codex Salmanticensis*," pp. 85–101. Other scholars have also questioned the early date of the collection: see John Carey, review of *Medieval Irish Saints' Lives*, by Richard Sharpe, *Speculum* 68 (1993), 260–62; and Ó Riain, "The O'Donoghue Lives of the Salamancan Codex," pp. 38–52. As far as later English-Irish relations are concerned, the provenance of the manuscript itself is interesting, on which see: Pádraig Ó Riain, "Codex Salmanticensis,": A Provenance *inter Anglos* or *inter Hibernos*?' in *'A Miracle of Learning': Studies in Manuscripts and Irish Learning. Essays in Honour of William O'Sullivan*, ed. Toby Barnard, Dáibhí Ó Cróinín and Katharine Simms (Ashgate, 1998), pp. 91–100.

[17] See, in particular, Kelly, *A Guide to Early Irish Law*; Ó Corráin, Breatnach, and Breen, "The Laws of the Irish," pp. 382–438; and Breatnach, "Lawyers in Early Ireland," pp. 1–13.

[18] Stokes and Strachan, eds. and trans., *Thesaurus Palaeohibernicus*, II.10–37.

[19] *The MacRegol or Rushworth Gospels*, with an introduction by W. O. Hassall, Major Treasures in the Bodleian Library 10 (Oxford, 1978).

[20] Stephen Allott, *Alcuin of York c. A.D. 732–804: His Life and Letters* (York, 1974), p. 15.

[21] Simon Keynes and Michael Lapidge, trans., *Alfred the Great: Asser's Life of Alfred and Other Contemporary Sources (Harmondsworth, 1983)*, pp. 113–14. See also Dumville, *Three Men in a Boat*. Later unnamed compatriots were associated with a later ruler of Wessex, King Æthelstan (d. 939); of their activities, however, no more than traces remain: see Michael Lapidge, "Some Latin Poems as

Evidence for the Reign of Æthelstan," *Anglo-Saxon England* 9 (1981), pp. 61–98. On exchange of books between Ireland and England in Æthelstan's reign, see Herbert, "Crossing Historical and Literary Boundaries," p. 90, n. 13.

[22] For connections between English and Irish martyrologies, see J. E. Cross, "The Influence of Irish Texts and Traditions on the *Old English Martyrology*," *Proceedings of the Royal Irish Academy* 81 C (1981), pp. 173–92; Ó Riain, *Anglo-Saxon Ireland*, and references therein, particularly to earlier work by John Hennig. A revised version of this article appears as "The Northumbrian Urtext of the Martyrology of Tallaght" in Pádraig Ó Riain, *Feastdays of the Saints*, pp. 43–52.

[23] For a general account of this material see Ó Cathasaigh, "The Literature of Medieval Ireland to *c.* 800," I.9–31; and Ní Mhaonaigh, "The Literature of Medieval Ireland, 800–1200," I.32–73. See also Ní Mhaonaigh, "Of Bede's 'Five Languages and Four Nations'"; and Clancy, "Gaelic Literature in Ireland and Scotland, 900–1150," pp. 637–59.

[24] Kelly, *Audacht Morainn*.

[25] Irish legal material has been elucidated by Kelly, *A Guide to Early Irish Law*; a detailed analysis of the contents of the tracts can be found in Breatnach, *A Companion to the Corpus Iuris Hibernici*.

[26] Patrick Wormald, "Anglo-Saxon Society and Its Literature," in *The Cambridge Companion to Old English Literature*, ed. Malcolm Godden and Michael Lapidge (Cambridge: Cambridge University Press, 1991), pp. 1–22 at p. 9; see also Dumville, "'Beowulf' and the Celtic World," p. 120: "the attitudes of Irish clerics to – and their heavy involvement in – the cultivation of vernacular literature seems likely to have constituted a formative influence on the attitudes of their English counterparts."

[27] Among the contributors to this debate have been (in chronological order): Max Deutschbein, "Die sagenhistorischen und literarischen Grundlagen des *Beowulfepos*," *Germanisch-romanische Monatschrift* 1 (1901), pp. 103–19; Donahue, "Beowulf, Ireland and the Natural Good," pp. 263–77, and "Grendel and the Clanna Cain," pp. 167–75; Carney, *Studies in Irish Literature and History*; Puhvel, *Beowulf and Celtic Tradition*; Tristram, *Sex Aetates Mundi: Die Weltzeitalter bei den Angelsachsen und den Iren*; and Cronan, "'Beowulf,' the Gaels and the Recovery of the Pre-Conversion Past," pp. 137–80.

[28] Dumville, "'Beowulf' and the Celtic World," p. 158.

[29] Note, for example, the division into texts "of the Alfredian era and those of the Benedictine reform period and later," in Elaine Treharne and Phillip Pulsiano, "An Introduction to the Corpus of Anglo-Saxon Literature," in their *A Companion to Anglo-Saxon Literature* (Oxford, 2001), p. 4.

[30] See Ó Cathasaigh, "The Literature of Medieval Ireland."

[31] See Charles-Edwards, *Early Christian Ireland*, pp. 592–93.

[32] This is clearly an oversimplification since the degree of use of the vernacular depended above all on the practice of a given annalist; a shift can be seen to have taken place in individual compilations at different times: see Dumville, "Latin and

Irish in the *Annals of Ulster*," pp. 320–41, which includes a brief comparison of Irish and English vernacular annalistic writing (pp. 333–34).

[33] Ó hAodha, ed. and trans., *Bethu Brigte*.

[34] Stokes, ed. and trans., *Félire Óengusso Céli Dé*; the text was dated to 797–805/7 by Thurneysen ("Die Abfassung des Félire von Oengus," pp. 6–8), whereas Ó Riain has argued for a slightly later date of 828–833 ("The Tallaght Martyrologies Redated," pp. 21–38); this revised date has generated discussion, see Breatnach, "Poets and Poetry," pp. 74–75; and Dumville, "*Félire Oengusso*," pp. 19–48.

[35] See, for example, Carey, *King of Mysteries*, pp. 14–15.

[36] The prolific ninth-century scholar, John Scottus Eriugena appears to have been neither a cleric nor a monk: Charles-Edwards, *Early Christian Ireland*, p. 591 and nn. 27, 28. Although much of his scholarly life was spent in Francia, his early intellectual training must have been received in Ireland.

[37] AU 887.5; the term *fili* is broader in meaning than English "poet" with which it is frequently equated; "scholar" or "man of learning" are more appropriate translations.

[38] Best and O'Brien, eds., *The Book of Leinster formerly Lebor na Núachongbála*, III.516–23.

[39] See Ní Mhaonaigh, "The Literature Of Medieval Ireland," p. 37.

[40] These include *Lebor na Cert* (The Book of Rights) and the Psalter of Cashel; see Dillon, "On the Date and Authorship of the *Book of Rights*," pp. 239–49; and Ó Riain, "The Psalter of Cashel," pp. 111–12, 113–14, 116–17.

[41] Breatnach has argued that he was the author of a eulogy of St. Senán, *Amra Senáin*: "An Edition of *Amra Senáin*," pp. 20–23. For a discussion of Cormac's literary career, see Ní Mhaonaigh, "Cormac mac Cuilennáin: king, bishop and 'wondrous sage,'" *Zeitschrift für celtische Philologie* 58 (2011): 109–28.

[42] Stokes, ed., *Three Irish Glossaries*, pp. 1–44; for the association with Cormac, see Russell, "The Sounds of a Silence," pp. 1–30.

[43] On medieval Irish glossaries in general, see Russell, "Laws, Glossaries and Legal Glossaries in Early Ireland," pp. 85–115; "*Graece ... Latine*: Graeco-Latin Glossaries in Early Medieval Ireland," *Peritia* 14 (2000): 406–20; as well as his general introduction to the genre: *'Read it in a Glossary': Glossaries and Learned Discourse in Medieval Ireland.*

[44] Mac Cana, ed. and trans., "A Poem Attributed to Cormac mac Cuilennáin (†908)," pp. 207–17; the list ends with Cormac's own predecessor as king, Cenn nGegáin.

[45] Carey, ed. and trans., "An Edition of the Pseudo-Historical Prologue to the *Senchas Már*," pp. 1–32. For a discussion of the date of the text, see McCone, "Dubthach maccu Lugair and a Matter of Life and Death," pp. 1–35; and Carey, "The Two Laws in Dubthach's Judgement," pp. 1–18.

[46] Carey, "The Two Laws in Dubthach's Judgement," p. 18.

[47] "Nónbur trá doérglas dond ordugud-sin .i. Pátraic ⁊ Benignus ⁊ Cairnech, trí epscoip; Loegaire mac Néill rí Hérenn ⁊ Dáire rí Ulad ⁊ Corc mac Lugdech

rí Muman, trí ríg; Dubthach maccu Lugair ⁊ Fergus fili ⁊ Ros mac Trechim suí bélra Féne" (Nine men were chosen to arrange [the laws]: Patrick and Benignus and Cairnech, three bishops; Loegaire mac Néill king of Ireland and Dáire king of Ulster and Corc mac Lugdech king of Munster, three kings; [and] Dubthach maccu Lugair, and Fergus the poet, and Ros mac Trechim the expert in legal language): Carey, "An Edition of the Pseudo-Historical Prologue," pp. 12, 19 (§8). Dubthach is described as "rígfhili insi Érenn" (royal poet of the island of Ireland) at an earlier point in the text: Carey, "An Edition of the Pseudo-Historical Prologue," pp. 11, 18 (§4).

[48] Carey, "An Edition of the Pseudo-Historical Prologue," pp. 12, 19 (§8). *Nó-fis* derives from *noí-fis* (literally, nine-knowledge), a fanciful etymology of *nós* (a custom or law) of a type commonly concocted in medieval Irish texts: see Carey, "An Edition of the Pseudo-Historical Prologue," p. 26.

[49] It also appears in another related glossary *Dúil Dromma Cetta*, for both of which see Carey, "An Edition of the Pseudo-Historical Prologue," p. 26; and Binchy, "The Pseudo-Historical Prologue to the *Senchas Már*," p. 22.

[50] This is the phrase used in the eighth-century law tract *Córus Béscnai*, "The Prescribed Arrangement of Custom," in Binchy, ed., *Corpus Iuris Hibernici*, II.529.4; see also McCone, *Pagan Past and Christian Present*, pp. 25–26. It is echoed in the Pseudo-Historical Prologue: McCone, "Dubthach maccu Lugair," pp. 21–23.

[51] AU 679.2.

[52] Binchy, *Corpus Iuris Hibernici*, I.250.37–38.

[53] Binchy, *Corpus Iuris Hibernici*, I.250.42.

[54] Binchy, *Corpus Iuris Hibernici*, I.251.2–3. Discussions of the narrative include Mac Cana, "The Three Languages and the Three Laws," pp. 62–66; Slotkin, "Medieval Irish Scribes and Fixed Texts," pp. 439–40; McCone, "Zur Frage der Register im frühen Irischen," pp. 61–67, and *Pagan Past and Christian Present*, pp. 23–24. Note also McManus's observation, with reference to the *Etymologiae* of Isidore of Seville, that "the statement that Cenn Fáelad lost 'his brain of forgetting' ... might indeed be interpreted to mean that he learned to read and write." In *A Guide to Ogam*, p. 184, n. 4.

[55] Charles-Edwards, "Language and Society among the Insular Celts," p. 722.

[56] Calder, ed. and trans., *Auraicept na nÉces*, pp. 6–7 (lines 63–78).

[57] Dumville, "'Beowulf' and the Celtic World," p. 147.

[58] Dumville, "'Beowulf' and the Celtic World," pp. 147–48. Niles has discussed the possibility of Irish influence more generally on the Cædmon story: "Bede's Cædmon: 'The Man Who Had No Story'" (Irish Tale-Type 2412B)," *Folklore* 117, no. 2 (2006): 141–55.

[59] Binchy, *Corupus Iuris Hibernici*, 586.14; 2212.3.

[60] McCone, *Pagan Past and Christian Present*, p. 23.

[61] The attribution was accepted by some earlier scholars; for discussion and references, see Ahlqvist, ed. and trans., *The Early Irish Linguist,* pp. 18–19.

[62] Ahlqvist, *Early Irish Linguist*, p. 40 and n. 3.

[63] Ahlqvist, *Early Irish Linguist*, p. 47.

[64] Ahlqvist, *Early Irish Linguist*, p. 48.

[65] Ahlqvist, *Early Irish Linguist*, p. 47.

[66] By way of example, we may note the following typical passage: "Insce trá: cis lir insci do-chuisin? Ni ansae: a tri .i. ferinsce ocus baninsce ocus deminsce lasin nGoídil .i. mascul ocus femen ocus neutur lasin Laitneoir" (Gender then: how many genders are there? Not difficult: three, namely "man gender," "woman gender," and "non-gender," according to the Irishman, masculine, feminine and neuter according to the Latinist): Ahlqvist, *Early Irish Linguist*, p. 49.

[67] See McManus, *Guide to Ogam*, pp. 27–31.

[68] McManus, *Guide to Ogam*, p. 31.

[69] McManus, "Ogam," p. 13. See also Harvey, "Early Literacy in Ireland," pp. 1–15.

[70] See McManus, *Guide to Ogam*, pp. 148–66.

[71] Note, for example, the following passage: "Attaat di ernail forsind apgitir Laitindai .i. guttai ocus consana. Attat dano di ernail forsin beithi-luis-nin ind oguim .i. feda ocus táebomnae " (There are two categories in the Latin alphabet, namely vowels and consonants. There are two categories in the Ogam alphabet, namely vowels and consonants ...): Ahlqvist, *Early Irish Linguist*, p. 48. The term *beithe-luis-nin* derives from the names designating three letters of the ogam alphabet: *beithe* (birch), *luis* (herb), *nin* (fork).

[72] Sims-Williams has drawn attention to the use of an ogam authorial inscription in a copy of a late tenth-century book by Byrhtferth of Ramsey: "Byrhtferth's Ogam Signature," pp. 283–91; reprinted in his *Studies on Celtic Languages*, pp. 169–77.

[73] See McManus, *Guide to Ogam*, pp. 129–40.

[74] The date of the manuscript is a matter of continuing debate centering on whether one of the main two scribes of the manuscript, M, or a later one, H, can be identified with Máel Muire mac Celéchair, who died in 1106. However, the length of time separating the scribes does not appear to have been great: see, Ó Concheanainn, "The Reviser of Leabhar na hUidhre," pp. 277–88, and "*Aided Nath Í* and the Reviser of Leabhar na hUidhre," pp. 146–62; Oskamp, "Mael Muire: Compiler or Reviser?," pp. 177–82; Mac Eoin, "The Interpolator H in Lebor na hUidre," pp. 39–46; and Caoimhín Breatnach's review of that volume, *Éigse* 29 (1996), 200–8, at 206–7. A recent study of the manuscript by Herbert takes as its working hypothesis, "that Lebor na hUidre is an eleventh-century Clonmacnoise product": Herbert, "Crossing Historical and Literary Boundaries," p. 92. On H's working methods, see Toner, "Scribe and Text in *Lebor na hUidre*," pp. 106–20; and Dooley, *Playing the Hero*, pp. 64–100. See further the essays in Ó hUiginn, *Lebor na hUidre*.

[75] I follow Poppe here in using the term "pseudo-historical" to cover "a significant part of what is traditionally called medieval Irish 'literature,' namely the nar-

rative texts of the so-called Mythological, History (or King), and Ulster (or Heroic) cycles:" Poppe, "Reconstructing Medieval Irish Literary Theory," pp. 33–34.

[76] Best and Bergin, eds., *Lebor na hUidre*. The contents, and other aspects of the manuscript, have been discussed by Ó Concheanainn, "Textual and Historical Associations of Leabhar na hUidhre," pp. 65–120, and "Leabhar na hUidhre: Further Textual Associations," pp. 27–91. See also now the essays in Ó hUiginn, *Lebor na hUidre*. For discussion of some of the homiletic material in the manuscript, see Boyle, "Neoplatonic Thought in Medieval Ireland," pp. 216–30, and "Eschatological Justice in *Scéla Laí Brátha*," pp. 39–54.

[77] For a brief description, see Best and Bergin, eds., *Lebor na hUidre*, p. xiii.

[78] Ó Concheanainn, "Textual and Historical Associations," p. 75.

[79] Herbert, "Crossing Historical and Literary Boundaries," pp. 91–93.

[80] See the various essays in Ó hUiginn, *Lebor na hUidre*.

[81] There are also references to *araile libair* (other books) and *in aliis libris*: Best and Bergin, eds., *Lebor na hUidre*, lines 7953 and 474, respectively.

[82] Despite its name, Mac Cana argued that the codex was written at the important monastery of Bangor, which had an association with Druimm Snechtai: "Mongán mac Fiachnai and *Immram Brain*," pp. 103–06.

[83] See Ó Concheanainn, "Textual and Historical Associations," pp. 84–86, with references to previous discussion.

[84] The list of texts it most likely contained is discussed by Carey, "On the Interrelationship of Some *Cín Dromma Snechtai* Texts," pp. 71–72, building on work by Thurneysen, *Die irische Helden- und Königsage bis zum siebzehnten Jahrhundert*, p. 17.

[85] Carey, "On the Interrelationship of Some *Cín Dromma Snechtai* Texts," p. 91, gives a summary of the dates of the texts.

[86] Mac Mathúna has argued for the later date on the basis of his reading of the linguistic evidence of one of the tales contained in the manuscript: *Immram Brain*, pp. 425–58; Kim McCone's analysis of the textual transmission of the latter text and its sister narrative, *Echtrae Chonnlai*, leads him to conclude that "an eighth-century date for the tantalizing *Cín* remains perfectly possible although a tenth-century one cannot be excluded": *Echtrae Chonnlai and the Beginnings of Vernacular Narrative Writing in Ireland*, p. 67.

[87] Ó Concheanainn, "Textual and Historical Associations," p. 83.

[88] For a description of these manuscripts, see Stokes and Strachan, eds. and trans., *Thesaurus Palaeohibernicus*, I.xiii–xxvi and II.ix–xl.

[89] Stokes and Strachan, eds. and trans., *Thesaurus Palaeohibernicus*, II.244–47, and II.xxvi for a description of the manuscript. On the text itself, see Ó Néill, "The Background to the *Cambrai Homily*," pp. 137–47; and Stancliffe, "Red, White and Blue Martyrdom," pp. 21–46. Other bilingual texts include the incantations against various ailments preserved in an eighth- or ninth-century St. Gall manuscript: Stokes and Strachan, eds. and trans., *Thesaurus Palaeohibernicus*, II.xxvii and II.248–49.

[90] See, for example, Ford's analysis of the nature poem, *Dom-fharcai fidbaide fál*, linking the frequent occurrence of pronouns therein with the grammatical content of the adjacent Latin text: "Blackbirds, Cuckoos and Infixed Pronouns," pp. 162–70. For a similar approach to another marginal stanza, see Ahlqvist, "*Is acher in gaíth ... úa Lothlind*," pp. 23–25. On the relative status of the two languages, see Charles-Edwards, "Language and Society," p. 721.

[91] Stokes and Strachan, eds. and trans., *Thesaurus Palaeohibernicus*, II.xxxii–xxxiv and II.293–96. The poem on the celebrated cat, Pangur Bán, has been much anthologized; see, for example, Murphy, ed. and trans., *Early Irish Lyrics*, pp. 2–3; and Greene and O'Connor, eds. and trans., *A Golden Treasury of Irish Poetry*, pp. 81–83. For discussion of the poem, see Toner, "'Messe ocus Pangur Bán,'" pp. 1–22; and Lauran Toorians, "Reclusive Blackbirds and a Scholarly 'White Fuller': Two Notes on Irish 'Nature Poetry,'" *Cambrian Medieval Celtic Studies* 61 (2011): 87–90.

[92] Stokes and Strachan, eds. and trans., *Thesaurus Palaeohibernicus*, II.xxiv and II.296. Elizabeth Boyle discusses this poem in "Lay Morality, Clerical Immorality, and Pilgrimage in Tenth-Century Ireland: *Cethrur macclérech and Epscop do Gáedelaib*," *Studia Hibernica* 39 (2013): 9–48, at 42–48. On pilgrimage more generally, see Hughes, "The Changing Theory and Practice of Irish Pilgrimage," *Journal of Ecclesiastical History* 11 (1960): 143–51.

[93] Notable exceptions include the late seventh-century liturgical manuscript, "The Antiphonary of Bangor," and the ninth-century Patrician collection, "The Book of Armagh:" see Griggs and Warren, ed., *The Antiphonary of Bangor*; and Gwynn, ed., *Liber Ardmachanus*. For discussion of books produced in Ireland but transmitted elsewhere, including Northumbria, see Sharpe, "Books from Ireland, Fifth to Ninth Centuries," pp. 1–55.

[94] Best and Bergin, eds., *Lebor na hUidre*, line 474.

[95] Best and Bergin, eds., *Lebor na hUidre*, line 7953.

[96] Charter evidence provides a parallel from Anglo-Saxon England, since only those charters which "found their way at some point to ecclesiastical archives" have survived: Wormald, "Anglo-Saxon Society," p. 10.

[97] For an account of Ireland's earliest extant literature, see Ó Cathasaigh, "The Literature of Medieval Ireland."

[98] Carney, "The Dating of Early Irish Verse Texts," pp. 177–216. See also his, "The Dating of Archaic Irish Verse," pp. 39–55, in which he argues for a fifth-century date for a collection of Leinster poems. For lucid arguments against this early date, see Ó Corráin, "Irish Origin Legends and Genealogies," pp. 59–67. See also Breatnach, "Poets and Poetry," pp. 75–76.

[99] *Birgit bé bithmaith* (Brigit, ever excellent woman), also known as Ultán's hymn after the seventh-century bishop to whom it is attributed in some manuscripts: Stokes and Strachan, eds. and trans., *Thesaurus Palaeohibernicus*, II.325–26; *Fo réir Choluimb céin ad-fías* (As long as I speak [may I be] obedient to Colum), and *Tiughraind Bhécáin* (The last verses of Bécán), both attributed to the

seventh-century poet, Bécán mac Luigdech: Kelly, ed. and trans., "A Poem in Praise of Columb Cille," pp. 1–34, and "Tiughraind Bhécáin," pp. 66–98. A seventh-century date appears to fit the linguistic evidence in the case of all three poems.

[100] *Imbu maccán cóic bliadnae* (When I was a five-year old boy); *Tair cucum a Maire boíd* (Come to me, loving Mary); and *A Maire, a grian ar clainde* (Mary, sunshine of our people), in Carney, ed. and trans., *The Poems of Blathmac son of Cú Brettan.*

[101] McNamara and Herbert, eds. and trans., "A Versified Narrative of the Childhood Deeds of the Lord Jesus," I.455–83.

[102] Carney, *The Poems of Blathmac.*

[103] Thurneysen accepts the ascription in his edition of the poems: "Colmān mac Lēnēni and Senchān Torpēist," pp. 193–209. This cleric-poet has been compared with Cædmon by Ireland, "The Poets Cædmon, and Colmán mac Lénéni," pp. 172–82.

[104] Stokes, ed. and trans., "The Bodleian Amra Choluimb Chille," pp. 30–55, 132–83, 248–87, 400–37. While the core of this text may be from the late sixth or early seventh century, Jacopo Bisagni has shown that it was revised and enlarged in the ninth century: "The Language and Date of Amrae Coluimb Chille," pp. 1–11.

[105] Michael Lapidge, "The School of Theodore and Hadrian," *ASE* 15 (1986): 45–72; and Wormald, "Anglo-Saxon Society," p. 9.

[106] See pp. 11–12, in this volume.

[107] Lapidge and Herren, trans., *Aldhelm: The Prose Works*, p. 163: "Why, I ask, is Ireland, whither assemble the thronging students by the fleet-load, exalted with a sort of ineffable privilege, as if here in the fertile soil of Britain, teachers who are citizens of Greece and Rome cannot be found?"; see further Love, pp. 11–12, in this volume.

[108] Lapidge, "Aldhelm and the 'Epinal-Erfurt Glossary'"; see also his "The Career of Aldhelm," pp. 15–69; and Love, p. 12, in this volume.

[109] On prostitutes and pagan stories, see Lapidge and Herren, trans., *Aldhelm: The Prose Works*, pp. 154–55; and Love, p. 12, in this volume.

[110] McCone, *Echtrae Chonnlai*; and Mac Mathúna, *Immram Brain*; on their date, see McCone, *Echtrae Chonnlai*, pp. 29–47.

[111] McCone, *Echtrae Chonnlai*, pp. 121, 132 (§3).

[112] McCone, *Echtrae Chonnlai*, pp. 121, 132 (§3).

[113] Carey, "The Rhetoric of *Echtrae Chonlai*," pp. 45–46.

[114] McCone, *Echtrae Chonnlai*, pp. 122, 178 (§11). Carey sees the woman as "a pre-Christian harbinger of Christian revelation" ("The Rhetoric of *Echtrae Chonlai*," pp. 57–58), whereas for McCone she is a symbol of the Church (*Echtrae Chonnlai*, pp. 100–04).

[115] McCone, *Echtrae Chonnlai*, pp. 121, 130 (§1).

[116] See, for example, Vendryes, ed., *Airne Fíngein*, p. 1; and Nic Dhonnchadha, ed., *Aided Muirchertaig meic Erca*, p. 1.

[117] Carney first proposed this reading of the tale: "The Deeper Level of Early Irish Literature," pp. 160–71; it was expanded upon by Carey, "The Rhetoric of *Echtrae Chonlai*."

[118] Breatnach has dated it to between 678 and 683: "The Ecclesiastical Element in the Old-Irish Legal Tract *Cáin Fhuithirbe*," pp. 439–59.

[119] See, for example, Ó Corráin, Breatnach, and Breen, "The Laws of the Irish"; Ó Corráin, "Irish Vernacular Law and the Old Testament," pp. 284–307; Breatnach, "Canon Law and Secular Law in Early Ireland," pp. 439–59, and his "Lawyers in Early Ireland."

[120] For a comprehensive introduction to the material, see Kelly, *Guide to Early Irish Law*; and Breatnach, *Companion to the Corpus Iuris Hibernici*.

[121] *Cáin Aicillne* (The Law of Base Clientship); *Cáin Lánamna* (The Law of Couples): Thurneysen, ed. and trans., *Studies in Early Irish Law*, pp. 1–75. *Cáin Iarraith* (The Law of the Fosterage-fee); *Bechbretha* (Bee-judgements): Charles-Edwards and Kelly, eds. and trans., *Bechbretha*. *Catshlechta* (Sections Concerning Cats) and *Conshlechta* (Sections Concerning Dogs).

[122] *Bretha Comaithchesa* (The Judgements of Neighborhood).

[123] Binchy, "Bretha Crólige (The Judgements of Sick-maintenance)," pp. 1–77; and Binchy, "Bretha Déin Chécht (The Judgements of Dían Cécht)," pp. 1–20.

[124] *Córus Bésgnai* (The Arrangement of Customary Behavior).

[125] It includes *Cáin Fhuithirbe* and the two *Bretha Nemed* (Judgements Concerning Privileged Persons) texts: *Bretha Nemed Toísech* (The First *Bretha Nemed*), and *Bretha Nemed Dédenach* (The Last *Bretha Nemed*).

[126] For a description of *rosc*, see Breatnach, "Zur Frage der *roscada* im Irischen," pp. 197–205.

[127] See, for example, McCone, *Echtrae Chonnlai*, p. 123 (§14), where a three-stanza, syllabic poem stands in contrast to the *rosc* used elsewhere. Other examples of this parallel usage are cited by Carey, "The Rhetoric of *Echtrae Chonlai*," p. 59.

[128] The tenth-century tale, *Orgain Denna Ríg* (The Destruction of Dinn Ríg), for example, concludes with a contemporary *rosc*: Greene, ed., *Fingal Rónáin and Other Stories*, p. 23; for discussion, see Ó Cathasaigh, "The Oldest Story of the Laigin," pp. 13–17.

[129] Henry, ed. and trans., "Verba Scáthaige," pp. 191–207.

[130] Murphy, "On the Dates of Two Sources," pp. 145–51.

[131] Fínnechta, for example, appears under a playfully etymologized form of his name: *ībthius Snechta Fīna fhirfess*; "Snechta Fína [Snow of Wine < *fín* (wine) and *snechta* (snow); Fínnechta being interpreted as Fínshnechta] who shall pour shall drink it": Murphy, "On the Dates of Two Sources," pp. 147, 149.

[132] For the text, see Hull, ed. and trans., "Apgitir Chrábaid," pp. 44–89. Its date continues to be debated; see, for example, Ó Néill, "The Date and Authorship of *Apgitir Chrábaid*," pp. 203–15; and McCone, "Prehistoric, Old and Middle Irish," pp. 34–35.

[133] The translation of the phrase (which occurs in a list of the kinds of

activities engaged in at the "Fair" of Carmain) is by Gwynn, ed. and trans., *The Metrical Dindshenchas*, III.20–21 (line 239). *Fid*, literally "wood," is used to mean "letter," usually a letter of the ogam alphabet. A text entitled *De Dúilib Feda* lists all the ogam supplementary characters (*forfeda*): Calder, *Auraicept na nÉces*, pp. 270–71.

[134] *Apgitir Chrábaid*, for example, draws on the work of John Cassian: Ó Néill, "Date and Authorship of *Apgitir Chrábaid*."

[135] Herbert, "Crossing Historical and Literary Boundaries."

[136] Herbert, "Crossing Historical and Literary Boundaries," p. 99.

[137] Herbert and Ó Riain, eds. and trans., *Betha Adamnáin*. The date of this and other compositions indicate that learning in some form continued in the Viking era, suggesting that the greater proliferation of extant texts from the eleventh century could also reflect "on-going activity emerging into visibility in a more stable era": Herbert, "Crossing Historical and Literary Boundaries," p. 88.

[138] For a general account of the genre, see Herbert, "Hagiography," pp. 79–90, and her article, "Latin and Vernacular Hagiography of Ireland from the Origins to the Sixteenth Century," III.327–60.

[139] McNamara, *The Apocrypha in the Irish Church*, p. 2. For a general account of this material, see also Dumville, "Biblical Apocrypha and the Early Irish," pp. 229–338. A list of relevant texts has been compiled by O'Leary, "The Apocrypha and Their Transmission," accessed via www.ucc.ie/celt/Apocrypha.pdf.

[140] For this description and a general account of the text, see Carey, *A Single Ray of the Sun*, pp. 75. For more detailed commentary, an edition, and translation of the text, see his *Apocrypha Hiberniae II, Apocalyptica 1*.

[141] For an edition, see Stokes, ed., *Saltair na Rann*; Carey translates three cantos in *King of Mysteries*, pp. 98–124; the story of Adam and Eve as related in the text has been edited and translated by Greene and Kelly, *The Irish Adam and Eve Story from Saltair na Rann*, Vol. 1; Vol. 2 by Murdoch consists of commentary. A prose version also exists: Dillon, ed. and trans., "Scél Saltrach na Rann," pp. 1–43.

[142] The text commonly known as "The Book of Invasions" is available in an unsatisfactory edition by Macalister, *Lebor Gabála Érenn*, 5 vols; see also the introduction to the reprint of this edition: Carey, *A New Introduction to Lebor Gabála Érenn*. For commentary on the narrative, see Carey, *The Irish National Origin-Legend*, and his "*Lebor Gabála* and the Legendary History of Ireland," pp. 32–48; as well as Scowcroft, "*Leabhar Gabhála* Part I," pp. 81–142, and "*Leabhar Gabhála* Part II," pp. 1–66.

[143] Gwynn, *Metrical Dindshenchas*, III.20–1 (line 265); this is another of the activities said to have occurred at the Fair of Carmain.

[144] The poems attributed to these poets are listed in Carey, *A New Introduction*, p. 5, nn. 11–14.

[145] For some evidence of this, see Carey, *A New Introduction*, p. 6.

[146] The *Historia regum* is, of course, very different both in purpose and in tone from the *Lebor Gabála*. Notwithstanding this, Byrhtferth did have some

connection with the world of Irish learning since he used ogam letters on an authorial inscription, as noted above: see Sims-Williams, "Byrhtferth's Ogam Signature." R. R. Davies astutely compared *Lebor Gabála Érenn* to Henry of Huntingdon's *Historia Anglorum*: "The Peoples of Britain and Ireland, 1100–1400: IV, language and historical mythology", *Transactions of the Royal Historical Society* 6.VII (1997), pp. 1–24 at p. 20; see further Máire Ní Mhaonaigh, "Seanchas traidisiúnta, idirnáisiúnta: cruthú na staire in Éirinn san aonú agus sa dara haois déag," in *Litríocht na Gaeilge ar fud an Domhain I: Cruthú, Caomhnú agus Athbheochan*, ed. Máirín Nic Eoin, Meidhbhín Ní Úrdail, and Regina Uí Chollatáin (Dublin, 2015), 1–21.

[147] For a brief introduction to this material, see Mac Niocaill, *The Medieval Irish Annals*, and Ó Corráin, "Annals, Irish," I.69–75. For a more detailed account of the genre, see Evans, *The Present and the Past in Medieval Irish Chronicles*, and McCarthy, *The Irish Annals*. The views of the latter remain contested: see, for example, the review of the volume by Charles-Edwards, *Studia Hibernica* 36 (2009–10): 207–10.

[148] For an account and attempted reconstruction of this source, see Charles-Edwards, trans., *The Chronicle of Ireland*, 2 vols. See also Flechner, "The Chronicle of Ireland: Then and Now," pp. 422–54.

[149] Stokes, ed. and trans., *The Annals of Tigernach*; Hennessy, ed. and trans., *Chronicum Scotorum*; Murphy, ed. and trans., *The Annals of Clonmacnoise*.

[150] Grabowski and Dumville, *Chronicles and Annals of Mediaeval Ireland and Wales*. The Munster collection has been edited and translated by Mac Airt, *The Annals of Inisfallen*.

[151] Ó hInnse, ed. and trans., *Miscellaneous Irish Annals*; see also Mac Niocaill, *Medieval Irish Annals*, pp. 26–29.

[152] Gwynn, "Cathal Óg mac Maghnusa and the Annals of Ulster," *Clogher Record* 2, no. 2 (1958): 230–43; 2, no. 3 (1959): 370–84. The Annals of Loch Cé have been edited and translated by Hennessy, *The Annals of Loch Cé*, 2 vols.

[153] O'Donovan, ed. and trans., *Annála Rioghachta Éireann*.

[154] AU 1012.2.

[155] Much of it by later copyists, including a stanza on another defeat of Máel Sechnaill's men, also in 1013: AU 1013.5.

[156] AU 1014.1; this is discussed in Ní Mhaonaigh, *Brian Boru*, pp. 54–65.

[157] See Máire Ní Mhaonaigh, "*Cogad Gáedel re Gallaib* and the Annals: A Comparison," *Ériu* 47 (1996): 101–26.

[158] Radner, ed. and trans., *The Fragmentary Annals of Ireland*.

[159] AU 867.7; Radner, *The Fragmentary Annals of Ireland*, pp. 128–29 (§348). An earlier attack on York is recorded uniquely in Irish sources: Radner, *The Fragmentary Annals of Ireland*, pp. 118–19 (§330).

[160] The terminal nature of the king's illness is mentioned no less than three times in the passage: Radner, *The Fragmentary Annals of Ireland*, pp. 166–73 (§429).

[161] Radner, *The Fragmentary Annals of Ireland*, pp. 166–73 (§429).

[162] Wainwright, "Ingimund's Invasion," pp. 145–69; his view is endorsed by Radner, *The Fragmentary Annals of Ireland*, pp. 206–7. Herbert has examined the entry in the context of a broader study of the Fragmentary Annals, the results of which she presented at a workshop at St. Catherine's College, Cambridge, July 2008, as part of the Arts and Humanities Research Council-funded event, "Crossing Conquests: Literary Culture in Eleventh-Century England."

[163] Radner, *The Fragmentary Annals of Ireland*, pp. 168–69 (§429). In an earlier section of the narrative, he adopted a different approach: having noted the return to Scandinavia of Amlaíb (Norse, Óláfr) to assist his father in battle, he remarks, "since it would be lengthy to tell the cause of the conflict, and since it is of little relevance to us, although we have knowledge of it, we forego writing it, for our task is to write about whatever concerns Ireland, and not even all of that" (uair ba fada ra inisin cúis a cogaidh ocus ara laighead tremdhírgeas cugainn cidh again na bheith a fhios, fagbhaim gan a scribeann, úair atá ar n-obair im neoch as d'Erinn do scribeann ocus cidh ní iad-saidhe uile): Radner, *The Fragmentary Annals of Ireland*, pp. 144–45 (§400).

[164] The term *Lochlannaig* is used for Scandinavians generally before coming to signify the inhabitants of Norway: see Ní Mhaonaigh, "Literary Lochlann," in *Cànan & Cultar. Language and Culture: Rannsachadh na Gàidhlig* 3, ed. Wilson McLeod, James E. Fraser and Anja Gunderloch (Edinburgh, 2006), pp. 25–37; and Colmán Etchingham, "The Location of Historical *Laithlinn/Lochla(i)nn*," in *Proceedings of the Seventh Symposium of Societas Celtologica Nordica*, ed. Mícheál Ó Flaithearta, Acta Universitatis Upsaliensis, Studia Celtica Upsaliensia (Uppsala, 2007), pp. 11–31. In this text, it is employed in opposition to *Danair* to specify a particular group of Scandinavians, thus Radner translates it "Norwegians."

[165] Radner, *The Fragmentary Annals of Ireland*, pp. 90–95 (§235): "is íad na Danair rug búaidh ocus cosgar tria rath Padraicc, ge ro badar na Lochlannaig tri chuttruma risna Danaroibh, nó ceithre cudruma" (it is the Danes who took victory and spoils through the grace of Patrick although the Norwegians were three or four times the number of the Danes). Their partial piety is cited as a reason for this preference: "uair as amhlaidh ra bhattar na Danair, ocus cinele crabhaidh aca, .i. gabhaid sealad fri fheóil ocus fri mhnáibh ar chrabhudh" (for the Danes were like that, and they had kinds of piety – that is, they abstained from meat and from women for a while, for the sake of piety). On the nuanced portrayal of Vikings in this texts, see Downham, "The Good, the Bad and the Ugly," pp. 28–40.

[166] In the context of the Crusades, its resonance would have been all the greater; for examples of such echoes in other texts, see Ní Mhaonaigh, "Pagans and Holy Men," pp. 143–61.

[167] She is similarly depicted in an account of another Viking-Saxon encounter later in the text in which her cunning cleverness (*gliocas*) is specifically commended: Radner, *The Fragmentary Annals of Ireland*, pp. 180–81 (§459).

[168] These include *imda na ndaleman* (the chamber of those distributing drink), *imda Tulchinne drúith* (the chamber of Tulchinne the jester), *imda na*

muccidi (the chamber of the swineherds), and *imda Chúscraid meic Conchobair* (the chamber of Cúscraid son of Conchobar): Best and Bergin, eds., *Lebor na hUidre*, pp. 231–32. For an edition of the tale without translation, see Knott, *Togail Bruidne Da Derga*. There is an earlier edition with translation by Stokes, ed. and trans., "The Destruction of Da Derga's Hostel." It has been analyzed by O'Connor, *The Destruction of Da Derga's Hostel*.

[169] Best and Bergin, eds., *Lebor na hUidre*, p. 233; Stokes, ed. and trans., "Destruction of Da Derga's Hostel," p. 291.

[170] Best and Bergin, eds., *Lebor na hUidre*, p. 233; Stokes, ed. and trans., "Destruction of Da Derga's Hostel," p. 291; the trio has been discussed by Tremaine, "The Three Saxon Princes," pp. 50–54.

[171] Stokes, ed. and trans, "Destruction of Da Derga's Hostel," p. 291, n. 3.

[172] The passage in question is found in an interpolation in *Lebor na hUidre* made by scribe H, whose date is debated, as noted above, n. 74.

[173] Todd, ed. and trans., *Cogadh Gaedhel re Gallaibh*, pp. 136–37.

[174] See Máire Ní Mhaonaigh, "*Cogad Gáedel re Gallaib*: Some Dating Considerations," *Peritia* 9 (1995): 354–77, esp. pp. 375–76.

[175] Meyer, ed. and trans., "The Oldest Version of Tochmarc Emire," pp. 446–47; van Hamel, ed., *Compert Con Culainn and Other Stories*, p. 48 (§64.6). The first element of the name is a representation of the Germanic element "Wulf."

[176] "Caireand Casdub, ingen Sgail Bailb, ri Saxan, máthair Neill" (Curly-black haired Cairenn, the daughter of silent Sgal, king of the Saxons, was Niall's mother): Stokes, ed. and trans., "The Death of Crimthann Son of Fidach," pp. 190–91. Alternative variants of the Saxon king's name, namely "Saxaill," occur in another version (Stokes, ed. and trans., "Death of Crimthann Son of Fidach," p. 190, n. 1); "Sacheill" is the form found in Niall's earlier death-tale: Meyer, ed. and trans., "How King Niall of the Nine Hostages Was Slain," p. 88. For this and other examples of Saxons in medieval Irish literature, see Ní Mhaonaigh, "The Outward Look," pp. 381–97.

[177] Two versions of the tale survive, one prose, one metrical: see Stokes, "Death of Crimthann Son of Fidach," pp. 190–203, and the poem edited and translated by Joynt, "Echtra mac Echdach Mugmedóin," pp. 91–111. It has been discussed by Downey, "Intertextuality in *Echtra mac nEchdach Mugmedóin*," pp. 77–104.

[178] On the various versions of this text, see Ní Mhaonaigh, "Níall Noígíallach's Death-Tale," pp. 178–91.

[179] See Toner, "The Transmission of *Tochmarc Emire*," pp. 71–88. The version of the text edited by Meyer ("Oldest Version") has been dated to the eighth century; the version edited by van Hamel (*Compert Con Culainn*) is the later one.

[180] There are two references to *Cín Dromma Snechtai* in the text: Best and Bergin, eds., *Lebor na hUidre*, line 8005, *Slicht Libair Dromma Snechta inso* (This is the version of The Book of Druimm Snechtai) and 8025, *Slicht na cíni béos* (This is still the version of the *Cín*). This summary version is sometimes referred to as *Orgain Brudne Uí Dergae* (The Slaughter of Ua Derga's Hostel), the title

used in *Lebor na hUidre*, to distinguish it from the longer tale. For an account of its transmission, see West, "Leabhar na hUidhre's Position in the Manuscript History," pp. 61–98; see also Ó Cathasaigh, "On the *Cín Dromma Snechta* Version of *Togail Brudne Uí Dergae*," pp. 103–14.

[181] Herbert, "Crossing Historical and Literary Boundaries," p. 98.

[182] See Herbert, "Crossing Historical and Literary Boundaries," pp. 99–100.

[183] Stokes, ed. and trans., "Death of Crimthann Son of Fidach," pp. 174–89.

[184] As argued by Ó Corráin, "Legend as Critic," pp. 33–35. On the basis of tendentious claims which undermine Munster's right either to Túadmumu or to Osraige (Stokes, ed. and trans., "Death of Crimthann Son of Fidach," pp. 186–89), Ó Corráin has suggested that the text belongs to the period between 1114 and 1130 when Tairdelbach Ua Conchobair was attempting to destroy the power base of the Munster dynasty, Uí Briain.

[185] Ó Riain, ed., *Cath Almaine*, p. xxiv. There is an earlier edition with translation by Stokes, "The Battle of Allen," pp. 41–70.

[186] "Dofuric araid nÓrlaim meic Ailello ocus Medba i Tamlachtai Órlaim fri Dísiurt Lóchait antúaid bicán oc béim feda and" (He [Cú Chulainn] came upon the charioteer of Órlam, son of Ailill and Medb, at a place called Tamlachta Órlaim a little to the north of Dísert Lochait where he was cutting wood): O'Rahilly, ed. and trans., *Táin Bó Cúailnge: Recension I*, pp. 27 (lines 870–72), 149; cf. O'Rahilly, ed. and trans., *Táin Bó Cúalnge from the Book of Leinster*, pp. 33 (lines 1219–21), 171–72.

[187] O'Rahilly, *Táin Bó Cúailnge: Recension I*, pp. 192 (line 3365), 215; cf. O'Rahilly, *Táin Bó Cúalnge from the Book of Leinster*, pp. 107 (line 3889), 243.

[188] O'Rahilly, *Táin Bó Cúailnge: Recension I*, pp. 61 (lines 195–97), 179.

[189] The fight of the bulls at the end of the text gives rise to a series of place-names all of which are readily identifiable; one of the two animals, Donn Cúailnge, drops the loin (*lúan*) of the other, In Findbennach, at a particular place "whence the name Áth Luain" (gorop de dá tá Áth **Lúain** [Athlone, Co. Westmeath; the ford of the loin]); he subsequently goes to Trim, Co. Meath [Áth **Troimm**, "the ford of the liver"] where he deposited In Findbennach's liver (goro fácaib a **thromm** ind Fhinbennaig and); he then threw In Findbennach's thigh as far as Port Lárge (ra chuir a **láraic** de co Port **Large** [Waterford, thigh-harbor]), before throwing his rib-cage as far as Dublin (ra chuir a **chlíathaig** úad go Dublind), "which is called Áth Cliath" (rissa ratter Áth **Cliath**): O'Rahilly, *Táin Bó Cúalnge from the Book of Leinster*, pp. 135–36 (lines 4903–09), 272; cf. O'Rahilly, *Táin Bó Cúailnge: Recension I*, pp. 124, 237.

[190] For a discussion of the topography of one particular section of *Táin Bó Cúailnge*, see Muhr, "The Location of the Ulster Cycle," pp. 149–58.

[191] Gwynn, *Metrical Dindshenchas*, III.76–76, from a poem concerning the Liamuin in Leinster.

[192] For a series of such explanations of a particularly humorous kind, see Thurneysen, ed., *Scéle Mucce Meic Dathó*, pp. 10, 12, 13–14 (§§10, 12, 14).

[193] See Arbuthnot, ed. and trans., *Cóir Anmann*. There are some place-names also in the tract which she discusses in "Short Cuts to Etymology," pp. 79–88.

[194] Prose and metrical versions are found alongside one another in many of the manuscripts, but have unfortunately been edited separately: see Gwynn, *The Metrical Dindshenchas*, and Gwynn, ed. and trans., "The Dinnshenchas in the Book of Uí Maine," pp. 68–94; Stokes, ed. and trans., "The Prose Tales in the Rennes Dindshenchas"; Stokes (ed. and trans.), "The Bodleian Dinnshenchas," pp. 467–516, and "The Edinburgh Dinnshenchas," pp. 471–97.

[195] See Arbuthnot, *Cóir Anmann*, pp. 45–47.

[196] For an introduction to the Glossary tradition, see Russell, "Laws, Glossaries and Legal Glossaries," and *'Read it in a Glossary.'*

[197] See Baumgarten, "Etymological Aetiology in Irish tradition," pp. 115–22; and Arbuthnot, "Medieval Etymology," pp. 1–20.

[198] Best and O'Brien, eds., *The Book of Leinster Formerly Lebor na Núachongbála*, p. 1119 (lines 32881–83), which has been edited and translated by Murray, "The Finding of the *Táin*," pp. 17–24 (with references to discussion of the tale); for other manuscript versions, see Meyer, ed., "Die Wiederauffindung der Táin Bó Cúalnge," pp. 2–6. The exchange is also recorded in the ninth-century collection, the Triads of Ireland: "Trí hamrai la Táin Bó Cúailnge .i. in cuilmen dara héisi i nÉrinn ..." (Three wonders concerning *Táin Bó Cúailnge*, i.e., the "summit of knowledge" came to Ireland in its stead ...): Meyer, ed. and trans., *The Triads of Ireland*, pp. 8–9 (§62).

[199] The full quote from a poem attributed to Cináed ua hArtacáin (d. 975), reads as follows: "Fianna batar i nEmain/ ir-Raith Chruachan, i Temair/ il-Luachair luatis curaid/ i n-Alind, i n-Íarmumain" (Champions who dwelt in Emain [Ulster], in Rathcroghan [Connacht], in Tara [Leinster], in Luachair [Munster] which heroes used to celebrate, in Allen, in West Munster): Whitley Stokes, ed. and trans., "On the Deaths of Some Irish Heroes," *Revue celtique* 23 (1902): 303–48 at 304–05 (§1).

[200] See, for example, Greenwood, "Some Aspects of the Evolution of Táin Bó Cúailnge," pp. 47–54.

[201] Hogan, ed. and trans., *Cath Ruis na Ríg for Bóinn*. For an analysis of the tale, see Patrick Wadden, "*Cath Ruis na Ríg for Bóinn*: History and Literature in Twelfth-Century Ireland," *Aiste* 4 (2014): 11–44.

[202] Hogan, *Cath Ruis na Ríg*, pp. 14–15.

[203] Meyer, ed. and trans., *Aislinge Meic Conglinne*, pp. 124–25; for discussion of this section of the tale which occurs only in the shorter version, see Herbert, "Crossing Literary and Historical Boundaries," p. 101. There is a later edition of the longer version of the tale (without translation) by Jackson, *Aislinge Meic Con Glinne*.

[204] His name is explained as "non-refusable" in the longer version of the tale: "... uair ni thanic remi ocus ní ticc dia eissi bu duilge aer no molad, conid aire atbertha Anera friss, iarsinni ní feta éra fair" (since there had not come before him

and will not come after him one whose satire or praise was harder to bear, and on account of that he was called Anéra [*an-* negative particle; *éra* "refusal"], because of that there was no refusing him): Meyer, *Aislinge Meic Conglinne*, pp. 8–9.

[205] Meyer, *Aislinge Meic Conglinne*, pp. 8–9; he is termed *ollam maith* (a good *ollam* [the highest grade of scholar]) in the shorter version of the tale: Meyer, *Aislinge Meic Conglinne*, pp. 114–15.

[206] The bed that awaited him there was "full of lice and flees" (ba mílach dergnatach): Meyer, *Aislinge Meic Conglinne*, pp. 10–11; his ration amounted to "a small cup of church whey-water, two sparks of fire in the middle of a wisp of oaten straw and two sods of fresh peat" (cuachan .i. corcca do médgusci na heclaise, ocus da óibell tened im medón suipp sílcátha corcca ocus da fhót do úrmónaid): Meyer, *Aislinge Meic Conglinne*, pp. 14–15.

[207] According to the repulsive abbot, Manchín, "our counsel will be none other than to crucify him tomorrow, for my honor and that of St. Finbarr and of the Church" (nib a comarile aile acht a chrochad imbarach imm enech-sa ocus enech Barra ocus ina heclaisi): Meyer, *Aislinge Meic Conglinne*, pp. 18–19.

[208] Meyer, *Aislinge Meic Conglinne*, pp. 128–29.

[209] For examples of these, see Peter Dronke, "Profane Elements in Literature," in *Renaissance and Renewal in the Twelfth Century*, ed. Robert L. Benson and Giles Constable (Oxford, 1982), pp. 569–92; *Aislinge meic Conglinne* in its European context is discussed briefly in Ní Mhaonaigh, "Pagans and Holy Men," pp. 159–61.

[210] Mac Cana, "The Rise of the Later Schools of *Filidheacht*," pp. 126–46; Simms, "An eaglais agus filí na scol," pp. 21–36.

[211] The precise instruction of the pair of guardian angels is as follows: "... ocus scríbthar na scéla sin i támlorguibh filed ocus i mbriathraibh ollaman, ór budh gairdiugudh do dronguibh ocus do degdáinibh deridh aimsire éisdecht frisna scéluib sin" (... and have these stories written on poets' tablets in refined language, so that the hearing of them will provide entertainment for the lords and commons of later times): Stokes, ed., "Acallamh na Senórach," p. 9; Dooley and Roe, trans., *Tales of the Elders of Ireland*, p. 12. For discussion, see Ní Mhaonaigh, "Pagans and Holy Men," pp. 147–48. For general comment on the text, see Nagy, *Conversing with Angels and Ancients*; and Parsons, "The Structure of *Acallam na Senórach*," pp. 11–39 (with further references). On the body of literature of which the *Acallam* forms a part, see also the essays in *The Gaelic Finn Tradition*, edited by Arbuthnot and Parsons.

[212] These include a late fourteenth-century manuscript, the *Book of Ballymote*, written by a number of scribes attached to a law school of Clann Aedhagáin, probably in the house of a local ruler, Tomaltach Mac Donnchaidh: see Ó Concheanainn, "The Book of Ballymote," pp. 15–25. The *Book of Lecan* was written in the house of its principal scribe, Gilla Ísu Mór Mac Fhirbhisigh (d. 1418); one of his pupils, Murchadh Riabhach Ó Cuindlis, who contributed to the *Book of Lecan*, was the sole scribe of another early fifteenth-century manuscript, *Leabhar*

Breac ("Speckled Book"): see Ó Concheanainn, "The Scribe of the Leabhar Breac," pp. 64–79.

[213] Johnston discusses the world of medieval Irish learning in *Literacy and Identity in Early Medieval Ireland.*

[214] In 871, Cú Roí "a learned abbot and the most expert in the histories of the Irish" (abbas, sapiens et peritissimus historiarum Scotticarum) died: AU 871.6. Of his work nothing has remained. A variety of texts ascribed to an almost exact contemporary of Ælfric, Aibertach mac Cosse Dobráin (d. 1016), has survived; he too was a monastic official (*airchinnech*) of Ros Ailithir, Co. Cork: AU 1016.8.

[215] These include Cormac mac Cuilennáin and a slightly earlier ninth-century bishop of Cork, Domnall, an excellent scribe (*scriba optimus*): AU 876.4. An eleventh-century bishop, Patrick, to whom a significant corpus of material has been attributed, was educated in Worcester during the time of Wulfstan II; for his postulated writings see, Gwynn, ed. and trans., *The Writings of Bishop Patrick*; see also Elizabeth Boyle, "The Authorship and Transmission of *De tribus habitaculis animae*," *The Journal of Medieval Latin* 22 (2012): 49–65. One of the scribes of the Book of Leinster was Finn, bishop of Kildare, on whose identity, see Bhreathnach, "Two Contributors to the Book of Leinster," pp. 105–07.

[216] A prominent example is Flann Mainistrech, of Monasterboice, whom we have already encountered, "eminent lector and master of the historical lore of Ireland" (airdfer leighinn ocus sui senchusa Erenn): AU 1056.8.

[217] Several of those belonging to Monasterboice and Armagh, including *In Lebor Buide* (The Yellow Book) and *In Lebor Gerr* (The Short Book), are listed in a passage by Scribe H in *Lebor na hUidre*, for discussion of which, see Herbert, "Crossing Historical and Literary Boundaries," pp. 92–93.

[218] He is thus described in his obit: AU 975.4.

[219] Gwynn, *Metrical Dindshenchas*, I.52–53: "Amlaíb Átha Cliath cétaig/ rogab rígi i mBeind Étair/ tallus lúag mo dúane de/ ech d'echaib ána Aichle" (Amlaíb of hundred-strong Dublin, who gained the kingship in Bend Étair, I bore off from him as price of my song a horse of the horses of Achall). For discussion, see Ní Mhaonaigh, "Friend and Foe," pp. 399–400, and references therein.

[220] AU 1024.3.

[221] Peters, ed. and trans., "Die irische Alexandersage," pp. 71–264.

[222] Gearóid Mac Eoin, "Das Verbalsystem von *Togail Troí* (H.2.17)," *Zeitschrift für celtische Philologie* 28 (1960–1): 73–136, 149–223 at 202. See also Mac Gearailt, "*Togail Troí*," pp. 71–85.

[223] For a general introduction to this material, see Ní Mhaonaigh, "Classical Compositions in Medieval Ireland," pp. 1–19; Poppe, "Mittelalterliche Übersetzungsliteratur im insular-keltischen Kulturraum," pp. 33–58; and most recently Ralph O'Connor, "Irish Narrative Literature and the Classical Tradition, 900–1300," in his *Classical Literature and Learning in Medieval Irish Narrative*, Studies in Celtic History 34 (Woodbridge, 2014), pp. 1–22.

[224] See Poppe, "Reconstructing Medieval Irish Literary Theory," p. 39, n. 32.

See also Clarke, "An Irish Achilles and a Greek Cú Chulainn," pp. 238–51.

[225] See Brent Miles, *Heroic Saga and Classical Epic in Medieval Ireland*; and the essays in O'Connor, *Classical Literature and Learning*.

[226] A prose and metrical catalogue of the names of famous women, known as the *Banshenchas*, has been preserved: Dobbs, ed. and trans., "The Ban-shenchus." For discussion of the text, see Ní Bhrolcháin, "The Manuscript Tradition of the Banshenchas," pp. 109–35; and Connon, "The *Banshenchas* and the Uí Néill Queens of Tara," pp. 98–108.

[227] See, for example, the list of mothers of Irish saints, as well as the litany of Irish saints preserved in the *Book of Leinster*, alongside saints' genealogies: O'Sullivan, *The Book of Leinster Formerly Lebar na Núachongbála*, VI.1692–705; Ó Riain, ed., *Corpus genealogiarum sanctorum Hiberniae*.

[228] Stokes, *Félire Óengusso*, p. 24 (§165); "Atbath borg tromm Temra/ la tairthim a flathe/ col-lín corad sruithe/ maraid Ard mór Machae" (Tara's mighty burgh perished at the death of her princes; with a multitude of venerable champions the great height of Machae [Armagh] abides).

[229] Best and Bergin, eds., *Lebor na hUidre*, pp. 278–87.

[230] "Creit do Dia ocus do náemPatraic, a Loegairi ..." (Believe in God and in holy Patrick, Láegaire ...): Best and Bergin, eds., *Lebor na hUidre*, pp. 280 (line 9301), 287 (line 9535); the latter example in the hand of Scribe H.

[231] Best and Bergin, eds., *Lebor na hUidre*, p. 288 (lines 9549–65).

[232] Best and Bergin, eds., *Lebor na hUidre*, p. 285 (lines 9462–63).

[233] Meyer, ed. and trans., *The Death-Tales of the Ulster Heroes*, pp. 8–11 (§12) (version A).

[234] Stokes, ed., "Acallamh na Senórach," p. 41; Dooley and Roe, *Tales of the Elders of Ireland*, p. 45.

[235] The direct involvement of Diarmait in the manuscript's creation has been refuted by Ó Corráin, "The Education of Diarmait Mac Murchada," pp. 75–76. Sympathy with Diarmait is evident in a note made in 1166 by one of the manuscript's scribes, Áed Úa Crimthainn of the monastery of Terryglass: "A ri nime is mor in gnim doringned i nHerind indiu (.i. Kl Aug) .i. Diarmait mac Dondchada meic Murchada ri Lagen ocus Gall do innarba do fheraib Herend dar muir. Uch, uch, a Chomdiu, cid dogen" (O King of Heaven, dreadful is the deed that has been perpetrated in Ireland today [i.e., the calends of August], namely, Diarmait son of Donnchad Mac Murchada, king of Leinster and the Foreigners, has been banished overseas by the men of Ireland. Alas, alas, O Lord, what shall I do?): Best, Bergin, and O'Brien, *The Book of Leinster Formerly Lebar na Núachongbála*, I.xvii. See also Mac Eoin, "The Provenance of the Book of Leinster," pp. 42–70.

[236] The phrase occurs in the *Triads of Ireland* which claims that the monastery of Ros Ailithir is the home of *legend hÉrenn*; it may designate specifically ecclesiastical learning, as to various ecclesiastical centers are ascribed other branches of learning: "féinechas hÉrenn Clúain hÚama ... senchas hÉrenn Imblech Ibair ... brethemnas hÉrenn Sláine" (the law of Ireland – Cloyne; the lore of Ireland

– Emly; the judgement of Ireland – Slane): Meyer, *Triads of Ireland*, pp. 2–3 (§§12, 15, 17, 21).

[237] This contribution was submitted for publication in 2007; I have made minor changes since then and have added bibliographical references to material published after that date, but it has not been substantially rewritten. I have benefitted much from comments made on an earlier draft by Dr. Elizabeth Boyle and Dr. Helen Imhoff, as well as by my colleague and fellow-author in this volume, Dr. Rosalind Love.

Bibliography

This is a highly selective bibliography, drawing primarily on the works cited in the accompanying article, arranged under headings designed to assist those not necessarily familiar with the material. The headings are as follows:

1. RESOURCES
   - *Bibliographies*
   - *Dictionary*
   - *Place-Names*

2. PRIMARY SOURCES
   - *Compendia*
   - *Genealogies*
   - *Glossaries*
   - *History and Pseudo-History*
     - *Annalistic Compilations*
     - *Other Texts*
   - *Law and Wisdom Literature*
   - *Manuscripts*
   - *Narrative Literature*
   - *Poets and Poetry*
   - *Saints' Lore*
   - *Miscellaneous Other Texts*

3. SECONDARY SOURCES
   - *Contacts between Ireland and Anglo-Saxon England*
   - *Medieval Ireland: An Introduction*
   - *Glossaries*
   - *Grammar, Language, and Literacy*
   - *Historical and Pseudo-Historical Writing*
   - *Law*
   - *Manuscripts*
   - *Narrative Literature*
   - *Poetry*
   - *Saints' Lore*
   - *Miscellaneous Other Texts*

Resources

Bibliographies

Baumgarten, Rolf, ed. *Bibliography of Irish Linguistics and Literature 1942–71.* Dublin: Dublin Institute for Advanced Studies, 1986; available in electronic form at http://bill.celt.dias.ie/.

Best, R. I., ed. *Bibliography of Irish Philology and of Printed Irish Literature.* Dublin: Browne and Nolan for H.M.S.O., 1913.

——. ed. *Bibliography of Irish Philology and Manuscript Literature: Publications 1913–1941.* Dublin: Dublin Institute for Advanced Studies, 1942.

Bibliography of British and Irish History. Institute of Historical Research. http://www.rhs.ac.uk/bibl/ (includes an option to search for "Irish material" only).

Celtic Studies Bibliography. Celtic Studies Association of North America (CSANA). http://celtic.cmrs.ucla.edu/csana/csanabib.html.

Dictionary

Quin, E. G., *et al.*, ed. *Dictionary of the Irish Language Based Mainly on Old and Middle Irish Materials.* Dublin: Royal Irish Academy, 1913–76; compact edition, 1983; available in electronic form at http://www.dil.ie/ (which includes much additional material).

Place-Names

Hogan, Edmund. *Onomasticon Goedelicum.* Dublin: Hodges, Figgis & Co., 1910; available in electronic form at http://www.ucc.ie:8080/cocoon/doi/locus.

Locus Project. University College Cork, Ireland. http://www.ucc.ie/locus/.

Ó Riain, Pádraig, Diarmaid Ó Murchadha, and Kevin Murray, eds. *Historical Dictionary of Irish Placenames: Foclóir Stairiúil Áitainmneacha na Gaeilge.* 5 fascicles (Names in A, B and C to 'Cnucha'). London: Irish Texts Society, 2003–13, ongoing).

Primary Sources

Compendia

Carey, John, trans. *King of Mysteries: Early Irish Religious Writing.* Dublin: Four Courts Press, 1998.

Celtic Digital Initiative: Text Archive. University College Cork, Ireland. http://sulis.ucc.ie/cdi/textarchive-search.php.

Corpus of Electronic Texts. University College Cork, Ireland. http://www.ucc.ie/celt/search.html.

Greene, David, and Frank O'Connor, eds. and trans. *A Golden Treasury of Irish Poetry A.D. 600 to 1200.* London, Melbourne and Toronto: Macmillan, 1967.

Murphy, Gerard, ed. and trans. *Early Irish Lyrics: Eighth to Twelfth Century.* Oxford: Clarendon Press, 1955.

Stokes, Whitley, and John Strachan, eds. and trans. *Thesaurus Palaeohibernicus: A Collection of Old-Irish Glosses, Scholia, Prose and Verse.* 2 vols. Cambridge: Cambridge University Press, 1903.

Thesaurus Linguae Hibernicae. University College Dublin, Ireland. http://www.ucd.ie/tlh/captured.html.

Genealogies

O'Brien, M. A., ed. *Corpus genealogiarum Hiberniae.* Vol. 1. Dublin: Dublin Institute for Advanced Studies, 1962.

Ó Riain, Pádraig, ed. *Corpus genealogiarum sanctorum Hiberniae.* Dublin: Dublin Institute for Advanced Studies, 1985.

Glossaries

Russell, Paul, Sharon Arbuthnot, and Pádraic Moran, eds. *Early Irish Glossaries Database*. http://www.asnc.cam.ac.uk/irishglossaries/.

Stokes, Whitley, ed. and trans. *Three Irish Glossaries*. London: Williams and Norgate, 1862.

History and Pseudo-History

Annalistic Compilations

The Annals of Clonmacnoise

Murphy, Denis, ed. and trans. *The Annals of Clonmacnoise being Annals of Ireland from the Earliest Period to A.D. 1408*. Dublin: University Press for the Royal Society of Antiquaries of Ireland, 1896; reprinted Felinfach: Llanerch, 1993.

The Annals of the Four Masters

O'Donovan, John, ed. and trans. *Annála Rioghachta Éireann: Annals of the Kingdom of Ireland by the Four Masters from the Earliest Period to the Year 1616*. 7 vols. Dublin: Hodges and Smith, 1851; 3rd ed., Dublin: De Búrca Rare Books, 1990.

The Annals of Inisfallen

Mac Airt, Seán, ed. and trans. *The Annals of Inisfallen (MS. Rawlinson B. 503)*. Dublin: Dublin Institute for Advanced Studies, 1951.

The Annals of Loch Cé

Hennessy, William M., ed. and trans. *The Annals of Loch Cé: A Chronicle of Irish Affairs from A.D. 1014 to A.D. 1590*. 2 vols. London: Longmans, 1871.

The Annals of Ulster

Mac Airt, Seán, and Gearóid Mac Niocaill, eds. and trans. *The Annals of Ulster (to A.D. 1131), Part I, Text and Translation*. Dublin: Dublin Institute for Advanced Studies, 1983.

The Annals of Tigernach

Stokes, Whitley, ed. and trans. *The Annals of Tigernach*. 2 vols. Felinfach: Llanerch, 1993; reprinted from "The Annals of Tigernach." *Revue celtique* 16 (1895): 374–419; 17 (1896): 6–33, 119–263, 337–420; 18 (1897): 9–59, 150–97, 267–303, 374–90.

The Chronicle of Ireland

Charles-Edwards, Thomas, trans. *The Chronicle of Ireland*. 2 vols. Translated Texts for Historians 44. Liverpool: Liverpool University Press, 2006.

Chronicum Scottorum

Hennessy, William M. *Chronicum Scotorum: A Chronicle of Irish Affairs from the Earliest Times to A.D. 1135; with a Supplement Containing the Events from 1141 to 1150.* London: Longmans, Green, Reader, and Dyer, 1866.

The Fragmentary Annals of Ireland

Radner, Joan N., ed. and trans. *The Fragmentary Annals of Ireland.* Dublin: Dublin Institute for Advanced Studies, 1978.

Miscellaneous Irish Annals

Ó hInnse, Séamus, ed. and trans. *Miscellaneous Irish Annals (A.D. 1114–1437).* Dublin: Dublin Institute for Advanced Studies, 1947.

Other Texts

***Acallam na Senórach*, "The Colloquy of the Ancients"**

Dooley, Ann, and Harry Roe, trans. *Tales of the Elders of Ireland.* Oxford: Oxford University Press, 1999.

Stokes, Whitley. "Acallamh na Senórach." In *Irische Texte mit Übersetzungen und Wörterbuch* 4:1, edited by Whitley Stokes and Ernst Windisch. Leipzig: S. Hirzel, 1900.

***Banshenchas*, "Women-Lore"**

Dobbs, Margaret, ed. and trans. "The Ban-shenchus." *Revue celtique* 47 (1930): 283–339; 48 (1931): 162–233; 49 (1932): 437–89.

***Cocad Gáedel re Gallaib*, "The Irish-Viking War"**

Todd, James Henthorn, ed. and trans. *Cogadh Gaedhel re Gallaibh: The War of the Gaedhil with the Gaill, or The Invasions of Ireland by the Danes and Other Norsemen.* London: Longmans, Green, Reader, and Dyer, 1867.

***Cóir Anmann*, "The Fitness of Names"**

Arbuthnot, Sharon, ed. and trans. *Cóir Anmann: A Late Middle Irish Treatise on Personal Names.* 2 vols. (59, 60). London: Irish Texts Society, 2005 and 2007.

***Dindshenchas*, "Place-Name Lore"**

Gwynn, E. J., ed. and trans. *The Metrical Dindshenchas.* 5 vols. Todd Lecture Series 8–12. Dublin: Royal Irish Academy, 1903–35.

——. ed. and trans. "The Dinnshenchas in the Book of Uí Maine." *Ériu* 10 (1926–28): 68–94.

Stokes, Whitley, ed. and trans. "The Bodleian Dinnshenchas." *Folklore* 3 (1892): 467–516.

——. "The Edinburgh Dinnshenchas." *Folklore* 4 (1893): 471–97.

Stokes, Whitley, ed. and trans. "The Prose Tales in the Rennes Dindshenchas." *Revue celtique* 15 (1894): 272–336, 418–84; 16 (1895): 31–83, 135–67, 269–83.

***Lebor Gabála Érenn*, "The Book of Invasions"**

Macalister, R. A. S., ed. and trans. *Lebor Gabála Érenn*. 5 vols. (34, 35, 39, 41, 44). London: Irish Texts Society, 1938–56.

***Lebor na Cert*, "The Book of Rights"**

Dillon, Myles, ed. and trans. *Lebor na Cert: The Book of Rights*. Dublin: Irish Texts Society, 1962.

***Saltair na Rann*, "The Psalter of the Quatrains"**

Dillon, Myles, ed. and trans. "Scél Saltrach na Rann." *Celtica* 4 (1958): 1–43.

Greene, David, and Fergus Kelly, eds. and trans. *The Irish Adam and Eve Story from Saltair na Rann*. Commentary by Brian O. Murdoch. 2 vols. Dublin: Dublin Institute for Advanced Studies, 1976.

Stokes, Whitley, ed. *Saltair na Rann*. Oxford: Clarendon Press, 1883.

Sex Aetates Mundi

Ó Cróinín, Dáibhí, ed. and trans. *The Irish "Sex Aetates Mundi".* Dublin: Dublin Institute for Advanced Studies, 1983.

Tristram, Hildegard L. C., ed. and trans. *Sex Aetates Mundi: Die Weltzeitalter bei den Angelsachsen und den Iren: Untersuchungen und Texte*. Anglistische Forschungen 165. Heidelberg: C. Winter, 1985.

Triads

Meyer, Kuno, ed. and trans. *The Triads of Ireland*. Todd Lecture Series 13. Dublin: Hodges, Figgis, & Co., 1906.

Law and Wisdom Literature

***Audacht Morainn*, "Morann's Testament"**

Kelly, Fergus, ed. and trans. *Audacht Morainn*. Dublin: Dublin Institute for Advanced Studies, 1976.

***Bechbretha*, "Judgments Concerning Bees"**

Charles-Edwards, Thomas, and Fergus Kelly, eds. and trans. *Bechbretha*. Early Irish Law Series 1. Dublin: Dublin Institute for Advanced Studies, 1983.

***Bretha Crólige*, "The Judgments of Sick-Maintenance"**

Binchy, Daniel A., ed. and trans. "*Bretha Crólige*." *Ériu* 12 (1934): 1–77.

***Bretha Déin Chécht*, "The Judgments of Dían Cécht"**

Binchy, Daniel A., ed. and trans. "*Bretha Déin Chécht.*" *Ériu* 20 (1966): 1–20.

***Bretha Nemed*, "Judgments Concerning Privileged Persons"**

Breatnach, Liam, ed. and trans. "The First Third of *Bretha Nemed Toísech.*" *Ériu* 40 (1989): 1–40.

Gwynn, E. J., ed. "An Old Irish Tract on the Privileges and Responsibilities of Poets." *Ériu* 13 (1942): 1–60, 220–36.

***Bríathra Flainn Fhína maic Ossu*, "The Words of Flann Fína mac Ossu [Aldfrith]"**

Ireland, Colin A., ed. and trans. *Old Irish Wisdom Texts Attributed to Aldfrith of Northumbria: An Edition of Bríathra Flainn Fhína maic Ossu.* Tempe, AZ: Medieval and Renaissance Texts and Studies, 1999.

***Cáin Lánamna*, "The Law of Couples"**

Thurneysen, Rudolf, ed. and trans. "*Cáin Lánamna.*" In *Studies in Early Irish Law*, by Rudolf Thurneysen, Nancy Power, Myles Dillon, Kathleen Mulchrone, Daniel A. Binchy, August Knoch, and John Ryan, 1–75. Dublin: Hodges, Figgis, & Co., 1936.

Canon Law

Binchy, Daniel A., ed. *Corpus Iuris Hibernici ad fidem codicum manuscriptorum recognovit.* 6 vols. Dublin: Dublin Institute for Advanced Studies, 1978.

Wasserschleben, Hermann, ed. *Die irische Kanonensammlung.* Leipzig: Bernhard Tauchnitz, 1885.

***Senchas Már*, "Pseudo-Historical Prologue"**

Carey, John, ed. and trans. "An Edition of the Pseudo-Historical Prologue to the *Senchas Már.*" *Ériu* 45 (1994): 1–32.

Manuscripts

Early Manuscripts at Oxford University. Oxford University Libraries. http://image.ox.ac.uk.

Irish Script on Screen. Dublin Institute for Advanced Studies. http://www.isos.dias.ie/.

The Antiphonary of Bangor

Warren, F. W., ed., and W. Griggs, transcriber. *The Antiphonary of Bangor: An Early Irish Manuscript in the Ambrosian Library at Milan.* 2 vols. Henry Bradshaw Society 4 and 10. London: Harrison and Sons, 1893 and 1895.

Liber Ardmachanus

Gwynn, John, ed. *Liber Ardmachanus: The Book of Armagh*. Dublin: Hodges, Figgis, & Co., 1913.

***Lebor na hUidre*, "The Book of the Dun Cow"**

Best, R. I., and Osborn Bergin, eds. *Lebor na hUidre: Book of the Dun Cow*. Dublin: Royal Irish Academy, 1929.

***Lebor na Nuachongbála*, "The Book of Oughvall"**

Best, R. I., Osborn Bergin, M.A. O'Brien, and A. O'Sullivan, eds. *The Book of Leinster formerly Lebor na Núachongbála*. 6 vols. Dublin: Dublin Institute for Advanced Studies, 1954–83.

Narrative Literature

***Aided Conchobair*, "The Death-Tale of Conchobar"**

Meyer, Kuno, ed. and trans. "The Death of Conchobar." In *The Death-Tales of the Ulster Heroes*, 2–21. Todd Lecture Series 14. Dublin: Hodges, Figgis, & Co., 1906.

***Aided Crimthainn meic Fidaig*, "The Death-Tale of Crimthann mac Fidaig"**

Stokes, Whitley, ed. and trans. "The Death of Crimthann Son of Fidach, and the Adventures of the Sons of Eochaid Muigmedón." *Revue celtique* 24 (1903): 174–89.

***Aided Muirchertaig meic Erca*, "The Death-Tale of Muirchertach mac Erca"**

Nic Dhonnchadha, Lil, ed. *Aided Muirchertaig meic Erca*. Mediaeval and Modern Irish Series 19. Dublin: Dublin Institute for Advanced Studies, 1964.

Stokes, Whitley, ed. and trans. "The Death of Muirchertach mac Erca." *Revue celtique* 23 (1902): 395–437.

***Aided Néill Noígiallaig*, "The Death-Tale of Niall of the Nine Hostages"**

Meyer, Kuno, ed. and trans. "How King Niall of the Nine Hostages was Slain." *Otia Merseiana* 2 (1900–01): 84–92.

***Airne Fíngein*, "Fíngen's Night-watch"**

Vendryes, Jospeh, ed. *Airne Fíngein*. Mediaeval and Modern Irish Series 15. Dublin: Dublin School of Celtic Studies, 1953.

***Aislinge Meic Con Glinne*, "The Vision of Mac Con Glinne"**

Meyer, Kuno, ed. and trans. *Aislinge Meic Conglinne, The Vision of Mac Conglinne: A Middle-Irish Wonder Tale*. London: Nutt, 1892.

Jackson, Kenneth Hurlstone, ed. *Aislinge Meic Con Glinne*. Dublin: Dublin Institute for Advanced Studies, 1990.

The Alexander Saga

Peters, Erik, ed. and trans. "Die irische Alexandersage." *Zeitschrift für celtische Philologie* 30 (1967): 71–264.

***Baile Chuind Chétchathaig*, "The Ecstasy of Conn of the Hundred Battles"**

Murphy, Gerard, ed. and trans. "On the Dates of Two Sources Used in Thurneysen's Heldensage." *Ériu* 16 (1952): 145–51.

***Cath Almaine*, "The Battle of Allen"**

Ó Riain, Pádraig, ed. *Cath Almaine*. Mediaeval and Modern Irish Series 25. Dublin: Dublin Institute for Advanced Studies, 1978.

Stokes, Whitley, ed. and trans. "The Battle of Allen." *Revue celtique* 24 (1903): 41–70.

***Cath Ruis na Ríg*, "The Battle of Ros na Ríg"**

Hogan, Edmund, ed. and trans. *Cath Ruis na Ríg for Bóinn; with Preface, Translation and Indices*. Todd Lecture Series 4. Dublin: Royal Irish Academy, 1892.

***De Faillsiugud Tána Bó Cualinge*, "Concerning the Revelation of 'The Cattle-Raid of Cúalnge'"**

Meyer, Kuno, ed. "Die Wiederauffindung der Táin Bó Cúalnge." In *Archiv für celtische Lexikographie*. Vol. 3, edited by Whitley Stokes and Kuno Meyer, 2–6. Halle: M. Niemeyer, 1907.

***Echtrae Chonnlai*, "The Adventure of Connlae"**

McCone, Kim, ed. and trans. *Echtrae Chonnlai and the Beginnings of Vernacular Narrative Writing in Ireland: A Critical Edition with Introduction, Notes, Bibliography and Vocabulary*. Maynooth Medieval Irish Texts 1. Maynooth: Dept. of Old and Middle Irish, National University of Ireland, Maynooth, 2000.

***Echtra mac nEchach Muigmedóin*, "The Adventure of the Sons of Éochaid Mugmedón"**

Joynt, Maud. "Echtra mac Echdach Mugmedóin." *Ériu* 4 (1908–10): 91–111.

Stokes, Whitley, ed. and trans. "The Death of Crimthann son of Fidach, and the Adventures of the Sons of Eochaid Muigmedón." *Revue celtique* 24 (1903): 190–203.

***Fled Bricrend*, "Bricriu's Feast"**

Henderson, George, ed. and trans. *Fled Bricrend, The Feast of Bricriu: An Early Gaelic Saga Transcribed from Older MSS. into the Book of the Dun Cow, by Moelmuiri mac mic Cuinn na mBocht*. Irish Texts Society 2. London: Nutt, 1899.

Immram Brain, "The Voyage of Bran"

Mac Mathúna, Séamas, ed. and trans. *Immram Brain: Bran's Journey to the Land of the Women*. Tübingen: M. Niemeyer, 1985.

Orgain Denna Ríg, "The Destruction of Dind Ríg"

Greene, David, ed. "Orgain Denna Ríg." In *Fingal Rónáin and Other Stories*, 16–26. Mediaeval and Modern Irish Series 16. Dublin: Dublin Institute for Advanced Studies, 1955.

Stokes, Whitley, ed. and trans. "The Destruction of Dind Ríg." *Zeitschrift für celtische Philologie* 3 (1901): 1–14.

Scéla Mucce Meic Dathó, "The Story of Mac Dathó's Pig"

Thurneysen, Rudolf, ed. *Scéla Mucce Meic Dathó*. Mediaeval and Modern Irish Series 6. Dublin: Dublin Institute for Advanced Studies, 1935.

Táin Bó Cúailnge. "The Cattle-Raid of Cúailnge"

O'Rahilly, Cecile, ed. and trans. *Táin Bó Cúailnge: Recension I*. Dublin: Dublin Institute for Advanced Studies, 1976.

——. ed. and trans. *Táin Bó Cúalnge from the Book of Leinster*. Dublin: Dublin Institute for Advanced Studies, 1980.

Táin Bó Fraích, "The Cattle-Raid of Fráech"

Meid, Wolfgang, ed. and trans. *Die Romanze von Froech und Findabair*. Innsbrucker Beiträge zur Kulturwissenschaft. Innsbruck: Institut für vergleichende Sprachwissenschaft der Universität Innsbruck, 1970.

Tochmarc Emire, "The Wooing of Emer"

Meyer, Kuno, ed. and trans. "The Oldest Version of Tochmarc Emire." *Revue celtique* 11 (1890): 433–57.

Van Hamel, A. G., ed. "Tochmarc Emire." In *Compert Con Culainn and Other Stories* 16–68. Mediaeval and Modern Irish Series 3. Dublin: Dublin Institute for Advanced Studies, 1933.

Togail Bruidne Da Derga, "The Destruction of Da Derga's Hostel"

Knott, Eleanor, ed. *Togail Bruidne Da Derga*. Mediaeval and Modern Irish Series 8. Dublin: Dublin Institute for Advanced Studies, 1936.

Stokes, Whitley, ed. and trans. "The Destruction of Da Derga's Hostel." *Revue celtique* 22 (1901): 9–61, 165–215, 282–329, 390–437.

Poets and Poetry

***Auraicept na nÉces*, "The Poets' Primer"**

Ahlqvist, Anders, ed. and trans. *The Early Irish Linguist: An Edition of the Canonical Part of the Auraicept na nÉces, with Introduction, Commentary and Indices.* Commentationes Humarum Litterarum 73. Helsinki: Societas Scientiarum Fennica, 1983.

Calder, George, ed. and trans. *Auraicept na nÉces: The Scholars' Primer.* Edinburgh: Grant, 1917.

Cormac mac Cuilennáin

Mac Cana, Proinsias, ed. and trans. "A Poem Attributed to Cormac mac Cuilennáin (†908)." *Celtica* 5 (1960): 207–17.

Blathmacc mac Con Brettan

Carney, James, ed. and trans. *The Poems of Blathmac son of Cú Brettan Together with the Irish Gospel of Thomas and a Poem on the Virgin Mary.* Irish Texts Society 47. London and Dublin: Irish Texts Society, 1967.

Colmán mac Lénéni

Thurneysen, Rudolf, ed. "Colmān mac Lēnēni and Senchān Torpēist." *Zeitschrift für celtische Philologie* 19 (1933): 193–209.

Gospel of Thomas

McNamara, Martin, and Máire Herbert, eds. and trans. "A Versified Narrative of the Childhood Deeds of the Lord Jesus." In *Apocrypha Hiberniae I: Evangelia Infantiae.* Vol 1, edited by Martin McNamara, Caoimhín Breatnach, John Carey, Máire Herbert, Jean Daniel Kaestli, Brian Ó Cuív, and Diarmuid Ó Laoghaire, 455–83. Corpus Christianorum Series Apocryphorum 13. Turnhout: Brepols, 2001.

***Uraicecht na Ríar*, "The Instruction of the Grades"**

Breatnach, Liam, ed. and trans. *The Poetic Grades in Early Irish Law.* Early Irish Law Series 2. Dublin: Dublin Institute for Advanced Studies, 1987.

***Verba Scáthaige* 'Scáthach's Words'**

Henry, P. L., ed. and trans. "*Verba Scáthaige.*" *Celtica* 21 (1990): 191–207.

Saints' Lore

Adomnán

Herbert, Máire, and Pádraig Ó Riain, eds. and trans. *Betha Adamnáin: The Irish Life of Adamnán.* Irish Texts Society 54. London: Irish Texts Society, 1988.

Brigit

Colgan, John. *Vita I: Triadis thaumaturgae actae*, pp. 527–42. Louvain, 1647.

——. *Vita II: Acta SS Feb 1*, pp. 135–41. Louvain, 1658.

Ó hAodha, Donncha, ed. and trans. *Bethu Brigte* ["The Life of Brigit"]. Dublin: Dublin Institute for Advanced Studies, 1978.

Columba

Anderson, A. O., and M. O. Anderson, eds. and trans. *Adomnán's Life of Columba.* 2 vols. London: Nelson, 1968.

Sharpe, Richard, trans. *Adomnan of Iona, Life of St. Columba.* Harmondsworth: Penguin Books, 1995.

***Amra Choluim Chille*, "Columba's Eulogy"**

Kelly, Fergus, ed. and trans. "*Fo réir Choluimb céin ad-fías*, 'As long as I speak [may I be] obedient to Colum': A Poem in Praise of Columb Cille." *Ériu* 24 (1973): 1–34.

Stokes, Whitley, ed. and trans. "The Bodleian Amra Choluimb Chille." *Revue celtique* 20 (1899): 30–55, 132–83, 248–87, 400–37.

***Tiugraind Bécáin*, "The Last Verses of Bécán"**

Kelly, Fergus, ed. and trans. "Tiughraind Bhécáin." *Ériu* 26 (1975): 66–98.

Patrick

Bieler, Ludwig, ed. *The Patrician Texts in the Book of Armagh.* Scriptores Latini Hiberniae 10. Dublin: Dublin Institute for Advanced Studies, 1979.

Mulchrone, Kathleen, ed. *Bethu Phátraic* ["The Life of Patrick"]: *The Tripartite Life of Patrick.* Dublin: Hodges, Figgis, & Co., 1939.

Senán

Breatnach, Liam, ed. and trans. "*Amra Senáin* 'Senán's Eulogy': An Edition of *Amra Senáin*." In *Sages, Saints and Storytellers: Celtic Studies in Honour of Professor James Carney*, edited by Donnchadh Ó Corráin, Liam Breatnach, and Kim McCone, 7–31. Maynooth: An Sagart, 1989.

***Félire Óengusso*, "The Calendar of Óengus"**

Stokes, Whitley, ed. and trans. *Félire Óengusso Céli Dé: The Martyrology of Oengus the Culdee.* Henry Bradshaw Society 29. London: Harrison and Sons, 1905.

Genealogies of Saints

Ó Riain, Pádraig, ed. *Corpus genealogiarum sanctorum Hiberniae.* Dublin: Dublin Institute for Advanced Studies, 1985.

Miscellaneous Other Texts

***Aipgitir Chrábaid*, "The Alphabet of Piety"**

Hull, Vernam, ed. and trans. "Apgitir Chrábaid: The Alphabet of Piety." *Celtica* 8 (1968): 44–89.

***In Tenga Bithnua*, "The Evernew Tongue"**

Carey, John, ed. and trans. *Apocrypha Hiberniae II, Apocalyptica 1: In Tenga Bithnua, The Ever-New Tongue*. Turnhout: Brepols, 2009.

Writings of Bishop Patrick

Gwynn, Aubrey, ed. and trans. *The Writings of Bishop Patrick, 1074–1084*. Scriptores Latini Hiberniae 1. Dublin: Dublin Institute for Advanced Studies, 1955.

Secondary Sources

Contacts between Ireland and Anglo-Saxon England

Cronan, Dennis. "'Beowulf,' the Gaels and the Recovery of the pre-Conversion Past." *Anglo-Saxon* 1 (2007): 137–80.

Cross, J. E. "The Influence of Irish Texts and Traditions on the *Old English Martyrology*." *Proceedings of the Royal Irish Academy* 81 (1981): 173–92.

Donahue, Charles. "Beowulf, Ireland and the Natural Good." *Traditio* 7 (1949): 263–77.

——. "Grendel and the Clanna Cain." *Journal of Celtic Studies* 1 (1950): 167–75.

Dumville, David N. "'Beowulf' and the Celtic World: The Uses of the Evidence." *Traditio* 37 (1981): 109–60.

——. *Three Men in a Boat: Scribe, Language and Culture in the Church of Viking-Age Europe*. Inaugural Lecture. Cambridge: Cambridge University Press, 1997.

Holtz, Louis. "Les grammairiens hiberno-latins: Étaient-ils des Anglo-Saxons?" *Peritia* 2 (1983): 170–84.

Hughes, Kathleen. "Evidence for Contacts between the Churches of the Irish and the English from the Synod of Whitby to the Viking Age." In *England Before the Conquest: Studies in Primary Sources Presented to Dorothy Whitelock*, edited by Peter Clemoes and Kathleen Hughes, 49–67. Cambridge: Cambridge University Press, 1971.

Ireland, Colin. "The Poets Cædmon, and Colmán mac Lénéni: The Anglo-Saxon Layman and the Irish Professional." In *Heroic Poets and Poetic Heroes in Celtic Traditions: A Festschrift for Patrick F. Ford*, edited by Joseph Falaky Nagy and Leslie Ellen Jones, 172–82. Celtic Studies Association of North America Yearbook 3–4. Dublin: Four Courts, 2005.

Moisl, Hermann. "The Bernician Royal Dynasty and the Irish in the Seventh Century." *Peritia* 2 (1983): 103–26.

Ní Mhaonaigh, Máire. "The Outward Look: Britain and Beyond in Medieval Irish Literature." In *The Medieval World*, edited by Peter Linehan and Janet L. Nelson, 381–97. London: Routledge, 2001.

——. "Of Saxons, a Viking and Normans: Colmán, Gerald and the Monastery of Mayo." In *Anglo-Saxon/Irish Relations before the Vikings*, edited by James Graham-Campbell and Michael Ryan, 411–26. Oxford: Oxford University Press, 2009.

——. "Of Bede's 'Five Languages and Four Nations': The Earliest Writing from Ireland, Scotland and Wales." In *The Cambridge History of Early Medieval English Literature*, edited by Clare A. Lees, 99–119. Cambridge: Cambridge University Press, 2012.

Ó Cróinín, Dáibhí. "Rath Melsigi, Willibrord, and the Earliest Echternach Manuscripts." *Peritia* 3 (1984): 17–49; including an Appendix by Thomas Fanning, "Appendix: Some Field Monuments in the Townlands of Clonmelsh and Garryhundan, Co Carlow," pp. 43–49.

Ó Riain, Pádraig. *Anglo-Saxon Ireland: The Evidence of the Martyrology of Tallaght*. H. M. Chadwick Memorial Lectures 3. Cambridge: Dept. of Anglo-Saxon, Norse, and Celtic, University of Cambridge, 1993; reprinted as "The Northumbrian Urtext of the Martyrology of Tallaght." In *Feastdays of the Saints: A History of Irish Martyrologies*, 43–52. Subsidia hagiographica 86. Brussels: Société des Bollandistes, 2006.

——. "Codex Salmanticensis: A Provenance *inter Anglos* or *inter Hibernos*?" In *"A Miracle of Learning": Studies in Manuscripts and Irish Learning. Essays in Honour of William O'Sullivan*, edited by Toby Barnard, Dáibhí Ó Cróinín, and Katharine Simms, 91–100. Aldershot, UK: Ashgate, 1998.

Orschel, Vera. "Mag nEó na Sacsan: An English Colony in Ireland in the Seventh and Eighth Centuries." *Peritia* 15 (2001): 81–107.

Puhvel, Martin. *Beowulf and Celtic Tradition*. Waterloo, Ontario: Wilfrid Laurier University Press, 1979.

Sims-Williams, Patrick. "Byrhtferth's Ogam Signature." In *Ysgrifau a Ckerddi cyflwynedig i Daniel Huws: Essays and Poems Presented to Daniel Huws*, edited by Tegwyn Jones and E. B. Fryde, 283–91. Aberystwyth: Llyfrgell Genedlaethol Cymru ar ran y Tanysgrifwyr, 1994; reprinted in *Studies on Celtic Languages before the Year 1000*, 169–77. Aberystwyth: Cambrian Medieval Celtic Studies Publications, 2007.

Smith, Julia M. H. "Writing in Britain and Ireland, *c.* 400 to *c.* 800." In *The Cambridge History of Early Medieval English Literature*, edited by Clare A. Lees, 19–49. Cambridge: Cambridge University Press, 2012.

Tremaine, Hadley P. "The Three Saxon Princes at the Destruction of Da Derga's Hostel." *Éire-Ireland* 4, no. 3 (1969): 50–54.

Wadden, Patrick. "The First English Invasion: Irish Responses to the Northumbrian Attack on Brega 684." *Ríocht na Midhe* 21 (2010): 1–33.

Wright, Charles D. *The Irish Tradition in Old English Literature*. Cambridge Studies in Anglo-Saxon England 6. Cambridge: Cambridge University Press 1993.

Yorke, Barbara. "Aldhelm's Irish and British Connections." In *Aldhelm and Sherborne: Essays to Celebrate the Foundation of the Bishopric*, edited by Katharine Barker and Nicholas Brooks, 164–80. Oxford: Oxbow Books, 2010.

Medieval Ireland: An Introduction

Boyle, Elizabeth, and Deborah Hayden, eds. *Authorities and Adaptations: The Reworking and Transmission of Textual Sources in Medieval Ireland*. Dublin: Dublin Institute for Advanced Studies, 2014.

Carey, John. *A Single Ray of the Sun: Religious Speculation in Early Ireland*. Andover and Aberystwyth: Celtic Studies Publications, 1999.

Carney, James. *Studies in Irish Literature and History*. Dublin: Dublin Institute for Advanced Studies, 1955.

Charles-Edwards, Thomas. "Language and Society among the Insular Celts AD 400–1000." In *The Celtic World*, edited by Miranda J. Green, 703–36. London and New York: Routledge, 1995.

——. *Early Christian Ireland*. Cambridge: Cambridge University Press, 2000.

Clancy, Thomas Owen. "Gaelic Literature in Ireland and Scotland, 900–1150." In *The Cambridge History of Early Medieval English Literature*, edited by Clare A. Lees, 637–59. Cambridge: Cambridge University Press, 2012.

Herbert, Máire. "Crossing Historical and Literary Boundaries: Irish Written Culture around the Year 1000." *Cambridge Medieval Celtic Studies* 53/54 (2007): 87–101.

Johnston, Elva. *Literacy and Identity in Early Medieval Ireland*. Studies in Celtic History 33. Woodbridge: Boydell Press, 2013.

McCone, Kim. *Pagan Past and Christian Present in Early Irish Literature*. Maynooth Monographs 3. Maynooth: An Sagart, 1991.

Ní Mhaonaigh, Máire. "The Literature of Medieval Ireland, 800–1200: From the Vikings to the Normans." In *The Cambridge History of Irish Literature*. Vol. 1, edited by Margaret Kelleher and Phil O'Leary, 32–73. Cambridge: Cambridge University Press, 2006.

Ó Cathasaigh, Tomás. "The Literature of Medieval Ireland to *c.* 800: St. Patrick to the Vikings." In *The Cambridge History of Irish Literature*. Vol. 1, edited by Margaret Kelleher and Phil O'Leary, 9–31. Cambridge: Cambridge University Press, 2006.

Ó Cróinín, Dáibhí, ed. *A New History of Ireland, I, Prehistoric and Early Ireland*. Oxford: Oxford University Press, 2005.

Poppe, Erich. "Reconstructing Medieval Irish Literary Theory: The Lesson of *Airec Menman Uraird maic Coisse*." *Cambrian Medieval Celtic Studies* 37 (1999): 33–54.

Thurneysen, Rudolf. *Die irische Helden- und Königsage bis zum siebzehten Jahrhundert*. Halle: M. Niemeyer, 1921.

Glossaries

Arbuthnot, Sharon J. "Glossary Entries, *DIL* and the Struggle with Meaning: Some Case Studies." *Studia Celtica* 42 (2008): 117–34.

Moran, Pádraic. "Hebrew in Early Irish Glossaries." *Cambrian Medieval Celtic Studies* 60 (2010): 1–21.

Russell, Paul. "The Sounds of a Silence: The Growth of Cormac's Glossary." *Cambridge Medieval Celtic Studies* 15 (1988): 1–30.

——. "Laws, Glossaries and Legal Glossaries in Early Ireland." *Zeitschrift für celtische Philologie* 51 (1999): 85–115.

——. *"Read it in a Glossary": Glossaries and Learned Discourse in Medieval Ireland.* Kathleen Hughes Memorial Lectures 6. Cambridge: Department of Anglo-Saxon, Norse, and Celtic, University of Cambridge, 2008.

Grammar, Language and Literacy

Baumgarten, Rolf. "Etymological Aetiology in Irish Tradition." *Ériu* 41 (1990): 115–22.

Harvey, Anthony. "Early Literacy in Ireland: The Evidence from Ogam." *Cambridge Medieval Celtic Studies* 14 (1987): 1–15.

Law, Vivien. *The Insular Latin Grammarians.* Studies in Celtic History 3. Woodbridge: Boydell Press, 1982.

Mac Cana, Proinsias. "The Three Languages and the Three Laws." *Studia Celtica* 5 (1970): 62–78.

——. "The Rise of the Later Schools of *Filidheacht*." *Ériu* 25 (1974): 126–46.

McCone, Kim. "Zur Frage der Register im frühen Irischen." In *Early Irish Literature – Media and Communication: Mündlichkeit und Schriftlichkeit in der frühen irischen Literatur*, edited by Stephen N. Tranter and Hildegard L. C. Tristram, 57–97. ScriptOralia 10. Tübingen: Gunter Narr Verlag, 1989.

McManus, Damian. "Ogam: Archaizing, Orthography and the Authenticity of the Manuscript Key to the Alphabet." *Ériu* 37 (1986): 1–31.

——. *A Guide to Ogam.* Maynooth Monographs 4. Maynooth: An Sagart, 1991.

Ó Corráin, Donnchadh. "The Education of Diarmait Mac Murchada." *Ériu* 28 (1977): 71–81.

Simms, Katharine. "An eaglais agus filí na scol." *Léachtaí Cholm Cille* 24 (1994): 21–36.

Historical and Pseudo-Historical Writing

Arbuthnot, Sharon. "Short Cuts to Etymology: Placenames in *Cóir Anmann*." *Ériu* 50 (1999): 79–88.

Carey, John. *A New Introduction to Lebor Gabála Érenn.* Irish Texts Society Subsidiary Series 1. London and Dublin: Irish Texts Society, 1993.

——. *The Irish National Origin-Legend: Synthetic Pseudohistory.* Quiggin Pamphlets on the Sources of Mediaeval Gaelic History 1. Cambridge: Department of Anglo-Saxon, Norse and Celtic, University of Cambridge, 1994.

——. "*Lebor Gabála* and the Legendary History of Ireland." In *Medieval Celtic Literature and Society*, edited by Helen Fulton, 32–48. Dublin: Four Courts Press, 2005.

Connon, Anne. "The *Banshenchas* and the Uí Néill Queens of Tara." In *Seanchas: Studies in Early and Medieval Irish Archaeology, History and Literature in Honour of Francis J. Byrne*, edited by Alfred P. Smyth, 98–108. Dublin: Four Courts, 2000.

Dillon, Myles. "On the Date and Authorship of the *Book of Rights*." *Celtica* 4 (1958): 239–49.

Downham, Clare. "The Good, the Bad and the Ugly: Portrayals of Vikings in 'The Fragmentary Annals of Ireland'." *Medieval Chronicle* 3 (2004): 28–40.

Dumville, David. "Latin and Irish in the *Annals of Ulster*, A.D. 431–1050." In *Ireland in Early Mediaeval Europe: Studies in Memory of Kathleen Hughes*, edited by Dorothy Whitelock, Rosamond McKitterick, and David Dumville, 320–41. Cambridge: Cambridge University Press, 1982.

——. and Kathryn Grabowski. *Chronicles and Annals of Mediaeval Ireland and Wales*. Studies in Celtic History 4. Woodbridge, UK: Boydell Press, 1984.

Evans, Nicholas. *The Present and the Past in Medieval Irish Chronicles*. Studies in Celtic History 27. Woodbridge: Boydell Press, 2010.

Flechner, Roy. "The Chronicle of Ireland: Then and Now." *Early Medieval Europe* 21, no. 4 (2013): 422–54.

Gwynn, Aubrey. "Cathal Óg mac Maghnusa and the Annals of Ulster." *Clogher Record* 2, no. 2 (1958): 230–43; 2, no. 3 (1959): 370–84.

Mac Niocaill, Gearóid. *The Medieval Irish Annals*. Medieval Irish History Series 3. Dublin: Dublin Historical Association, 1975.

McCarthy, D. P. *The Irish Annals: Their Genesis, Evolution and History*. Dublin: Dublin Historical Association, 2008.

Ní Bhrolcháin, Muireann. "The Manuscript Tradition of the Banshenchas." *Ériu* 33 (1982): 109–35.

Ní Mhaonaigh, Máire. "*Cogad Gáedel re Gallaib*: Some Dating Considerations." *Peritia* 9 (1995): 354–55.

——. "Friend and Foe: Vikings in Ninth- and Tenth-Century Irish Literature." In *Ireland and Scandinavia in the Early Viking Age*, edited by Howard B. Clarke, Máire Ní Mhaonaigh, and Raghnall Ó Floinn, 381–402. Dublin: Four Courts Press, 1998.

——. "Classical Compositions in Medieval Ireland: The Literary Context." In *Translations from Classical Literature:* Imtheachta Aeniasa *and* Stair Ercuil ocus a Bás, edited by Kevin Murray, 1–19. Irish Texts Society, Subsidiary Series, 17. London: Irish Texts Society, 2006.

——. "Pagans and Holy Men: Literary Manifestations of Twelfth-Century Reform." In *Ireland and Europe in the Twelfth Century: Reform and Renewal*, edited by Damian Bracken and Dagmar Ó Riain-Raedel, 143–61. Dublin: Four Courts Press, 2006.

——. *Brian Boru: Ireland's Greatest King?* Stroud: Tempus, 2007.

Ó Corráin, Donnchadh. "Irish Origin Legends and Genealogies: Recurrent Aetiologies." In *History and Heroic Tale: A Symposium*, edited by Tore Nyberg, Iørn Piø, Preben Meulengracht Sørensen, and Aage Trommer, 51–96. Odense: Odense University Press, 1985.

——. "Legend as Critic." In *The Writer as Witness: Literature as Historical Evidence*, edited by Tom Dunne, 23–38. Historical Studies 6. Cork: Cork University Press, 1987.

——. "Annals, Irish." In *Celtic Culture: A Historical Encyclopedia*. Vol. 1, edited by John T. Koch, 69–75. Santa Barbara, CA, Denver, CO, and Oxford: ABC-Clio, 2006.

Parsons, Geraldine. "The Structure of *Acallam na Senórach*." *Cambrian Medieval Celtic Studies* 55 (2008): 11–39.

Poppe, Erich. "Mittelalterliche Übersetzungsliteratur im insular-keltischen Kulturraum: Eine komparatistische Perspektive." In *Übersetzen im skandinavischen Mittelalter*, edited by Vera Johanterwage and Stefanie Würth, 33–58. Wien: Fassbaender, 2007.

Scowcroft, R. Mark. "*Leabhar Gabhála* Part I: The Growth of the Text." *Ériu* 38 (1987): 81–142.

——. "*Leabhar Gabhála* Part II: The Growth of the Tradition." *Ériu* 39 (1988): 1–66.

Wainwright, F. T. "Ingimund's Invasion." *English Historical Review* 247 (1948): 145–69.

Law

Binchy, Daniel A. "The Pseudo-Historical Prologue to the *Senchas Már*." *Studia Celtica* 10–11 (1975–76): 15–28.

Breatnach, Liam. "Canon Law and Secular Law in Early Ireland: The Significance of *Bretha Nemed*." *Peritia* 3 (1984): 439–59.

——. "The Ecclesiastical Element in the Old-Irish Legal Tract *Cáin Fhuithirbe*." *Peritia* 5 (1986): 439–59.

——. "Lawyers in Early Ireland." In *Brehons, Serjeants and Attorneys: Studies in the History of the Irish Legal Profession*, edited by Daire Hogan and W. N. Osborough, 1–13. Dublin: Irish Academic Press, 1990.

——. "On the Glossing of Early Irish Law-Texts, Fragmentary Texts, and Some Aspects of the Laws Relating to Dogs." In *Celtica Helsingiensia: Proceedings from a Symposium on Celtic Studies*, edited by Anders Ahlqvist, Glyn Welden Banks, Ritta Latvio, Harry Nyberg, and Tom Sjöblom, 11–20. Commentationes Humanarum Litterarum 107. Helsinki: Societas Scientiarum Fennica, 1996.

——. *A Companion to the Corpus Iuris Hibernici*. Early Irish Law Series 5. Dublin: Dublin Institute for Advanced Studies, 2005.

Carey, John. "The Two Laws in Dubthach's Judgement." *Cambridge Medieval Celtic Studies* 19 (1990): 1–18.

Kelly, Fergus. *A Guide to Early Irish Law*. Early Irish Law Series 3. Dublin: Dublin Institute for Advanced Studies, 1988.

McCone, Kim. "Dubthach maccu Lugair and a Matter of Life and Death in the Pseudo-Historical Prologue to the *Senchas Már*." *Peritia* 5 (1986): 1–35.

Ó Corráin, Donnchadh, Liam Breatnach, and Aidan Breen. "The Laws of the Irish." *Peritia* 3 (1984): 382–438.

——. "Irish Vernacular Law and the Old Testament." In *Irland und die Christenheit: Ireland and Christendom*, edited by Proinséas Ní Chatháin and Michael Richter, 284–307. Stuttgart: Klett-Cotta, 1987.

Manuscripts

Bhreathnach, Edel. "Two Contributors to the Book of Leinster." In *Ogma: Essays in Celtic Studies in Honour of Próinséas Ní Chatháin*, edited by Michael Richter and Jean-Michel Picard, 105–11. Dublin: Four Courts Press, 2002.

Breatnach, Caoimhín. Review of *Ulidia: Proceedings of the First International Conference on the Ulster Cycle of Tales*, edited by J. P. Mallory and Gerard Stockman. *Éigse* 29 (1996): 200–08.

Carey, John. "On the Interrelationship of Some *Cín Dromma Snechtai* Texts." *Ériu* 46 (1995): 71–92.

Mac Eoin, Gearóid. "The Interpolator H in Lebor na hUidre." In *Ulidia: Proceedings of the First International Conference on the Ulster Cycle of Tales*, edited by J. P. Mallory and Gerard Stockman, 39–46. Belfast: December Publications, 1994.

——. "The Provenance of the Book of Leinster." *Zeitschrift für celtische Philologie* 57 (2009–10): 42–70.

Ó Concheanainn, Tomás. "The Scribe of the Leabhar Breac." *Ériu* 24 (1973): 64–79.

——. "The Reviser of Leabhar na hUidhre." *Éigse* 15 (1974): 277–88.

——. "*Aided Nath Í* and the Reviser of Leabhar na hUidhre." *Éigse* 16 (1976): 146–62.

——. "The Book of Ballymote." *Celtica* 14 (1981): 15–25.

——. "Textual and Historical Associations of Leabhar na hUidhre." *Éigse* 29 (1996): 65–120.

——. "Leabhar na hUidhre: Further Textual Associations." *Éigse* 30 (1997): 27–91.

Oskamp, H. P. A. "Mael Muire: Compiler or Reviser?" *Éigse* 16 (1976): 177–82.

O'Sullivan, William. "Manuscripts and Palaeography." In *A New History of Ireland, I, Prehistoric and Early Ireland*, edited by Dáibhí Ó Cróinín, 511–15. Oxford: Oxford University Press, 2005.

Sharpe, Richard. "Books from Ireland, Fifth to Ninth Centuries." *Peritia* 21 (2010): 1–55.

Toner, Gregory. "Scribe and Text in *Lebor na hUidre*: H's Intentions and Methodology." In *Ulidia 2: Proceedings of the Second International Conference on the Ulster Cycle of Tales, National University of Ireland Maynooth 24–27 June 2005*, edited by Ruairí Ó hUiginn and Brian Ó Catháin, 106–20. Maynooth: An Sagart, 2009.

Narrative Literature

Arbuthnot, Sharon J., and Geraldine Parsons, eds. *The Gaelic Finn Tradition*. Dublin: Four Courts Press, 2012.

Carey, John. "The Rhetoric of *Echtrae Chonlai*." *Cambrian Medieval Celtic Studies* 30 (1995): 41–65.

Carney, James. "The Deeper Level of Early Irish Literature." *Capuchin Annual* 69 (1969): 160–71.

Clarke, Michael. "An Irish Achilles and a Greek Cú Chulainn." In *Ulidia 2: Proceedings of the Second International Conference on the Ulster Cycle of Tales, National University of Ireland Maynooth 24–27 June 2005*, edited by Ruairí Ó hUiginn and Brian Ó Catháin, 238–51. Maynooth: An Sagart, 2009.

Dooley, Ann. *Playing the Hero: Reading the Irish Saga Táin Bó Cúailnge*. Toronto: University of Toronto Press, 2006.

Downey, Clodagh. "Intertextuality in *Echtra mac nEchdach Mugmedóin*." In *Cín Chille Cúile. Texts, Saints and Places: Essays in Honour of Pádraig Ó Riain*, edited by John Carey, Máire Herbert, and Kevin Murray, 77–104. Aberystwyth: Celtic Studies Publications, 2004.

Greenwood, E. M. "Some Aspects of the Evolution of Táin Bó Cúailnge from TBC I to LL TBC." In *Ulidia: Proceedings of the First International Conference on the Ulster Cycle of Tales, Belfast and Emain Macha, 8–12 April 1994*, edited by J. P. Mallory and G. Stockman, 47–54. Belfast: December Publications, 1994.

Mac Cana, Proinsias. "Mongán mac Fiachnai and *Immram Brain*." *Ériu* 23 (1972): 102–42.

Mac Gearailt, Uaitéar. "*Togail Troí*: An Example of Translating and Editing in Medieval Ireland." *Studia Hibernica* 31 (2000–01): 71–85.

Miles, Brent. *Heroic Saga and Classical Epic in Medieval Ireland*. Studies in Celtic History 30. Cambridge: D. S. Brewer, 2011.

Muhr, Kay. "The Location of the Ulster Cycle: Part I Tóchustal Ulad." In *Ulidia: Proceedings of the First International Conference on the Ulster Cycle of Tales, Belfast and Emain Macha, 8–12 April 1994*, edited by J. P. Mallory and G. Stockman, 149–58. Belfast: December Publications, 1994.

Nagy, Joseph Falaky. *Conversing with Angels and Ancients: Literary Myths of Medieval Ireland*. Ithaca and London: Cornell University Press, 1997.

Ní Mhaonaigh, Máire. "Níall Noígíallach's Death-Tale." In *Cín Chille Cúile. Texts, Saints and Places: Essays in Honour of Pádraig Ó Riain*, edited by

John Carey, Máire Herbert, and Kevin Murray, 178–91. Aberystwyth: Celtic Studies Publications, 2004.
Ó Cathasaigh, Tomás. "On the *Cín Dromma Snechta* Version of *Togail Brudne Uí Dergae*." *Ériu* 41 (1990): 103–14.
——. "The Oldest Story of the Laigin: Observations on *Orgain Denna Ríg*." *Éigse* 33 (2002): 1–18.
O'Connor, Ralph. *The Destruction of Da Derga's Hostel: Kingship and Narrative Artistry in a Mediaeval Irish Saga*. Oxford: Oxford University Press, 2013.
——. ed. *Classical Literature and Learning in Medieval Irish Narrative*. Studies in Celtic History 34. Woodbridge: Boydell & Brewer, 2014.
Ó Riain, Pádraig, ed. *Fled Bricrenn: Reassessments*. Irish Texts Society Subsidiary Series 10. London and Dublin: Irish Texts Society, 2000.
Toner, Gregory. "The Transmission of *Tochmarc Emire*." *Ériu* 49 (1998): 71–88.
West, Máire. "Leabhar na hUidhre's Position in the Manuscript History of *Togail Bruidne Da Derga* and *Orgain Brudne Uí Dergae*." *Cambridge Medieval Celtic Studies* 20 (1990): 61–98.

Poetry

Ahlqvist, Anders. "*Is acher in gaíth ... úa Lothlind*." In *Heroic Poets and Poetic Heroes in Celtic Tradition: A Festschrift for Patrick K. Ford*, edited by Joseph Falaky Nagy and Leslie Ellen Jones, 19–27. Celtic Studies Association of North America Yearbook 3–4. Dublin: Four Courts Press, 2005.
Breatnach, Liam. "Zur Frage der *roscada* im Irischen." In *Metrik und Medienwechsel: Metrics and Media*, edited by Hiledgard L. C. Tristram, 197–205. ScriptOralia 35. Tübingen: G. Narr Verlag, 1991.
——. "Poets and Poetry." In *Progress in Medieval Irish Studies*, edited by Kim McCone and Katharine Simms, 65–77. Maynooth: Department of Old Irish, St. Patrick's College, 1996.
Carney, James. "The Dating of Early Irish Verse Texts." *Éigse* 19 (1982–83): 177–216.
——. "The Dating of Archaic Irish Verse." In *Early Irish Literature – Media and Communication: Mündlichkeit und Schriftlichkeit in der frühen irischen Literatur*, edited by Stephen N. Tranter and Hildegard L. C. Tristram, 39–55. ScriptOralia 10. Tübingen: G. Narr Verlag, 1989.
Ford, Patrick K. "Blackbirds, Cuckoos and Infixed Pronouns: Another Context for Early Irish Nature Poetry." In *Celtic Connections: Proceedings of the Tenth International Congress of Celtic Studies*, edited by Ronald Black, William Gillies, and Roibeard Ó Maolalaigh, 162–70. East Linton, Scotland: Tuckwell Press, 1999.
Ó Corráin, Donnchadh. "Early Irish Hermit Poetry?" In *Sages, Saints and Storytellers: Celtic Studies in Honour of Professor James Carney*, edited by Donn-

chadh Ó Corráin, Liam Breatnach, and Kim McCone, 251–67. Maynooth: An Sagart, 1989.

Toner, Gregory. "'Messe ocus Pangur Bán': Structure and Cosmology." *Cambrian Medieval Celtic Studies* 57 (2009): 1–22.

Saints' Lore

Breatnach, Caoimhín. "The Significance of the Orthography of Irish Proper Names in the *Codex Salmanticensis*." *Ériu* 55 (2005): 85–101.

Carey, John, Máire Herbert, and Pádraig Ó Riain, eds. *Studies in Irish Hagiography: Saints and Scholars*. Dublin: Four Courts Press, 2001.

Dumville, David. "Biblical Apocrypha and the Early Irish: A Preliminary Investigation." *Proceedings of the Royal Irish Academy* 73C (1973): 229–338.

——. "*Félire Oengusso*: Problems of Dating a Monument of Old Irish." *Éigse* 33 (2002): 19–48.

Hennig, John. "The Place of Irish Saints in Medieval English Calendars." *Irish Ecclesiastical Record* 82, no. 2 (1954): 93–106.

——. "Britain's Place in the Early Irish Martyrologies." *Medium Ævum* 26 (1957): 17–24.

Herbert, Máire. "Latin and Vernacular Hagiography of Ireland from the Origins to the Sixteenth Century." In *Hagiographies: International History of the Latin and Vernacular Hagiographical Literature in the West from its Origins to 1550*. Vol. 3, edited by G. Philippart, 327–60. Turnhout: Brepols, 2001.

——. "Hagiography." In *Progress in Medieval Irish Studies*, edited by Kim McCone and Katharine Simms, 79–90. Maynooth: Dept. of Old Irish, St. Patrick's College, 1996.

——. "The *Vita Columbae* and Irish Hagiography: A Study of *Vita Cainnechi*." In *Studies in Irish Hagiography: Saints and Scholars*, edited by John Carey, Máire Herbert, and Pádraig Ó Riain, 31–40. Dublin: Four Courts Press, 2001.

McCone, Kim. "Brigit in the Seventh Century: A Saint with Three Lives." *Peritia* 1 (1982): 107–45.

McNamara, Martin. *The Apocrypha in the Irish Church*. Dublin: Dublin Institute for Advanced Studies, 1975.

Ó Riain, Pádraig. "The Tallaght Martyrologies Redated." *Cambridge Medieval Celtic Studies* 20 (1990): 21–38.

——. *A Dictionary of Irish Saints*. Dublin: Four Courts Press, 2011.

——. "The O'Donoghue Lives of the Salamancan Codex: The Earliest Collection of Irish Saints' Lives?" In *Gablánach in Scélaigecht: Celtic Studies in Honour of Ann Dooley*, edited by Sarah Sheehan, Joanne Findon, and Westley Follett, 38–52. Dublin: Four Courts Press, 2013.

Sharpe, Richard. "Vitae S. Brigitae: The Oldest Texts." *Peritia* 1 (1982): 81–106.

——. *Medieval Irish Saints' Lives: An Introduction to Vitae Sanctorum Hiberniae.* Oxford: Clarendon Press, 1991.

Thurneysen, Rudolf. "Die Abfassung des Félire von Oengus." *Zeitschrift für celtische Philologie* 6 (1906): 6–8.

Miscellaneous Other Texts

Boyle, Elizabeth. "Neoplatonic Thought in Medieval Ireland: The Evidence of *Scéla na Esérgi.*" *Medium Ævum* 78, no. 2 (2009): 216–30.

——. "Eschatological Justice in *Scéla Laí Brátha.*" *Cambrian Medieval Celtic Studies* 59 (2010): 39–54.

McCone, Kim. "Prehistoric, Old and Middle Irish." In *Progress in Medieval Irish Studies*, edited by Kim McCone and Katharine Simms, 7–53. Maynooth: Dept. of Old Irish, St. Patrick's College, 1996.

Ó hUiginn, Ruairí, ed. *Lebor na hUidre: Codices Hibernenses Eximii I.* Dublin: Royal Irish Academy, 2015.

Ó Néill, Pádraig. "The Background to the *Cambrai Homily.*" *Ériu* 32 (1981): 137–47.

——. "The Date and Authorship of *Apgitir Chrábaid*: Some Internal Evidence." In *Irland und die Christenheit, Ireland and Christendom: The Bible and the Missions*, edited by Próinséas Ní Chatháin and Michael Richter, 203–15. Stuttgart: Klett-Cotta, 1987.

Ó Riain, Pádraig. "The Psalter of Cashel: A Provisional List of Contents." *Éigse* 22 (1987): 107–30.

Stancliffe, Clare. "Red, White and Blue Martyrdom." In *Ireland in Early Medieval Europe: Studies in Memory of Kathleen Hughes*, edited by Dorothy Whitelock, Rosamond McKitterick, and David Dumville, 21–46. Cambridge: Cambridge University Press, 1982.

Typeset in Garamond Premier Pro
Composed by Martine Maguire-Weltecke

Medieval Institute Publications
College of Arts and Sciences
Western Michigan University
1903 W. Michigan Avenue
Kalamazoo, MI 49008-5432
http:/ /www.wmich.edu/medieval/mip